A Guide to Effective Studying and Learning

D1616403

A Guide to Effective Studying and Learning

Practical Strategies from the
Science of Learning

MATTHEW G. RHODES

ANNE M. CLEARY

EDWARD L. DeLOSH

New York   Oxford
OXFORD UNIVERSITY PRESS

Oxford University Press is a department of the University of Oxford.
It furthers the University's objective of excellence in research, scholarship,
and education by publishing worldwide. Oxford is a registered trade mark of
Oxford University Press in the UK and certain other countries.

Published in the United States of America by Oxford University Press
198 Madison Avenue, New York, NY 10016, United States of America.

© 2020 by Oxford University Press

For titles covered by Section 112 of the US Higher Education
Opportunity Act, please visit www.oup.com/us/he for the latest
information about pricing and alternate formats.

All rights reserved. No part of this publication may be reproduced, stored in
a retrieval system, or transmitted, in any form or by any means, without the
prior permission in writing of Oxford University Press, or as expressly permitted
by law, by license, or under terms agreed with the appropriate reproduction
rights organization. Inquiries concerning reproduction outside the scope of the
above should be sent to the Rights Department, Oxford University Press,
at the address above.

You must not circulate this work in any other form
and you must impose this same condition on any acquirer.

Library of Congress Cataloging-in-Publication Data

Names: Rhodes, Matthew (Matthew G.), author. | Cleary, Anne (Anne M.),
author. | DeLosh, Edward (Edward L.), author.
Title: A guide to effective studying and learning : practical strategies from
the science of learning / by Matthew G. Rhodes, Anne M. Cleary, and
Edward L. DeLosh.
Description: New York, NY : Oxford University Press, [2020] | Includes
bibliographical references and index.
Identifiers: LCCN 2018041430 (print) | LCCN 2018055741 (ebook) |
ISBN 9780190864507 (ebook) | ISBN 9780190214470 (soft cover)
Subjects: LCSH: Study skills. | Learning. | Learning—Social aspects. | Memory.
Classification: LCC LB2395 (ebook) | LCC LB2395 .R54 2020 (print) |
DDC 371.30281—dc23
LC record available at https://lccn.loc.gov/2018041430

1 3 5 7 9 8 6 4 2
Printed by LSC Communications, Inc., United States of America

TABLE OF CONTENTS

....

Preface   xi
Acknowledgements   xv

CHAPTER 1   **What Should Guide You in Learning
How to Learn?**   1
Learning Objectives   1
Everyone Has an Opinion   3
The Perils of Intuition   6
Turning to Science for Guidance on What Helps Learning   11
Learning How to Learn   13
Putting It All Together   14
Tips You Can Use   14
Discussion Questions   15
Suggestions for Further Reading   15
Credits   16

CHAPTER 2   **A Science-Based Approach to Life and Learning**   17
Learning Objectives   17
Belief, Myth, and Common Sense   19
The Approach of Science   21
The Cycle of Science   22
An Example of the Cycle of Science in Action   23
The Benefits of a Scientific Approach to Information   27
Evaluating Claims Using Science   29
Common Errors in Science-Based Thinking   31
Putting It All Together   34

Tips You Can Use 35
Discussion Questions 35
Suggestions for Further Reading 36
Credits 36

CHAPTER 3 **Research Methods in the Science of Learning** 37
Learning Objectives 37
Experimental Methods in Research
    on Learning and Memory 38
Variables in Experimental Research 40
The True Experiment 41
Threats to Experiments 44
Nonexperimental Methods in Psychology 47
Combining Experimental and Descriptive Methods 51
Putting It All Together 54
Tips You Can Use 55
Discussion Questions 55
Suggestions for Further Reading 56
Credits 56

CHAPTER 4 **Metacognition: Understanding Your Own
Memory** 57
Learning Objectives 57
Metacognition: What Is It Good For? 61
Toward an Accurate Understanding of Our Learning 65
Delay: The Joys of Waiting 67
Test: The Value of Testing 72
Two Bonus Methods of Improving Your
    Understanding of Your Own Learning 73
Putting It All Together 75
Tips You Can Use 76
Discussion Questions 77
Suggestions for Further Reading 77
Credits 78

CHAPTER 5 **Can You Expand On That? Boosting
Learning and Retention by Elaborating** 79
Learning Objectives 79
Repetition and Rote Memorization 81
Quality of Processing 85
Interim Summary: Taking Stock of What You've Learned 87

Elaboration   87
How Does Elaboration Help?   96
Putting It All Together   98
Tips You Can Use   98
Discussion Questions   99
Suggestions for Further Reading   100
Credits   100

CHAPTER 6   **Imagery: The Benefits of Imagery on Learning and Training**   101
Learning Objectives   101
Introducing the Method of Loci:
    The "Memory Palace"   102
Imagery for Studying: The Keyword Mnemonic   107
Imagery for Performance Training: Imagining Doing
    Things Improves Performance   111
Putting It All Together   120
Tips You Can Use   120
Discussion Questions   121
Suggestions for Further Reading   122
Credits   122

CHAPTER 7   **Organization: The Importance of Organization for Remembering**   123
Learning Objectives   123
Research on Organization and Memory   125
Applying Organization in Your Own Learning   128
Organization and Cognitive Processing   133
Ease Others' Cognitive Load: Use Organization
    for Effective Communication   141
Putting It All Together   144
Tips You Can Use   145
Discussion Questions   145
Suggestions for Further Reading   146
Credits   146

CHAPTER 8   **Give It a Break! Spacing Your Study and Practice**   149
Learning Objectives   149
The Science of Spaced Study and Practice   151
So Study More Frequently?   152

Space Within a Session? Across Sessions?   153
How Much Spacing?   155
Interim Summary: Taking Stock
    of What You've Learned   158
Cramming   158
What About Problem-Solving?   161
And Skill-Learning?   161
Is it Good or Bad to Mix Things Up?   163
Putting It All Together   165
Tips You Can Use   166
Discussion Questions   167
Suggestions for Further Reading   168
Credits   168

CHAPTER 9   **Learning to Love Testing**   169
Learning Objectives   169
Testing Enhances Memory:
    Did We Know This All Along?   171
Testing the Benefits of Testing   173
A World of Testing Benefits   174
Interim Summary: Understanding the
    Benefits of Testing   180
A Guide to Effectively Using Testing   181
Putting It All Together   188
Tips You Can Use   188
Discussion Questions   189
Suggestions for Further Reading   190
Credits   190

CHAPTER 10   **Cues You Can Use: How to Jog Your Memory**   191
Learning Objectives   191
The Power of Cues   192
Why Do Cues Matter?   193
A World of Cues   195
Context in Context: A Principle and a Caveat   201
The Best Cues for Studying Are . . .   203
Putting It All Together   209
Tips You Can Use   210
Discussion Questions   211

Suggestions for Further Reading   211
Answers to Demonstration 10.1   211
Credits   212

CHAPTER 11   **Learning Is More Than Remembering:
Understanding, Discovery, and Innovation**   213
Learning Objectives   213
Insight   215
How Mechanisms of Memory Affect Understanding   215
Escaping the Grip of the Wrong Mindset   217
The Importance of Spaced Attempts   219
Giant Mental Leaps: The Role of Analogy   223
Can You Sense an Impending Moment of Insight?   230
Putting It All Together   231
Tips You Can Use   231
Discussion Questions   233
Suggestions for Further Reading   233
Credits   234

CHAPTER 12   **Social Aspects of Learning:
Learning in a Group Context**   235
Learning Objectives   235
The Promises and Perils of Collective
Knowledge at the Individual Level   237
The Promises and Pitfalls of Social
Interaction on Learning   242
To Collaborate or Not to Collaborate?   247
Putting It All Together   252
Tips You Can Use   253
Discussion Questions   253
Suggestions for Further Reading   254
Credits   254

Glossary   255
References   259
Index   278

PREFACE

....

Our motivation to write this book stemmed from the fact that a large gap exists between books on the science of learning and books offering practical advice for people on to how to learn. It also stemmed from our own experiences with our students in college classes. Time after time, each of us has experienced a conversation with a distraught student expressing genuine puzzlement at having received a bad grade on a test. One of the most common complaints that we hear from students is something along the lines of "I do not understand how I did so poorly on the test. I studied really hard and I honestly felt like I was well prepared!" In these cases, when we ask *how* the student prepared for the exam, the most common answer seems to be "I read and reread my notes, and as I was looking through my notes, I really felt like I knew this stuff. I don't know how I could have done so poorly."

Being both college course instructors and researchers in learning and memory ourselves, we were well-positioned to begin developing methods of combatting this disconnect between impressions of learning and actual learning among students. We were also well-positioned to devise methods of helping students to become better, more effective learners, in addition to becoming better assessors of their own learning. It started with writing this book.

Indeed, while scientific research on learning has been taking place for well over a century, one relatively new pattern to emerge in the past few decades is documentation of a pervasive disconnect between what people believe helps their learning and what actually does help learning.

Part of the disconnect occurs because people have erroneous beliefs about learning and about how to improve it. However, another part of the disconnect is that people's in-the-moment impressions during learning can lead them astray. This disconnect occurs both in gauging their learning and in gauging what is an effective learning technique. Very often, the factors that help learning are the opposite of the ones that lead to the most positive in-the-moment impressions while attempting to learn. Thus, one of the most challenging aspects of learning how to learn is overcoming the inclination to rely on in-the-moment impressions. A student in one of our classes put it best when describing the subjective experience of shifting to some of the science-based techniques in this book (such as testing) from the more intuitive techniques that students tend to use (such as rereading the material). The student described the science-based techniques as not feeling like they were going to work. In other words, while engaged in these techniques, it does not seem like the technique is going to be effective. However, come test time, suddenly it is surprisingly apparent that they worked. The student said, "It almost feels like sneaky learning—the learning just sneaks up on you."

This is the challenge faced by learners and educators alike: Because in-the-moment impressions while studying are often the opposite of what is most effective, it can be difficult to get students to believe in these techniques until they have the opportunity to practice them (skeptically) and then see first-hand that they do work come exam time. Our advice to you is this: Give the techniques in this book a chance beyond your impressions while using them. Keep using them, even if they feel like they are not going to work, and watch what happens.

Approach

Our approach in writing this book was to practice what we preach about learning through the way the book is written and organized. To do so, we implemented many of the very learning strategies that are the subject matter of this book. For example, because one strategy for effective learning is spaced repetition of subject matter, we strategically incorporated spaced repetition of important concepts across chapters to help reinforce learning of earlier material from the book. Another strategy for effective learning involves elaborating on the material. A very simple method for using elaboration in your everyday learning is a technique called *elaborative interrogation*. Elaborative interrogation involves simply asking yourself the question "why?" periodically while reading through new material, listening to a talk or a lecture, or reviewing your notes. We incorporate this very simple learning strategy throughout the book using what we call Elaborative Interrogation Arrows. You will see these arrows asking you to ponder "why?" seemingly strewn throughout the book (though they are actually strategically placed). As you read through this book, you may even find it useful to try to identify all of the different ways in which we try to incorporate the very strategies that we discuss in this book within the structure and organization of the book itself, and embedded in its content.

Our book differs from other books on learning in a number of other important ways as well. First, it emphasizes science as the source of information on learning how to learn. There are a lot of claims out in the world about how to learn. Many of them are not supported by science and thus are not valid claims. Second, both because it can be difficult to sift through and evaluate the many claims that are out there in the world about learning, and because the scientific literature on the science of learning is overwhelming, this book condenses and distills the science into usable, practical tips for enhancing learning that are grounded in science. Our focus is on adult learning of all types, and ways in which adults can improve upon their everyday attempts at learning new things by engaging in methods supported by scientific studies of learning. At the same time, the book attempts to equip the reader with the skills necessary to critically evaluate claims about learning.

Organization of this Book

This book starts out by dispelling some common myths about learning (some of which you may come to the book believing yourself), and by emphasizing the need for the scientific approach in assessing the validity of claims in general (about anything, really), and not just learning. We then turn to one of the major factors that often leads people to spend their time engaging in the wrong activities when trying to better learn: The disconnect between people's impressions of their learning and the factors that actually help learning. Here, we emphasize that contrary to many popular opinions, learning itself is not intuitive. One must learn to overcome beliefs and impressions about learning and instead turn toward methods that science has shown are effective. These science-based techniques might not feel initially like they are going to have an impact on your learning, but if you accept the science and persist with them, you will likely find that they are effective. Then, chapter by chapter, we cover the many techniques and strategies that science has shown are effective for enhancing learning, one by one. Each chapter then culminates with a series of tips and practical recommendations for implementing the ideas and skills discussed in the chapter.

ACKNOWLEDGEMENTS

....

We were very fortunate to have the support of our university's central administration in our various efforts to improve student learning, including the development and adminis-tration of our groundbreaking all-university course, Science of Learning, for which we now use this book. For this, we are especially grateful to Drs. Alan Lamborn and Paul Thayer, without whom this course may have never taken off. We are also grateful for the feedback of many reviewers, colleagues, and students, who all helped to shape this book.

Special thanks go to the following reviewers who read and provided thoughtful insights on our chapters.

William S. Altman
SUNY Broome Community College

Jeffrey S. Anastasi
Sam Houston State University

Andrew C. Butler
Washington University in St. Louis

Alan Castel
University of California, Los Angeles

Stephen Chew
Samford University

Giovanna Cicillini
William Paterson University

Corinne Corte
Arizona State University

Pete Delaney
University of North Carolina at Greensboro

John Dunlosky
Kent State University

Jason Finley
Fontbonne University

Scott Gabriel
Viterbo University

Jason Geller
*University of
Alabama–Birmingham*

Dorsha E. Goodman
Bowie State University

Charla R. Hall
*Southeastern Oklahoma
State University*

Valerie Jahns
*University of Wisconsin
Colleges*

Sean Kang
Dartmouth College

Carmalita M. Kemayo
*University of Illinois
Springfield*

Nate Kornell
Williams College

Gary Muir
St. Olaf College

Michael Polgar
*Pennsylvania State
University*

Adam Putnam
Carleton College

Jerry Rudmann
Irvine Valley College

Bennett L. Schwartz
*Florida International
University*

Uma Tauber
Texas Christian University

CHAPTER 1

....

What Should Guide You in Learning How to Learn?

....

Learning Objectives
- Reading this chapter will help you:
  - Appreciate the limitations of your intuitions about learning.
  - Identify flaws in common-sense ideas about learning.
  - Understand how to approach claims about learning.

....

Imagine this scenario. You are a student taking five classes and, over the next seven days, will have an important exam in each class. After pondering whether you are at the center of a cruel, intra-university conspiracy to eliminate most of your free time, you get down to the business of preparing for the exams. The content you will need to learn is all over the place. You will have a midterm in art history, unit exams in chemistry and political science, an open-book essay exam in American history, and one of ten regular exams (really, these are long quizzes) in calculus.

Although you do not see your future life revolving around each of these subjects, you enjoy the classes and truly want to master the material. And you are optimistic that a byproduct of this interest in mastering the material is that the exams will go well. But a question keeps gnawing at you: How should you study? Should you spend a separate day studying for each exam? With so many different classes and so many different exam dates, is it okay to wait until the night before an exam to study? Should you look over the material for each and every course every day that you study? Is it effective to reread and maybe rewrite your notes? Or better yet, what *is* effective? Does it help to have someone quiz you or can you quiz yourself? How much time should you spend studying? Should you take lots of breaks while studying, or should you concentrate on studying in large blocks of time?

The best answers to these questions are not obvious. Indeed, part of what makes learning how to learn so difficult is that much of what is best for learning is not common sense. You could search the Internet for guidance on how to learn and will probably find yourself overwhelmed with an abundance of often-conflicting, and frequently false, information that claims to be guidance. How do you know which claims about studying to ignore and which to adapt? For example, are learning styles important for your learning? Do so-called brain-training games help you to become better at learning?

Each of your authors has had the experience of being approached by a bewildered student, deeply disappointed about a recent score on an exam. Often this student will swear that he or she had studied diligently and mastered the material. Because of all of that hard work, the student is confused and dismayed that performance on the exam did not match the efforts exerted.

There is no reason to doubt the sincerity of this claim. And who would not be sympathetic to a diligent student who is working hard but not seeing this work translate into true learning? However, there is often a common thread running through these experiences. The student is absolutely sure that the methods of studying used should have produced the desired outcome—a good score on the exam. Yet those efforts did not produce the desired outcome.

One core fact can account for the discrepancy between the perception of learning and actual learning: *There is often a large difference between what you feel is best for learning and what are the best strategies for learning.* Fortunately, well over 100 years of scientific research has provided a very good understanding of how best to learn, be it differential equations for a calculus exam, ruminations on the Treaty of Versailles, the complete cast of characters from *Modern Family*, or how to hit a curveball. However, one reason the science of learning does not reach as many people as it should is precisely because *the factors that help learning are not intuitive.* The goal of this book is to bring the science to the everyday learner, in ways that will be accessible and useful no matter what your background and no matter what you are trying to learn.

Everyone Has an Opinion

There is certainly no shortage of opinions on what makes for optimal learning. Each of your authors knows students who swear that learning is best with loud music playing the background, using a particular color of highlighter, during the morning/afternoon/evening, or after a shower!

In addition to these scattered anecdotes, surveys provide interesting information regarding students' thoughts about learning. For example, on the first day of a recent class, one of your authors surveyed students' opinions about learning. The results of the survey showed, for example, that 35 of 47 students endorsed the statement "Adherence to a student's learning style (such as visual learner, auditory learner, etc.) is very important to effective learning," on a rating scale of 1 ("strongly disagree") to 5 ("strongly agree"), with an average rating of 3.83. In the same survey, 22 out of 47 students endorsed the statement "Brain-training games are a good way to sharpen your mind to become a better learner."

Twenty-six out of 47 students also endorsed the statement "Repeating information over and over again is an effective way to commit it to memory." Along similar lines, 21 of 47 students endorsed the statement "One way that I often try to remember something is to say it to myself over and over again." How about you? Do you often try to remember something by saying it over and over to yourself? Before reading any further, try Demonstrations 1.1a through 1.1d.

Your authors recently conducted an experiment and tested 29 participants who did exactly what you just did—they learned pairs of words by repeating them over and over (repetition) and other word pairs by forming an image of two objects interacting (imagery). Just after studying each list, the participants then predicted the percentage of words they would remember. Finally, they took a test for the words, allowing a comparison between the predictions and how much they could actually remember.

Those data are shown in Figure 1.1. Participants' predictions (left side of the graph) indicated that they believed imagery would give them only a very small advantage over repetition. That is, they made slightly

DEMONSTRATION 1.1a

First, try to memorize the word pairs below by repeating each pair over and over to yourself three times. For example, if the pair is pitcher–lizard, simply say "pitcher-lizard-pitcher-lizard-pitcher-lizard." Do not use any other method of remembering. Just repeat them over and over to yourself.

fish–truck	squirrel–playground	bed–squash
flower–house	dish–elephant	lake–lamp
carpet–hammer	hose–desk	piano–foot
horse–candle	car–banana	chess–beef
wheel–apple	tree–umbrella	
window–bird	teapot–statue	

DEMONSTRATION 1.1b

Now, without looking at the list at the top of the page, try writing down the second word from each pair from memory. For example, if it says, "pitcher–_____" you would write down "lizard."

tree–_____   flower–_____

chess–_____   dish–_____

fish–_____   wheel–_____

lake–_____   car–_____

couch–_____   piano–_____

horse–_____   window–_____

hose–_____   teapot–_____

squirrel–_____

DEMONSTRATION 1.1c

Next, try to memorize the word pairs below by forming an image in your mind of the two interacting. For example, if the pair is "pitcher–lizard," you might form an image of a lizard swimming around inside of a glass water pitcher, or a pitcher that is in the shape of a lizard. Do not use any other method of remembering. Just form images of each item within the pair interacting.

gate–tiger	bee–fog	dove–leather
coffee–paint	button–lawn	balloon–pool
bike–hat	frog–pistol	clover–oatmeal
egg–brick	couch–garden	sign–port
sink–doll	boat–pencil	
rose–shoe	frame–jacket	

DEMONSTRATION 1.1d
Now, without looking at the prior page go ahead and write down the second word from each pair from memory. For example, if it says, "pitcher–_____" you would write down "lizard."

coffee–_____

gate–_____

egg–_____

bike–_____

button–_____

frog–_____

rose–_____

couch–_____

sign–_____

boat–_____

frame–_____

dove–_____

sink–_____

bee–_____

balloon–_____

clover–

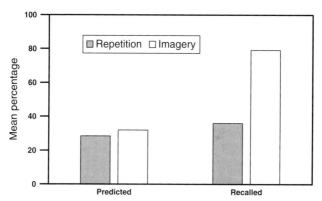

FIGURE 1.1 The predicted percentage of words remembered and the actual percentage of words remembered (from an experiment conducted by the authors).

higher predictions of memory for imagery (white bars) than for repetition (gray bars). But the data for the mean percentage of items recalled (right side) shows a much more dramatic difference in favor of imagery, one that the participants clearly did not anticipate. In fact, the participants correctly remembered almost 2.5 times as many words associated with imagery (79%) than words that were simply repeated (32%)!

There are really two morals to this story. First, imagery can powerfully benefit learning under some circumstances (see Chapter 6 on imagery for much more on effectively using imagery in learning). Second, it is difficult to appreciate the benefits of imagery and, likewise, to understand that repetition is not all that useful for enduring learning. Indeed, although imagery was far better for learning than repetition, participants thought it would only produce a tiny advantage compared to repeating items over and over. This is a very important consideration when you try to decide what helps learning and what does not: *Intuitions about learning may often lead you astray.* The techniques that you *feel* are effective may not be effective. To add insult to this learning injury, learners may have little sense of what actually does help. Throughout this book we've included additional help in the form of elaborative interrogation arrows (see Box 1.1).

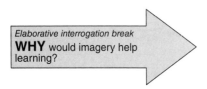

Elaborative interrogation break
WHY would imagery help learning?

The Perils of Intuition

Look at the two lines in Figure 1.2. Which line do you think is larger?

If you are like most people (and each of your authors), your gut reaction is that the upper line must be larger. In fact, the two lines are exactly the same length (go ahead, measure them). This is an example of the well-known Muller-Lyer visual illusion, whereby the arrows on the end of each line create the very powerful, but mistaken, sense that the two lines are not the same.

Individuals' moment-to-moment impressions during learning can similarly produce their own powerful illusions that may lead them to mistakenly believe their intuitions. This can be a troubling realization. Indeed, most people are a bit uncomfortable with the idea that their

---

BOX 1.1   A NOTE ON ELABORATIVE INTERROGATION ARROWS

In each chapter of this book, you will periodically see large arrows with questions inside them. These arrows are intended to prompt you to asking yourself a question about the reading and form answers that connect with the material. Researchers have shown that such **elaborative interrogation** can improve your learning of what you are reading (see Chapter 5 for more on this idea). For that reason, as you read this book, try taking a break by answering the questions in the arrows!

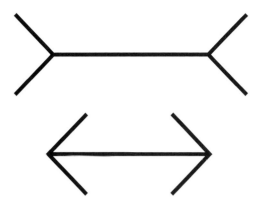

FIGURE **1.2** Which middle line is larger: the top or bottom?

intuitions or gut feelings about their own learning can be wrong. That may go some ways toward explaining why repeating something over and over gives the false impression that learning has taken place: that repetition *feels* like it is beneficial while you are doing it. The repeated information is, after all, highly accessible in the moment as it is repeated.

The problem lies in the fact that what feels helpful in the moment may not be very useful later on when you would like to remember that information (as on an exam). In fact, as you will see in this book, very often what feels helpful in the moment is actually the exact *opposite* of what is helpful, and vice versa! Repeating something over and over makes it feel very accessible and easy to bring to mind in the moment. After all, as you are repeating it, the information is currently in your mind, so it is currently very accessible. You may therefore think that it will be easy to remember later on.

The problem here is that the momentary feeling of accessibility while repeating information does not always predict your ability to later remember it (e.g., Benjamin, Bjork, & Schwartz, 1998). As another example, people often believe that they will have highly accurate memories for an emotional or important event. However, research shows that although learners may be confident in their memory under these circumstances, important events do not always lead to accurate memories (e.g., Talarico & Rubin, 2003). This type of misunderstanding is probably one of the greatest impediments to identifying what does and does not help learning. The moment-to-moment sense of whether you have truly learned something is often not a good indicator of actual learning.

Not only are intuitions about what helps learning often wrong, they are sometimes the *opposite* of what actually does help learning. For example, suppose you were in an art history class and charged with learning the style of several different artists. Your learning should be good enough that you could identify the artist even if you had never seen the painting before. Should you look at each artist's works in blocks before moving on to the next artist? For example, do you think it would be easier to learn Monet's style of painting if you studied many different Monet paintings in close succession, as in the top panel of Figure 1.3? (Note that in the top panel of Figure 1.3, three Monet paintings are presented together.) Or would it be better to mix up artists' paintings? For example, you could study a Degas, then a Van Gogh, a Cassatt, and so forth. The bottom panel of Figure 1.3 show what this kind of mixing might look like.

FIGURE 1.3 Which method would be better for learning a particular genre of painting or a particular artist's style of painting: seeing the paintings of that style or by that artist together, as in the top row, or seeing them interspersed among other paintings, as in the bottom row?

One group of researchers (Kornell & Bjork, 2008) addressed this very question in an experiment by varying the ways that their participants studied artists' works. Some of the paintings were studied in blocks, with several examples of paintings from the same artist presented together, before a sample of paintings from another artist, and so on. In other cases, paintings from different artists were randomly mixed together. The participants then took a test where they saw new paintings and had to identify the artist responsible for the work.

As you can see in Figure 1.4, their participants were much better at correctly identifying the artist when the paintings had been mixed together (white bar) than presented in blocks by a single artist (gray bar). However, participants seemed to be largely unaware of this. For example, after completing the test, participants were asked whether they learned more by having paintings blocked or mixed (they were also free to say each was equally effective). The vast majority of participants (78%) said that blocking was as good or better than mixing paintings!

This is a fascinating set of data. Participants were twice as likely to correctly identify an artist's painting after mixed learning than blocked learning, but nearly 4 out of every 5 participants thought that blocking was the best way to learn. Why would predictions be so out of tune with actual performance? One explanation is that the close succession of paintings from the same artist feels in the moment as if it is helping learning.

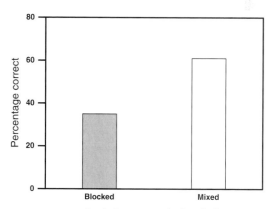

FIGURE 1.4 Average percentage of paintings correctly classified when studied in blocks or mixed (adapted from Kornell & Bjork, 2008).

In the moment, you can more easily see common patterns in the paintings when they are presented together than when they are interspersed among other paintings. Thus, it feels like learning is better when they are presented together. Yet people's learning performance suggests the opposite: Learning is actually better when the paintings are interspersed among those of other artists (see Chapter 8 for much more information on this topic).

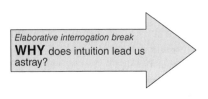

Elaborative interrogation break
WHY does intuition lead us astray?

It turns out that poor insight into the benefits of mixing learning is not an isolated finding. In one study (McCabe, 2011), students read descriptions of different learning scenarios. One scenario described learning artists by mixing their paintings together, while another scenario described learning about a set of artists by studying paintings from only a single artist at a time. The students were asked to rate how beneficial each scenario was for learning. Among the nearly 300 undergraduates tested, approximately 93% believed that learning was better if information was blocked (e.g., all paintings of a single artist presented at once) rather than mixed (e.g., interspersing paintings by multiple artists). Such misunderstandings do not apply only to college students. Consider work from a group of researchers (Morehead, Rhodes, & DeLozier, 2016), who gave this same scenario about learning paintings to approximately 140 instructors at a large university taking a survey about their knowledge of learning. Nearly 90% of these instructors regarded blocking as a better strategy than mixing materials.

Such cases of mistaken beliefs about learning are common. For example, other work shows that students readily endorse the value of highlighting text and believe that restudying material is more effective than testing (Hartwig & Dunlosky, 2012; Kornell & Bjork, 2007; McCabe, 2011; Morehead et al., 2016). What unites these findings? They all represent common-sense ideas about memory that are flat wrong. Highlighting provides little benefit to memory and testing is a more effective study strategy than rereading (see Dunlosky, Rawson, Marsh, Nathan, & Willingham, 2013, for a review). In the midst of so many mistaken beliefs, how do you identify the best information to guide your own decisions about learning?

Turning to Science for Guidance on What Helps Learning

Findings like the common-sense belief that highlighting consistently aids memory suggests that you cannot rely on your intuition for guidance on how best to learn. To what, then, should you turn? Is there an ultimate authority? Should you believe claims on the Internet of companies trying to sell you learning products and methods? How do you evaluate claims that certain techniques or products help learning? This is especially important because intuitions about learning may be compelling, but are often wrong about what actually helps learning. For example, do you feel that you have a particular learning style? Is your preferred learning style visual or auditory or kinesthetic? Does having an instructor who teaches to your preferred learning style actually help you to learn better? Have you ever actually tested this? A number of products have been developed based on this idea of preferred learning styles. But do they have merit? Chapters 2 and 3 will deal with critical thinking and the importance of science as a means of obtaining information about what does and does not work, or what is and is not effective for improving learning, including the issue of whether learning styles exist.

Since the Renaissance (A.D. 1300s–1600s), during which the scientific revolution is often said to have occurred, Western civilizations began turning toward the scientific process for answers to

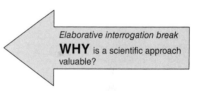

Elaborative interrogation break
WHY is a scientific approach valuable?

questions about how things work—or, put differently, for truth and understanding (see, e.g., Bynum, 2012). For example, the scientific process enabled people to understand that the Earth is not the center of the solar system (it actually revolves around the sun), and that the heart serves as a pump within a circulatory system (see Sternberg, 1999, for an excellent review of how the history of science fits together with the scientific study of mental processes).

People are generally quite willing to rely on science rather than intuition in many realms of knowledge. For example, although the Earth appears to be flat, most people are willing to rely on science to inform them that the Earth is actually spherical. People can accept

The earth may appear to be flat.

The earth is spherical.

that their intuition, what their first-person perspective discloses about the world, is actually wrong. However, the idea that you should rely on science instead of intuition to understand your mental processes, like those involved in learning, has been accepted much more slowly. When it comes to learning, many people believe that their intuitions and hunches are viable sources of information on how learning takes hold. However, these are often not sound sources of information. Just as the approach of science has given the world an accurate picture of the shape of the Earth, so can a scientific approach give you an accurate picture of learning.

Learning How to Learn

What does scientific research have to tell you about what *does* help learning? That is the purpose of this book—to help equip you with a repertoire of skills and habits that are rooted in scientific evidence to help you to become a better learner. If you are like many students, this will be the first time that you have been formally introduced to such skills and habits.

For example, Kornell and Bjork (2007) asked 472 UCLA students this question: "Would you say that you study the way you do because a teacher (or teachers) taught you to study that way?" Only 20% of Kornell and Bjork's participants said that they had been taught to study. Hartwig and Dunlosky (2012) gave this same question to a group of 324 Kent State University students and similarly found that only 36% of students reported being taught how to study (see also Morehead el al., 2016). This suggests that there is not only a significant need to provide high-quality information about learning, but also a wonderful opportunity to enhance student success. That is the goal of this book.

You do not need to be an aspiring competitive memorizer to benefit from this book. Nor do you need to be a college student majoring in psychology, or even enrolled in college, to benefit. You need only to have an interest in enhancing and improving your learning. No matter what your hobbies or profession, some type of learning is involved and you will stand to benefit from improving your learning skills. Whether you are interested in expanding your knowledge in a new topic area or improving your athletic performance, acquiring a new skill or learning a new language, trying to learn people's names or remember your passwords, principles taken from the science of learning can help you.

Each of the chapters in this book provides an overview of a core topic in learning and end with practical tips that you can use. Among other things, you will find chapters on how to spread out your studying and the benefits of spreading out learning, how imagery can be used as a tool to help learning and training, how different ways of processing information impact your learning, effective methods of evaluating your own learning, and how testing is much more than an assessment tool, but is instead one of the most effective learning tools available. You will also find tips on how technology might be useful in helping you to incorporate these techniques into your everyday habits. In all, the goal of this book is not only to make you a well-informed learner, but to give you the tools to be a highly effective learner.

Putting it All Together

Humans are born as veritable learning machines, be it an infant rapidly learning the key features of their environment (such as the sound of a parent's voice), a young child mastering an entire language, an adolescent becoming a highly skilled soccer player, or an adult becoming an expert accountant. Although you were born to learn, these prior experiences, surprisingly, do not translate into deep insights about the nature of learning. Indeed, many individuals continue to engage in entirely ineffective learning strategies such as cramming, convinced that this is the right approach. Fortunately, many decades of scientific research on learning can provide key insights that can allow you to fully understand and use the learning machine at your disposal. This book is thus a how-to guide to that learning machine.

Tips You Can Use

1. **Ask for the evidence.** This book is rooted in the scientific literature on learning. That is, all the tips and strategies suggested are based on evidence from careful scientific studies on memory. Each of your authors follows this mantra any time a claim is made about memory: What is the evidence? As you read these chapters and think about your own learning, you should ask for the evidence every time an idea about learning is presented.
2. **Beware of in-the-moment impressions about your learning.** Techniques that feel in the moment like they are helping you learn are often the very opposite of what does help you learn. Do not rely only on impressions to gauge your learning and whether a technique is effective at helping you learn (see Chapter 4 on metacognition for much more information on this topic).
3. **Difficulty is good.** The nasty secret of research on learning is that many of the things that make learning feel easy are not actually all that good for durable, long-lasting learning. Instead, activities that do not feel very easy in the moment, activities that might make learning feel difficult, often lead to the best learning (e.g., Schmidt & Bjork, 1992; Soderstrom & Bjork, 2015). For example, you might recall that many people preferred blocked presentations of material

even though it clearly led to poorer learning (see Figure 1.4). The message is clear: What makes learning feel difficult and unpleasant is often what is best for learning.

4. **Learning is itself a skill.** The principles described in this book are highly effective for learning, but take time to master. Just as you likely were not an expert driver the first time you got behind the wheel, you should not expect high levels of proficiency the first time you attempt to mix some of the strategies suggested in this book, such as the value of spreading out learning and testing yourself. Instead, give yourself the chance to practice these ideas and develop the skills for applying them to all kinds of situations. Each of the chapters will provide you with tips and suggestions to accomplish this.

Discussion Questions

1. Misunderstandings of memory (and optimal methods of studying) appear to be widespread. What do you think accounts for these misunderstandings? That is, why is it so common for people to have misunderstandings of how memory operates?

2. How would you remedy the misunderstandings of memory discussed in this chapter? For example, consider the results from Kornell and Bjork (2008) showing that students believed seeing a block of paintings by the same artist would result in superior learning compared to studying a mix of different artists. The reality was different, as mixing paintings improved learning of artists' styles. How would you teach people that it would be better to mix artists' paintings?

3. What do you think are the best methods of learning? How do you think you developed this perspective on learning? Do you feel that your methods are consistent with research on learning?

4. A science-based approach is not only valuable to learning but valuable in virtually all aspects of life, from understanding what is healthy to eat to whether it will rain. How might you foster an approach to information grounded in science in your own life?

Suggestions for Further Reading

One of our motivations for writing this book is that although there are excellent textbooks on memory, these books are aimed at students of memory rather than individuals seeking a science-based, practical guide to studying. However, for those interested in a fuller appreciation of memory, including in-depth coverage of theoretical perspectives, there are several excellent books to choose from. We particularly like Bennett Schwartz's *Memory: Foundations and Applications* (2018) for its accessible prose and wide coverage of memory. *Memory* (2014) by Alan Baddeley, Michael Eysenck, and Michael Anderson is also highly recommended. In the popular press, two books stand out among many entries. Daniel Schacter's *Searching For Memory: The Brain, the Mind, and the Past* (1996) deftly combines science with deeper reflections on the importance of memory. *Make It Stick: The Science of Successful Learning* (2014) by Peter Brown, Henry Roediger, and Mark McDaniel provides a number of practical suggestions for memory improvement, couched in rigorous science and aimed at anyone with a general interest in enhancing their learning.

Credits

Page 8: (Figure 1.3) Everett - Art / Shutterstock
Page 12: (top) alybaba / Shutterstock
Page 12: (bottom) Triff / Shutterstock

CHAPTER 2

A Science-Based Approach to Life and Learning

....

Learning Objectives
- Reading this chapter will help you:
    - Identify common myths in thinking about the world and about learning.
    - Appreciate the advantages of a science-based approach to learning.
    - Explain the cycle of science.
    - Recognize common errors in thinking about learning.

....

Were you ever told to wash your hands before dinner? Most people have probably been given this order at some time in their life. But why wash your hands? An obvious reason is to remove the dirt and grime of the day before using your hands as supplementary utensils during a meal. However, there is a more important reason to wash your hands that only became known in the past 150 years. Your body is densely populated with micro-organisms, including a wide variety of bacteria. Some of these bacteria are helpful and a necessary part of healthy function, such as the bacteria in your gut that aids digestion. Other bacteria are harmful and take up residence on your skin through your day-to-day contact with the world and should be removed. Estimates suggest that your hands contain 5,000 to 5,000,000 colony-forming units per square millimeter of space (Boyce & Pittet, 2002; Guwande, 2002).

Figures such of these would have astounded the earliest practitioners of medicine. Rather than seeing disease as linked to the work of malignant

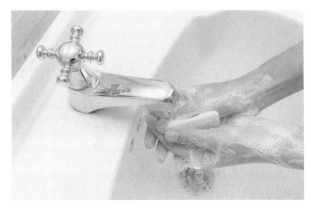

Washing hands can remove harmful bacteria that were only revealed by scientific advances from the late 1800s.

micro-organisms, many physicians focused well into the nineteenth century on the ancient Greek idea of balance or "humours" (blood, bile, and water) within the body (Bynum, 2008). It is because of this belief in humours that patients were frequently bled, so as to "rebalance" the body.

Today's physicians practice a very different kind of medicine from their early predecessors (you probably have not been offered a good bloodletting at the doctor's office). This reflects a science-based approach to medicine that revolutionized treatment and theories of disease. For example, Louis Pasteur and others such as Robert Koch were able to identify under their microscopes the tiny bacteria that often lead to disease. This work not only altered understanding of health, but produced a sea change in how medicine was practiced. One consequence was a greater emphasis on sterilization and efforts to prevent bacteria being introduced during medical procedures like surgery (Lister, 1867; 1870). Thus, part of the scientific legacy of Pasteur, Lister, and others is that hand-washing is now a central part of medical practice.

But of course, this is not a book about hand hygiene or medicine, but a book about learning. And just as a scientific approach guided developments in medical practice, so should a scientific approach guide how you learn. For example, should you copy notes or test yourself? Would you gain an advantage if you studied in the room where you will later take an exam? Does it help to study with friends, or should you do most studying on your own? Should you try to take classes that match your learning style? Should you spend time playing brain-training games?

DEMONSTRATION 2.1

For each of the following statements, indicate whether it is *something you believe in, something you're not sure about*, or *something you don't believe in*.

1. ESP or extrasensory perception
2. That houses can be haunted
3. Ghosts
4. Telepathy/communication between minds without using traditional senses

For each of the following statements, indicate whether you *agree* or *disagree*:

1. Strange behaviors are more common during a full moon.
2. Most people use only 10% of their brain.
3. Hypnosis is useful for helping witnesses accurately recall the details of a crime.
4. Our handwriting says something about our personality.

There are many ways to answer these questions. You could ask friends, seek advice on the Internet, solicit the opinions of your instructors, or reflect on your own experiences. But the best way to answer these questions is to consider what scientific research on learning can tell you about how to study. Accordingly, this chapter focuses on the approach of science and its applications in learning. Before reading on, try Demonstration 2.1.

Belief, Myth, and Common Sense

The items in Demonstration 2.1 have two things in common. First, each represents a widely held belief. For example, the first four items about the paranormal were taken from a larger Gallup survey (Moore, 2005). As you can see in Figure 2.1, 41% of the respondents in that study endorsed a belief in extrasensory perception (ESP), 37% believed that houses could be haunted, and about a third of respondents (32%) believed that humans are capable of seeing the future. In all, the Gallup survey asked about 10 different paranormal beliefs and found that approximately 75% of respondents endorsed at least one paranormal belief. The second set of questions also represents very popular beliefs. For example, approximately 59% of college-educated individuals agreed that people use only 10% of the brain (Herculano-Houzel, 2002), and 55% of a large sample of

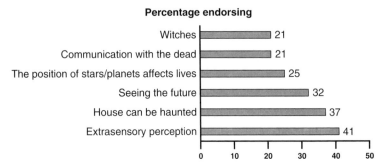

FIGURE 2.1 **The percentage of respondents endorsing each belief (adapted from Moore, 2005).**

adults agreed that hypnosis was useful for making memory more accurate (Simons & Chabris, 2011). Clearly, these beliefs have wide appeal and are consistent with many individuals' intuitions about the world.

In addition to engendering wide agreement, the statements in Demonstration 2.1 also have a second common feature: Each is a myth (e.g., hypnosis improves memory) or bit of folklore (e.g., ghosts) that is not supported by scientific evidence. There are probably many reasons for these widespread beliefs. For one, the paranormal is often the subject of compelling stories and movies that treat it as a real phenomenon. In other cases, the beliefs likely represent instances of mistaken information that have been passed down through an optimistic sense of individuals' untapped or unexplored potential (Lilienfeld, Lynn, Ruscio, & Beyerstein, 2010). For example, the myth that people use only 10% of the brain invites the tantalizing prospect that everyone has a large reservoir of untapped mental horsepower.

Indeed, part of what makes many myths difficult to overcome is that they often constitute widely accepted beliefs that are taken as intuitive, what might be termed **common sense**. History is replete with examples of information that was once regarded as common sense that appear very foolish and even ridiculous to modern sensibilities. For example, it was once taken as common sense that tomatoes were poisonous, women were unqualified to vote, and bathing more than few times a year harmed health.

Modern times also come with all kinds of common sense that is nothing more than bunk. For example, there is no health value to "detoxifying" your body with any of a variety of exotic purges, no matter the celebrity endorsing its healing powers. Major media moguls will not pay you to post a link on social media or forward an email. And retailers continue to make a great deal of money selling small magnets in bracelets that are viewed as supercures that enhance "blood flow" but do not affect even an atom of your body.

You might be familiar with common sense about studying. For instance, people often favor lots of studying in one period time (massing) over spreading out the same amount of studying across several sessions (spacing). Highlighting text and notes is very popular as a study aid but appears to have little effectiveness. Unfortunately, although wrong, these ideas are often regarded as common sense and frequently endorsed by students (e.g., Kornell & Bjork, 2007; Morehead et al., 2016).

You can avoid falling prey to these myths and relying strictly on common sense by always asking for evidence to support a claim. And in studying and in much of the rest of life, the best evidence comes from a scientific approach.

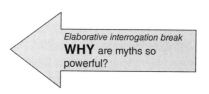

Elaborative interrogation break
WHY are myths so powerful?

The Approach of Science

What is science? Is it people in white lab coats who write down numbers on clipboards? Is it equations and test tubes and studious individuals in stuffy rooms peering into microscopes? Each of these questions represent stereotypes associated with science, but tell you nothing about the nature of science. Instead, science is best described as a method of collecting information that is driven by observation and experimentation.

Any **scientific approach** to information starts with the assumption that nature consists of laws or consistent principles that can be discovered. That is, nature is not a series of random events but operates in a lawful, orderly manner that can be studied systematically. As such, science has several goals:

1. **Measure and describe.** Science must focus on information that can be measured and, thus, described. Suppose you wanted to learn the Swahili word for "soil" (*ardhi*). Would it help to imagine

a man in large field of dirt painting on a canvas (making "art for he")? More generally, does thinking of an image help you learn information? Before this question can be answered, you first need a way to measure learning. Fortunately, many years of research have furnished excellent methods for measuring learning and memory.

2. **Understand and predict.** Uncovering the laws of nature allows an understanding of why phenomena occur. For example, one reason that imagery helps memory (see Figure 1.1 from Chapter 1) is that it allows learners to consider information in multiple formats. Therefore, information learned with an image can be remembered by thinking of a picture, the sound of a word, or a combination of the two. Based on this, you can also predict that your learning will improve if you can think of information in more than one format.

3. **Application and control.** Understanding the laws of nature allows this knowledge to be applied to enhance individuals' everyday lives. For example, a goal of writing this book is to provide a science-based approach that would help people optimize learning in all aspects of their life.

Thus, science moves from measuring and describing behavior to achieving an understanding of behavior that allows for accurate predictions about how processes interact so that the processes can be controlled. How are these goals actually put into practice?

The Cycle of Science

You may have the impression that the scientific method refers to a general set of procedures that all scientists employ. This has an element of truth—scientists do largely agree on the essential procedures—but it does not capture the nature of science. Science is really an orientation or set of methods for collecting information. There is general agreement on the four key elements that constitute the scientific process. These elements are:

1. **Induction.** Using existing data to develop general conclusions that form a statement about data that can be tested (a **hypothesis**).

2. **Deduction.** Based on a hypothesis (or hypotheses), make specific predictions about the outcome.

3. **Observation.** Collect data that allow the hypotheses to be tested.

4. **Verification.** Confirm whether the hypotheses are correct or falsified.

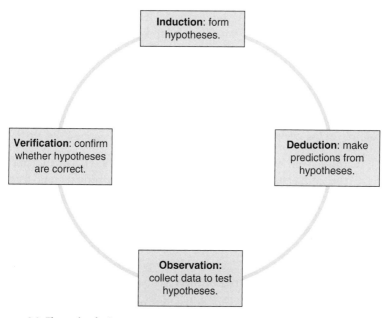

FIGURE **2.2 The cycle of science.**

These processes are best considered as a cycle of science (see Figure 2.2). That is, hypotheses lead to a set of predictions, which in turn generate data for observation. Once the hypotheses are subject to verification, they often beget additional hypotheses that start the cycle all over again.

Science in practice does not uniformly adhere to these steps. For example, verifying the results may alter the way data is collected, perhaps encouraging the investigator to collect different observations than originally intended. Other steps are also often involved such as reporting the results of scientific investigations in journals and books. However, the four elements in Figure 2.2 capture the fundamental components of the scientific method.

An Example of the Cycle of Science in Action

Is feedback important for learning? For example, suppose you and a friend are studying for an upcoming test in your Italian class. Your friend gives you the English phrase "clown car," and you provide what you think is the correct translation into Italian (*auto di clowno*).

Should your friend give you feedback? If so, what is the best way to provide that feedback? Do you only need to know whether your answer is correct (*right/wrong feedback*)? Should you be given the correct answer as part of feedback (*correct answer feedback*)? (Incidentally, the correct translation of "clown car" is *auto di pagliaccio*.) Pashler, Cepeda, Wixted, and Rohrer (2005) reported an experiment examining whether the type of feedback provided influences learning and provide a strong example of the cycle of science in action.

1. **Induction.** Prior research (e.g., Guthrie, 1971) had indicated that *correct answer feedback* was better for learning than no feedback at all. However, it was not apparent whether *correct answer feedback* was superior to *right/wrong feedback*, particularly when the learner had to wait more than a few minutes to take a test. Because *right/wrong feedback* does not actually involve presenting the correct answer, Pashler at al. hypothesized that it would be less effective than *correct answer feedback*.

2. **Deduction.** In their study, Pashler et al. (2005) had participants learn foreign vocabulary words and tested their memory immediately and then again seven days later. They made two specific predictions.

   - **Prediction 1:** Participants given *correct answer feedback* will correctly remember more information immediately after studying than participants given *right/wrong feedback* or given *no feedback* at all.

   - **Prediction 2:** Participants given *correct answer feedback* will correctly remember more information after a seven-day delay than participants given *right/wrong feedback* or given *no feedback* at all.

   Thus, the researchers moved from a general hypothesis about the effects of feedback into specific predictions concerning different types of feedback and how long any benefits of feedback could be detected.

3. **Observation.** To test their hypothesis that *correct answer feedback* was superior to *right/wrong feedback* and *no feedback*, the researchers conducted an experiment (see Figure 2.3 for a diagram of this experiment). Participants first studied a set of 20 Lagunda words (the major language of Uganda), paired with its English translation (e.g., *leero*–today). Each pair was presented one at a time until all 20 pairs had been studied, with this procedure done

twice. Next, participants took a test on the pairs. For this test, participants were given the Lagunda word and tried to produce its English translation (e.g., *leero* means: ?). After an answer, some participants were told whether that answer was correct (*right/wrong feedback*). Other participants were given the correct answer (*correct answer feedback*), and a third group of participants received *no feedback* at all. Once this first test had been completed the researchers immediately administered a second test to determine whether feedback impacted learning. Once the second test was completed, participants left the experiment. They returned seven days later and completed a final test, done the same way as the tests on the first day (i.e., type in the English translation to a Lagunda word). The researchers measured learning as the

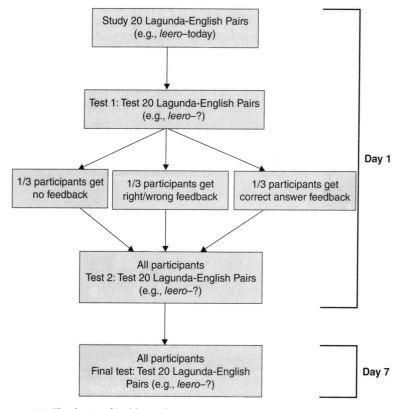

FIGURE 2.3 The design of Pashler et al.'s (2005) experiment on feedback.

number of words (correct translations) their participants could correctly recall on each test.

4. **Verification.** The major hypothesis of this experiment is that learning is best when participants are given *correct answer feedback*. Figure 2.4 is consistent with that hypothesis. Each of the specific predictions the researchers made can also be examined.

- **Prediction 1:** The first prediction stated that *correct answer feedback* was best for learning when memory was tested shortly after learning. Those data can be found by looking at performance on the first day from Test 1 to Test 2. In the experiment, participants receiving feedback were first given that feedback on Test 1 after supplying an answer. Because feedback was first introduced during Test 1, feedback can only influence performance starting on Test 2. Indeed, whereas memory is much better from Test 1 to Test 2 for correct answer feedback, memory actually stays about the same for the other types of feedback.

- **Prediction 2:** The second prediction stated that *correct answer feedback* would be best for the final test given seven days after learning. That prediction was also confirmed. Although all participants' memory was a little worse after seven days, the correct answer group had the best performance.

Thus, the researchers started with a general hypothesis about the benefits of giving the correct answer when providing feedback, generated

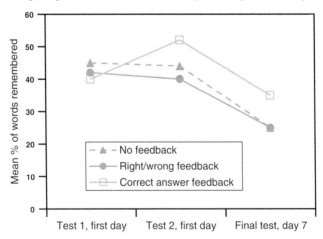

FIGURE 2.4 Learning outcomes for individuals given no feedback, right/wrong feedback, or correct answer feedback (adpated from Pashler et al., 2005).

specific predictions, and conducted an experiment as a test of their hypothesis. With science being a cycle, there are many more questions still to be asked. For example, the researchers also observed that feedback was more effective following an error than a correct answer. That observation has led other researchers to consider how feedback might change learning based on whether a correct answer was generated (e.g., Butler & Roediger, 2008; Sitzman, Rhodes, & Tauber, 2014) or how the kind of error made might affect whether an error can be corrected (Mullet & Marsh, 2016). These questions will, in turn, generate new hypotheses and new experiments that will continue the cycle of science.

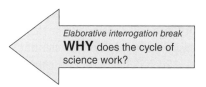

Elaborative interrogation break
WHY does the cycle of science work?

The Benefits of a Scientific Approach to Information

A scientific approach to information confers many advantages over other methods, such as using common sense. For one, by specifying hypotheses, investigators must clearly identify what they are studying and how it will be measured. Take this statement: *Sleep can help memory.* This is true to some extent, but it is imprecise. For example, what kind sleep enhances memory? How much sleep is necessary? What is meant by the term "memory"—memory for words, pictures, books, television shows? How is memory tested? A scientific approach forces investigators to be very specific about what is being tested and how it is measured.

Beyond that, science is a never-ending cycle of induction-deduction-observation-verification (Figure 2.2). The beauty in that approach is that rather than staying rooted in place, knowledge gained from science is always progressing and hence more likely to approach the correct answer to a question. For example, Pluto was long regarded as the ninth planet of the solar

An image of Pluto taken from NASA's *New Horizons* spacecraft.

system. That label goes back to a 1930 discovery by astronomer Clyde Tombaugh and remained scientific "fact" for over 70 years. However, in 2003, a larger object was discovered beyond Pluto that was initially thought to be a new planet. The ensuing debate among astronomers led them to reclassify Pluto as a dwarf planet (indeed, Pluto is only two-thirds the size of Earth's moon). Debate on the topic persists, with some continuing to deem Pluto a planet and others considering it one of a number of planetary objects beyond Neptune. As new information and understanding emerges, and the cycle of science proceeds, the status of Pluto will continue to be debated and discussed. Similar debates can easily be found in other scientific domains (see Box 2.1).

Such debates are also common within scientific research on learning and memory. You may be familiar with the finding that humans can learn and immediately remember about 7 bits of information at one time. This finding is referred to as Miller's Magic Number, named in honor of George Miller (1956), who reviewed many experiments and determined that humans could keep in mind and remember about 7±2 units of information (Miller called them *chunks*) at one time. The work was highly influential and even led phone companies to adopt a maximum of 7 digits for local phone numbers.

More recent research using different methods has refined this number, suggesting that you can immediately hold about 4±1 units of information at a time (Cowan, 2001). Miller was not "wrong"; he made a reasonable assessment of what was known at that time and spurred many other studies that sought to further understand the limited capacity of immediate memory. It was the progressive nature of science, the never-ending

---

BOX 2.1   SCIENTIFIC DEBATE

The cycle of science drives a never-ending debate in all scientific domains about a variety of issues. For example, paleontologists are at odds over whether dinosaurs predominantly had scales or feathers (e.g., Godefroit et al., 2014; Lingham-Soliar, 2014). Physicists continue to attempt to measure and characterize some of the tiniest particles (i.e., neutrinos) that make up the universe, with no consensus yet on their mass or whether that mass can even be accurately measured (e.g., Cho, 2017). In medicine, debate continues over issues such as when adults should be screened for certain types of diseases, such as prostate cancer (Fenton et al., 2018). These debates will continue as new findings emerge.

induction-deduction-observation-verification cycle, that altered and updated Miller's original finding and will bring about new insights in the years to come.

Elaborative interrogation break
WHY are debates good for science?

Evaluating Claims Using Science

Suppose you are on a cross-country flight and start a conversation with a passenger in the seat next to you. And suppose also that this individual cannot stop talking about the benefits of a brain-training game he and his family are using, raving that playing this game has made everyone in his family smarter and sharper.

You have probably already heard similar claims. In recent years, brain-training has become a multibillion dollar industry that is projected to keep growing (Simons et al., 2016). Claims vary by company, but often imply that playing these games (of course, for a subscription fee) can enhance attention, improve memory, increase intelligence, and generally make everyday living better. These benefits sound enticing—who would not want to be smarter, to be better at remembering names, to find life easier? But a key question lingers: Are these claims accurate? How should you evaluate these claims? What kind of evidence would you need to see to accept these claims? Go ahead, try thinking about what would be needed.

Do video games improve brain function?

When your authors pose these questions in class, students frequently answer along the lines of, "There would need to be a scientific study, like an experiment comparing people who were and were not given these brain-training games." Indeed, when evaluating a claim such this, your first recourse should be to ask whether information has been collected using the cycle of science (Figure 2.2) to address the claim.

This thought exercise also raises some other interesting issues that are worth considering. For example, what if a study existed that supported the claim? Does that study alone provide all of the evidence needed to support the claim? Standing alone, it probably does not. First, has the finding been reproduced (*replicated*, in the terminology of the scientific community) by others (Patil, Peng, & Leek, 2016)? By this standard, a finding is given greater weight if it has been replicated. Second, is there consensus in the field? That is, do a large number of studies from many different labs around the world converge on the same finding?

One great way to assess this is to look for a review paper. A review paper assembles and assesses the large body of scientific work that has been carried out on a topic. If the topic is one for which consensus is emerging, that should be apparent in the review article. If it is one still debated, that should also be apparent in the review article. An ideal type of review, **meta-analysis**, combines the findings from all prior studies on a topic and analyses those findings. A meta-analysis can portray patterns that emerge from a large number of published research studies to assess trends and highly replicable findings. If a meta-analysis supports a claim (such as the claim that testing benefits learning; indeed such a meta-analysis has been done by Rowland, 2014), it is much more compelling than if only a single study has reported the claim.

In regard to brain-training, there are several excellent review papers. Melby-Lervag and Hulme (2013) report a meta-analytic review of one particular type of training (see also Shipstead, Hicks, & Engle, 2012) and Simons et al. (2016) provide a wonderful overview of the entire brain-training literature. Their conclusion is that evidence for the broad claims made by brain-training games simply does not exist. They do not make people smarter, sharper, or make everyday living easier. The bottom line is that it pays to have a critical eye for evaluating claims about learning.

Common Errors in Science-Based Thinking

In their splendid book *50 Great Myths of Psychology* (2010), Scott Lilienfeld and colleagues lay out over 250 myths that pervade people's "understanding" of behavior. This includes several of the myths discussed previously, such as the belief that we only use 10% of our brain. Here are a few more myths:

> *An individual with amnesia often forgets their own name and identity.*
> *Criminal profilers are better at predicting criminal behavior than untrained college students.*
> *Ulcers are caused by stress.*
> *Subliminal messages influence what products you buy.*
> *If you are unsure of an answer on a test, stick with your first hunch.*

Did you find that you believed any of these statements to be fact? If you did, that is okay! These myths are interesting precisely because they represent mistaken, but widely held, beliefs. As noted in Chapter 1, learning and memory also comes with its own set of myths that people take to be common sense. For example, the myth that amnesia essentially wipes out memory of one's name and identity is so pervasive that one survey found nearly 8 out of 10 adults believed it (Simons & Chabris, 2011)! The larger point is not that such myths represent the intellectual shortcomings of a scattered few, but rather are a common feature of being human (Shermer, 2002). Critically evaluating claims is itself a skill that and one that takes training and practice.

The best antidote to myth in life and learning is an approach grounded in science. But there are some impediments to reasoning that are worth pointing out because they crop up so commonly when evaluating learning. Consider these five common errors.

1. **Being an authority does not automatically make a statement true.** Students sometimes tell your authors that they study the way they do because a trusted person in their life (teacher/ parent/minister) told them that highlighting/copying notes/ doing handstands leads to the best learning. However, an idea should not be accepted simply because it came from an authority. Instead, it is vital to ask for the evidence. Have there been experiments comparing individuals who did or did not highlight? Have

Beware of appeals to authority.

studies compared learning after individuals were assigned to a handstand or no-handstand condition? Although each of your authors has been studying memory for two decades or more, you should not take any recommendations made in this book on faith. Instead, the claims in this book will be backed by science-based evidence. You might also do your own digging into the scientific literature on many of the issues discussed in this book.

2. **Anecdotes are not evidence.** Everyone loves a good story. For example, you may have heard the yarn about two students who missed an exam, claiming a flat tire. As a make-up, their instructor put each student into a separate room and administered a two-question exam:

1. What is the chemical formula for water? (5 points)
2. Which tire? (95 points)

Although entertaining, this story is merely a bit lore that likely never happened. But it illustrates a broader point. No story counts as evidence, and 100 anecdotes cannot replace the value of a single experiment (Shermer, 2002). Sure, your roommate swears she aced her last test because she studied with a group of classmates, but what is the evidence that studying in a group positively influenced her learning? Instead, this question is best addressed with an experiment (see Chapter 3 for more on experiments).

3. **Common sense is not evidence.** A poor argument often begins with the following words: "Common sense tells us that . . ." The simple stipulation that a belief is common sense does not make that belief accurate (Lilienfeld et al., 2010). This does not mean that everything regarded as common sense is wrong. You are more likely to learn from your book if you read it rather than use it to swat flies; memory for words from a known language will generally exceed memory for words from an unknown language; and sleeping in class does not increase exam performance. However, much of what is deemed common sense (or intuition) is inaccurate, and does not qualify as a form of evidence. For example, common sense might dictate that seeing an object thousands of times would result in excellent memory for that object. However, several experiments have demonstrated very poor memory for common objects such as pennies (Nickerson & Adams, 1979). Common sense might also suggest that people would have an excellent, enduring memory for very important national events, such as the 2001 attacks on the World Trade Center. Again (and you can probably guess where this is going), common sense would be wrong (e.g., Talarico & Rubin, 2003). Thus, no amount of common sense can replace what we gain from well-controlled scientific research.

4. **Just because A and B are related does not mean A causes B.** Simply because two variables or two events are associated with each other does not mean that one causes the other. For example, the temperature of a city can likely be predicted by the amount of ice cream consumed in that city, such that the more ice cream consumed, the higher the temperature is likely to be. Could global warming be halted by eliminating ice cream? No. An ice cream cone is a more attractive proposition in hot than frigid weather, but the amount of ice cream consumed is unrelated to the temperature. That is, the two are associated, but have nothing to do with each other. So the next time someone makes a claim of doing well on an exam because they did X (swam, ran nude through the park, played Red Rover) when studying, ask yourself whether they are simply talking about two events that are related. And then tell them that this does not imply that one causes the other.

5. **Finding confirming information alone does not make a claim correct.** Humans are frequently driven by the tendency to

confirm what they already believe (Nickerson, 1998). For example, suppose you did have a friend who claimed that swimming changed her academic life, increasing her learning in all of her courses. As evidence, she admonishes you to go talk to her buddy who has had the same experience. And suppose that this buddy also confirms that swimming increased her learning. Does that make her claim correct? No. For one, as you have just learned, a few stories do not make for sound evidence. In addition, you need to do more than seek out information consistent with your friend's claim. That is, you need to determine whether there is information that would be inconsistent (disconfirm) with her claim. For example, can you find people who do not swim who also make good grades? Are there swimmers who have seen no improvement in grades? Thus, when evaluating a claim, seek out the alternative, the other side of the issue.

There are many more peculiarities of human thinking you should be on the lookout for (see Lilienfeld et al., 2010; Shermer, 2002), but having these five principles in mind will serve you well as you explore the science of learning.

Putting it All Together

You have an almost limitless array of information available to you to address any question you might ever want to ask. Some of these questions will engender straightforward answers, such as the chemical formula for sodium or the gestation period of an African elephant. Many of life's other questions, such as the molecular composition of octopus ink or the best methods of engineering safe roads, require more complex answers. The same can be said about which practices you should engage in to produce long-lasting, enduring learning. But regardless of the complexity of the query, you have a choice in how the question should be answered. You can seek a friend's knowledge, listen to a few compelling stories, rely on your common sense, or try any of a countless number of other strategies. The problem with these alternatives is that they are not as likely to get you close to the truth of the matter as an approach grounded in science. To be fair, science is no guarantee of truth. For example, you might recall the debates described in this chapter among scientists about the existence of Pluto or the capacity of memory. But the never-ending cycle of science will be your best source of information in understanding learning and in understanding much of life.

Tips You Can Use

1. **Follow the trail of the cycle of science.** When encountering a claim, it often helps to consider how the researchers have implemented the cycle of science. What hypothesis drove the investigation? What specific predictions did the researchers make? How did they test these predictions? Do the observations match those predictions? Considering research evidence in light of the step-by-step process of the cycle of science (Figure 2.2) can often make the approach and contribution of an area of research much clearer.

2. **Ask for the evidence.** No matter the claim, your starting point should always be this question: "What is the evidence?" Although many types of evidence are possible, your best source will be evidence gained from a scientific approach.

3. **Look for scientific consensus.** If a claim says that it is based on science or "science shows," but it appears to be based on a single study that is the only one to ever show the effect, be skeptical. Scientific consensus emerges when multiple studies from multiple sources report findings that are consistent with one another, tested under conditions that could reveal an inconsistency. Reviews, particularly meta-analytic reviews, are often an excellent place to seek such consensus.

4. **Common sense is not evidence.** The factors that help learning are often those that have the least intuitive appeal. Instead of relying on common sense or intuition, look for the evidence.

Discussion Questions

1. People hold a number of beliefs that are at odds with science. For example, Moore (2005) reported a broad survey that showed that 75% of respondents endorsed at least one paranormal belief. Why are these beliefs so prevalent? Is there anything that can be done to the spread of such beliefs?

2. "Opposites attract." Although this statement is often deemed to be common sense, it contradicts much of the scientific literature on relationships. Nonetheless, statements such as these often influence beliefs.

What distinguishes the approach of science from such common-sense approaches to evaluating information? What are the merits of a scientific approach? Are there any drawbacks?

3. The last decade or two have witnessed a significant increase in enrollment in classes that take place exclusively online (e.g., Allen & Seamen, 2010). Do you think learning is as effective, more effective, or less effective for such classes? Discuss how these questions might be evaluated using the cycle of science. That is, discuss how you might draw conclusions about the effect of online courses by using the scientific method encompassed by the cycle of science.

4. Discuss the five major impediments to scientific thinking, providing an example of each obstacle. How could you overcome these impediments in your own life?

Suggestions for Further Reading

You could spend the rest of your life investigating the scientific process. Indeed, there is an almost endless trove of writing and debate on conducting science. The classic works on how science is conducted and how it advances were authored by Karl Popper (1959) and Thomas Kuhn (1970). William Bynum (2012) and Geoffrey Gorham (2009) also provide highly accessible introductions to the history and philosophy of science. A virtue of understanding research in psychology is that one can readily identify approaches masquerading as science (what has been dubbed *pseudoscience*) and question long-held beliefs that are myth. Scott Lilienfeld and colleagues' wonderful book, *50 Great Myths of Psychology* (2010), superbly ferrets out many of the prevailing myths in psychology and provides a template for understanding how these myths came to exist. On a more general level, Michael Shermer's *Why People Believe Weird Things* (2002) is highly entertaining and a must-read for anyone concerned with understanding pseudoscience and superstition.

Credits

Page 18: Summer Photographer / Shutterstock
Page 27: NASA
Page 29: Rawpixel.com / Shutterstock
Page 32: goodluz / Shutterstock

CHAPTER 3

Research Methods in the Science of Learning

....

Learning Objectives
- Reading this chapter will help you:
  - Appreciate how research in the science of learning takes place.
  - Understand experimental methods in the science of learning.
  - Understand descriptive methods in the science of learning.
  - Distinguish between experimental and descriptive methods in the science of learning.
  - Know how to evaluate claims about learning.

....

Y ou probably have at least a general sense of what it means to do scientific research in disciplines like biology, chemistry, and astronomy. For example, you might be able to readily picture a scientist in her lab coat, looking into a microscope, mixing chemicals in test tubes, or peering into a telescope, jotting down observations and measurements. But what does it mean to do scientific research on human learning and memory?

As you will recall from Chapter 2, at a general level, science refers to an orientation toward gathering information that is centered on stating questions (hypotheses), making predictions, and then transparently testing those predictions as a way of advancing knowledge. This cycle of science (see Figure 2.2 in Chapter 2) allows for self-correction and

Scientists observe and measure as part of scientific methodology.

continued progress toward the ultimate goal of predicting and understanding the phenomenon of interest. The cycle of science applies to the science of learning and memory as well. Researchers in learning and memory use a number of different scientific methods; paramount among them is the experiment.

Experimental Methods in Research on Learning and Memory

Why do courses often have prerequisites? That is, why must you first take algebra, precalculus, and trigonometry before enrolling in calculus? One idea is that without knowing something about algebra and trigonometry, calculus would be a bewildering array of functions and proofs. Accordingly, prerequisites benefit learning because it is easier to learn new information when you can connect it with something you already know. Stated a bit more formally, linking new information to prior knowledge causes learning to improve. The emphasis on *cause* is no accident. A primary goal of **experimental research** is to establish the causes of behavior (Rosnow & Rosenthal, 2012). That is, experimental research allows a researcher to understand which variables or treatments cause which outcomes. Before reading on, try Demonstration 3.1.

If you are like most people, you probably found the paragraph very difficult to understand and challenging to remember. The sentences themselves make sense and are grammatical, but they seem almost randomly arranged.

Demonstration 3.1 is based on a classic experiment by Bransford and Johnson (1972), who were interested in how prior knowledge influences learning. To study this, they had college students read the same paragraph you just read. One group of participants simply read the paragraph; another group of participants were given some context prior to reading, being told that the paragraph was about washing clothes; finally, a third group of participants were informed that the paragraph was about washing clothes, but this information was only provided after they had read the paragraph. Once everyone had finished reading the paragraph, participants were asked to recall as much of the content as they could.

Figure 3.1 shows the results of this experiment. As you can see, the percentage of information recalled was greater when participants were told the paragraph was about washing clothes prior to reading the paragraph (the *context before* condition on the far right of the figure). However, providing context of this sort after reading did not change memory, even when compared with having no context at all.

This work has many of the hallmarks of good experimental research. The researchers varied the only condition they were interested

DEMONSTRATION 3.1

Please read this paragraph:

> The procedure is actually quite simple. First you arrange items into different groups. Of course one pile may be sufficient depending on how much there is to do. If you have to go somewhere else due to lack of facilities that is the next step; otherwise, you are pretty well set. It is important not to overdo things. That is, it is better to do too few things at once than too many. In the short run this may not seem important, but complications can easily arise. A mistake can be expensive as well. At first, the whole procedure will seem complicated. Soon, however, it will become just another facet of life. It is difficult to foresee any end to the necessity for this task in the immediate future, but then, one never can tell. After the procedure is completed one arranges the materials into different groups again. Then they can be put into their appropriate places. Eventually, they will be used once more and the whole cycle will then have to be repeated. However, that is part of life.

How well did you understand this paragraph? *Really well, somewhat, not at all*

Now, step away from your chapter and try writing down as much as you can remember from that paragraph. (This should only take two or three minutes.)

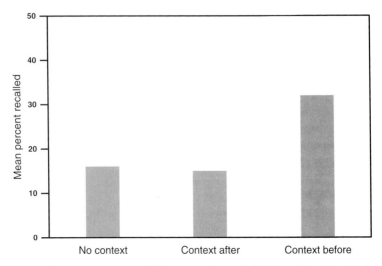

FIGURE 3.1 The mean percentage of ideas correctly recalled (adpated from Bransford & Johnson, 1972).

in—whether participants could make use of prior knowledge—and kept all other factors (such the paragraph participants read) the same. By keeping these other factors constant, Bransford and Johnson could pinpoint the effect of prior knowledge on learning. As such, they were able to establish that having a hint connecting information to prior knowledge (in this case, people's extensive knowledge of doing laundry) facilitates learning.

Variables in Experimental Research

Experiments are comprised of two classes of variables: Those that the experimenter manipulates (**independent variables**) and those that the experimenter measures (**dependent variables**).

Independent Variables

The independent variable is the treatment that is manipulated in an experiment. These variables are said to be "independent" because the experimenter determines the nature or amount of this variable independently of all other factors in the experiment. For example, in the Bransford and Johnson (1972) experiment, the researchers manipulated whether participants received context for the paragraph, while all other elements of the experiment were held constant. The different, specific ways that an independent variable is manipulated are the **levels** of the independent variable. In the Bransford and Johnson experiment there were three levels: *no context*, *context before*, and *context after*. Thus, Bransford and Johnson varied their treatment in three different ways. In addition to selecting the levels of an independent variable, experimenters also choose the way an independent variable is manipulated. A **between-subjects** manipulation means that participants are only exposed to a single level of an independent variable. Bransford and Johnson employed a between-subjects manipulation in their experiment, as different groups of participants received a different level of the independent variable. In contrast, a **within-subjects** manipulation entails that participants are exposed to all levels of an independent variable. For example, in Demonstration 1.1 from Chapter 1, you were asked to first learn a list of word pairs by repeating the pairs over and over to yourself; for the next list, you were asked to create an image linking each word. In that case, the independent variable was the type of strategy you used, with two levels: *repetition* and *interactive imagery*. This variable was manipulated within-subjects because you were exposed to all levels of the independent variable.

Dependent Variables

The dependent variable is what is being observed or measured by the experimenter. In this way, it is said to "depend" on the manipulation of the independent variable. Bransford and Johnson (1972) measured the number of ideas that participants recalled from the paragraph. Good dependent variables reflect measures that remain consistent (termed **reliability**). For example, a reliable dependent variable will yield the same outcome when an experiment is repeated using the same independent variables and levels.

The True Experiment

The experimental approach is often favored in science because it allows cause-and-effect relationships to be identified. That is, researchers want to determine what variables cause which outcomes. Experiments on learning allow researchers to identify variables that cause learning to improve, decline, or stay about the same.

Suppose you have an idea for an experiment. You find that you prefer quiet when you study, but your roommate prefers to work with episodes of *SpongeBob SquarePants* playing in the background. After quickly growing tired of hearing about a character who lives in a pineapple under the sea, you begin to think that listening to *SpongeBob* while studying might hurt learning compared to studying in quiet. So you set out to do an experiment to test your hypothesis. To do this, you find 20 friends who are willing to participate and ask them to learn a list of Swahili words and their English translations. Before they start learning this list, your participants choose whether they would like to study in quiet or with *SpongeBob* blaring in the background.

After studying the words, each group takes a test. To your slightly smug delight, the friends who study in quiet remember more than the friends who prefer *SpongeBob* in the background. Can you conclude that having *SpongeBob* playing in the background hinders learning?

Although this might be an appealing conclusion, you *cannot* say that listening to *SpongeBob* while studying is detrimental to learning. Instead, to draw cause-and-effect conclusions, you must conduct a **true experiment** that has each of the following:

1. An independent variable (i.e., a treatment that is manipulated).
2. **Random assignment** of participants to conditions, meaning that participants must be allocated to levels of an independent variable in a manner that is completely unbiased.

Consider the design used in this example. In that case, participants chose whether to study in quiet or with *SpongeBob* playing in the background. Any resulting differences in memory could be attributed to many different factors. It could be that *SpongeBob* hinders learning but it might also be that individuals who choose to study while listening to *SpongeBob* are simply different in the first place. That is, the superior memory performance under quiet conditions might have nothing to do with background noise and instead might reflect something about the individuals who choose those contexts.

To make this a true experiment, you could retain your original independent variable (type of background noise) and the same levels (quiet vs. *SpongeBob* playing). However, instead of permitting individuals to choose their favored study condition, you could use random assignment to assign your friends to the levels of the variable in a way that is unbiased. For example, you might flip a coin or use a random number generator to determine which level of the independent variable each participant was exposed to. By doing this, you would now be able to address whether a quiet study environment leads to (causes) better learning than studying while listening to the adventures of SpongeBob and Patrick.

Although a true experiment is the ideal approach to determine causality, scientists are sometimes interested in independent variables that cannot be randomly assigned. For example, suppose you were interested in whether middle-schoolers get as much of a benefit out of a practice test as do college students (cf. Carpenter, Pashler, & Cepeda, 2009). This would worthwhile to study, but it would be impossible to do under the auspices of a true experiment. In particular, it would be impossible to randomly assign an individual to be in middle school or college once they show up to your experiment. Experiments like this that focus on differences among people (e.g., gender, ethnicity, age) do not allow for random assignment, but these differences are often valuable to study. Such cases where an experiment is conducted, but random assignment to levels of an independent variable is not possible, are referred to as **quasi-experiments**.

Randomly assigning participants to levels of an independent variable is necessary to have a true experiment.

Elaborative interrogation break
WHY are experiments important?

Consider research on individuals who have a history of alcohol abuse. It is important to understand the effects of alcohol abuse and to establish effective treatments. However, to conduct a true experiment, one would have to randomly assign some individuals to chronically imbibe large amounts of alcohol for many years. This would be deeply unethical.

Instead, to understand whether years of alcohol abuse affects capacities like memory and attention, a quasi-experimental design could be used by selecting individuals with and without a history of alcohol abuse. In doing so, you could understand whether there is an association between alcohol abuse and memory. Causal conclusions are not warranted, though, because it is always possible there is some other characteristic of the groups, aside from alcohol abuse, that might account for any differences in memory. Typically, the best method of controlling for potential differences among participants is to select groups that are as similar as possible in every way aside from the variable or variables that are the focus of the study.

Threats to Experiments

Although an experiment is an ideal way to test scientific claims, it is important that the experiment is well conducted and can indicate whether a variable causes change in an outcome (i.e., whether levels of the independent variable affect the dependent variable). This goal is undermined when factors other than the independent variable(s) influence the results.

These additional, pesky factors that might alter the effect of the independent variable are called **extraneous variables**. For example, suppose your friend believes she has created a revolutionary new way to learn all the lines from classic episodes of *The Simpsons*. She tests this idea in an experiment with a local *Simpsons* fan group. These individuals are shown an episode and instructed to learn the lines hanging upside down on a trapeze (her revolutionary method), or through any other method of their choosing. However, when everyone is tested, your friend discovers that memory was the same between the two conditions.

Does this mean that her new method was ineffective? Maybe. But consider that all participants were sufficiently intense in their *Simpsons* fandom that they belonged to a club devoted to the exploits of Bart and Homer. In this case, they might already know the episodes so well that the method of learning would not matter. Thus an extraneous variable, like the specific participants who were tested, might explain the results. If that was the case, the experiment really does not say much about whether the independent variable caused a change in learning.

A careful experimenter seeks to control all other factors that might influence the dependent variable so as to understand whether an independent variable, and only that variable, causes a change in behavior. These pernicious other factors come in many forms. You have already read about one factor: the nature of the participants being studied. Other examples include whether the task adequately captures the behavior of interest or whether elements of the environment might influence the results. For example, a study of reading in kindergartners will probably not reveal much if the experiment's dependent variable relies on the children understanding a chapter from the Russian literary classic *War and Peace*. Likewise, an unreasonably hot room or loud environment might compromise performance in any experiment (unless that was the goal of the experiment).

Probably the most damaging extraneous variable that influences outcomes is a **confound**—any factor that varies with the manipulation of the independent variable and influences the dependent variable. For example, you might be familiar with the claim that listening to Mozart improves intelligence. This claim has no scientific support (it is a myth) but is based upon a famous experiment (Rauscher, Shaw, & Ky, 1993). Participants in that experiment answered questions used as part of a popular intelligence test that required them to imagine and identify the object that would be created by folding a paper in several ways. Just prior to answering the questions, the participants either listened to 10 minutes of relaxation instructions, sat in silence for 10 minutes, or spent 10 minutes listening to piano sonatas composed by Mozart. The results of the experiment showed that participants who listened to Mozart were better at the paper-folding task than participants who engaged in relaxation or sat silently, translating to an increase of about 8 to 9 IQ points. However, this difference in performance disappeared if there was a 10 to 15 minute delay before starting the paper-folding test.

These results seem relatively modest—listening to a few minutes of classical music temporarily improved performance on a test requiring imagining the object that would be created by folding a piece of paper. And with science being the self-correcting method that it is, other researchers became curious about the finding and ran additional experiments. But media claims following the publication of the original study far exceeded any conclusions that the original experiment ever drew. In fact, it spawned an industry selling products, often aimed at young children, claiming that

Does listening to Mozart improve intelligence?

listening to Mozart improved intelligence. There was only one problem with this claim: The original experiment had a significant confound.

As you will recall, a confound is any factor that varies with the manipulation of the independent variable and influences the outcome. You might have noticed that in the original experiment (Rauscher et al., 1993), two of the conditions encouraged participants to be calm, either through relaxation or sitting in silence. Other researchers hypothesized that listening to Mozart might simply be more exciting than mulling over the world in silence or engaging in deep relaxation. This excitement could temporarily boost alertness and make a participant just a little bit better on a task requiring concentration (like the paper-folding test).

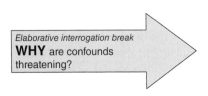

Elaborative interrogation break
WHY are confounds threatening?

To test the idea that classical music simply increased excitement, one group of researchers (Nantais & Schellenberg, 1999) had participants listen to a selection from Mozart and an excerpt from a story by Stephen King. After listening to each, the participants then took the paper-folding test. The number of items participants correctly answered on the paper-folding test is shown in Figure 3.2. As you can see, paper-folding performance was essentially the same in each condition. (No industry arose advocating that babies would be much smarter if they were just read Stephen King stories.)

Other research showed that statistically controlling for the amount of excitement induced by listening to Mozart completely eliminated any benefits (Thompson, Schellenberg, & Husain, 2001). Thus, manipulating

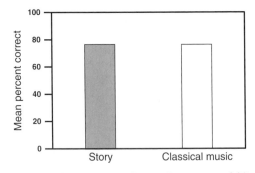

FIGURE 3.2 The percentage of items answered correctly on a paper-folding test after participants listened to classical music or heard a story (adapted from Nantais & Schellenberg, 1999).

whether individuals listened to classical music or sat in silence was confounded with the level of excitement. That is, the level of excitement participants felt also varied with exposure to classical music or silence. The moral of the story: Beware of confounds!

Nonexperimental Methods in Psychology

The experiment is the cornerstone of scientific approaches to learning and memory and underlies most of the advice in this book. But the experiment is not the only method available to science. Indeed, scientists are frequently interested in addressing research questions that do not require an experiment or for which an experiment would be impractical or impossible to conduct. In those cases, the goal is to describe behavior or identify associations between variables.

Correlational Designs

The most common nonexperimental approach in psychology is the **correlational design**, whereby researchers attempt to determine whether there is an association between two variables. That is, are changes in one variable associated with changes in another variable? One element that makes this type of design attractive is that relationships can be distilled into a single number—the correlation coefficient (see Box 3.1).

BOX 3.1   THE CORRELATION COEFFICIENT

The correlation coefficient is a measure of the association between two variables. They vary from −1.00 to +1.00, with a coefficient of 0.00 indicating that there is no relationship. Correlation coefficients are considered on two dimensions:

- **magnitude:** the strength or degree of the relationship. This is given by the absolute value of the coefficient. For example, a correlation of −0.95 is stronger than a correlation of +0.75.
- **sign:** the direction of the relationship.
  - *positive correlation*: as the value of one variable increases, so does the value of the other. For example, when class attendance increases, grades also increase.
  - *negative correlation*: as the value of one variable increases, the value of the other variable decreases. For example, Huff (1954) showed that as exposure to science increases, belief in the paranormal decreases.

A key feature of correlational research is that once a relationship between two variables has been identified, it is possible to make a prediction. For example, insurance companies use driving records to determine the rates they charge. Having a history of prior accidents is correlated with (i.e., predicts) a greater likelihood of future, similar events, increasing the amount that an insurance company will charge for a car policy.

It was correlational research that led to the original Surgeon General's report in 1964 on the dangers of smoking. A number of studies in the 1950s and 1960s had shown a strong, positive correlation association between lung cancer and smoking: The more an individual smoked, the more likely that individual would develop lung cancer. Could this conclusion have been drawn in a true experiment with humans? Consider the conditions necessary for a true experiment: an independent variable and random assignment. It would be highly unethical to randomly assign participants to either smoke or not smoke for years and to track the incidence of lung cancer. This highlights a key benefit of correlational designs—they permit researchers to examine associations between variables when a true experiment is not possible.

Does an association establish a cause-and-effect relationship? No! Correlation does not imply causation. Consider a ritual that takes place at the end of most college courses—the class evaluation. In the evaluation, students rate their like or dislike for the instructor, classroom, and course, among other dimensions. Does a student's grade predict their evaluation of the instructor? Cohen (1981) reviewed many studies on this issue and reported that the average correlation between the instructor rating and a student's grade was +0.43. That is, there was a moderate, positive correlation such that higher grades in a course were associated with better instructor ratings.

Does this mean that better instructors produce students with better grades who are also happier with their course? That is one possible interpretation, but consider a few others. Perhaps the instructor is awful but students base their ratings on their own achievement. Or, perhaps excellent students change the behavior of their instructors enough that the instructor gets a favorable rating. You can also likely think of other interpretations. The key problem is that the correlation coefficient only indicates that there is a relationship between two variables but it does not indicate whether one variable causes the other. So, to repeat one more time: Correlation does not imply causation!

Descriptive Methods

Other nonexperimental methods have the primary goal of describing behavior rather than assessing relationships between variables.

Naturalistic Observation

Suppose you were interested in how college students studied on their own time. One way to investigate this would be to invite some students to the library and ask them to study as they normally would. Would there be any problems with this approach? One possibility is that the students might alter their typical behavior, knowing that they were being observed. You might witness different behaviors if you were to simply sit down at the library and unobtrusively observe students while they study. By carefully observing behavior without directly interacting or intervening with the participants, you would be engaging in naturalistic observation. One of the most notable examples of naturalistic observation involved a group of researchers (Festinger, Reicken, & Schachter, 1956), who infiltrated a doomsday cult and observed reactions to a failed prophecy that the world was ending. Naturalistic observation was also famously used by Jane Goodall to understand the behavior of chimpanzees in the wild. Research in learning and memory makes minimal use of naturalistic observation, although there have been calls for greater understanding of students' behaviors in their "natural habitats" (Daniel & Poole, 2009).

Case Studies

The case study involves the intensive investigation of a single subject. This is typically done when there is something sufficiently unusual or rare about an individual that the phenomena of interest could not be easily studied on a larger scale. Probably the most studied individual in psychology was Henry Molaison, best known by the initials H. M. He suffered from severe epileptic seizures as a young man that required a surgical intervention that removed several parts of the brain that are very important in forming new memories. After that surgery in 1957, H. M. appeared largely unable to learn new information for the remainder of his life. Many researchers conducted case studies of H. M. and documented elements of his memory that were spared or damaged, providing important insights into the neural mechanisms of memory. Other case studies have focused on individuals with extraordinary memory abilities. For example, Parker, Cahill, and McGaugh (2006; see also LePort et al., 2012) documented a woman, A. J., who has a remarkable memory for dates and the events of her life.

Surveys

Do you prefer to study alone or in groups? Would you rather take a class online or in person? How quickly did you grow tired of reading about SpongeBob earlier in this chapter? This succession of questions mimics a survey, an instrument designed to gather detailed, self-reported information about people's attitudes, values, behaviors, and beliefs. You took a short survey at the beginning of Chapter 2 in Demonstration 2.1. Surveys are designed to gather a specific set of information about a large group of people. For example, there are a number of surveys that have asked students about their study behaviors (Hartwig & Dunlosky, 2012; Kornell & Bjork, 2007; Morehead et al., 2016).

Pros and Cons of Descriptive Methods

Each of these descriptive methods has their own benefits and limitations. Surveys are relatively easy to administer and allow lots of data to be gathered, but they rely on the sometimes faulty assumption that participants will accurately report on their attitudes, beliefs, or behaviors. Case studies allow intensive investigation of a single individual, permitting the researcher to document behaviors that are rare. However, because by its very nature the case study focuses on a single case, it is often unclear whether insights gathered from that individual apply to the behavior of others. Naturalistic observation allows the researcher to gain knowledge of behavior in that "natural context," but that can be undermined if individuals are aware they are being observed. More importantly, none of these methods pinpoint the *causes* of behavior—the true experiment is needed for that. But descriptive methods can generate the observations that lead to more carefully controlled research—they can, for example, produce hypotheses that researchers subsequently test in experiments—making them valuable tools for the researcher interested in learning and memory.

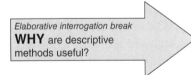

Elaborative interrogation break
WHY are descriptive methods useful?

Combining Experimental and Descriptive Methods

The choice of appropriate research methods is not an either/or proposition. That is, a preference for experiments does not mean that a survey is not a useful tool. In fact, many important questions in learning can only be addressed by using multiple methods. Work on learning styles provides an excellent example of a multifaceted approach combining descriptive and experimental methods.

Do you feel that you have a particular learning style? Is your preferred learning style visual or auditory or kinesthetic? Does having an instructor who teaches to your preferred learning style actually help you to learn better?

Students are often adamant that they have a particular learning style and that teaching to this style helps their learning. Consistent with this, one survey (Morehead et al., 2016) reported that the majority of college students believed that they have a particular learning style, a belief strongly shared by instructors. Similarly, one review (Howard-Jones, 2014) summarized evidence from surveys of teachers in five different countries; the vast majority (93%–97%) believed that learning outcomes were better when students were taught in their preferred learning style.

But recall that any claim should be approached by asking this question: What is the evidence? Fortunately, enough research has been done on learning styles to evaluate the claim.

The central hypothesis of learning styles is that learning will be best when an instructor's style of teaching matches a students' style of learning and will suffer when there is a mismatch. In fact, Figure 3.3 shows you what the data *would* look like if learning styles were real. If an individual were an auditory learner, then learning would be best when instruction was primarily verbal and would suffer when it was not verbal (e.g., if many pictures were used). Likewise, if an individual claimed to be a visual learner, learning should be best following visual instruction compared with verbal instruction.

One study (Massa & Mayer, 2006; see Figure 3.4 for a diagram of their procedure) evaluated this hypothesis by having students learn information in either their preferred or nonpreferred learning style. College students in this study took a variety of surveys and tests to evaluate their supposed learning style. For example, the students reported their SAT (Scholastic Aptitude Test) scores and completed tests that measured verbal and spatial

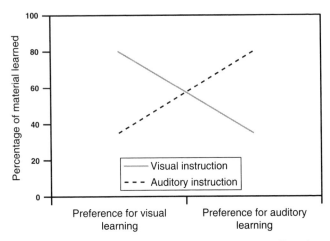

FIGURE 3.3 Hypothetical pattern of data if learning styles were true. If learning styles were true, this is the pattern of data that should be produced, with better learning when the mode of presentation (e.g., visual presentation) matches the style of learning. Research has failed to reveal such a pattern.

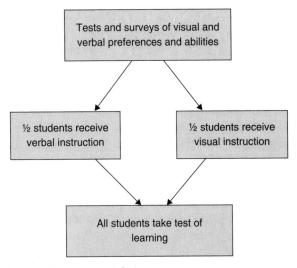

FIGURE 3.4 Massa and Mayer's (2006) design.

ability. Students also answered questions about their preferred learning style such as whether they preferred to learn with text or pictures.

Once all students' learning styles had been assessed, the researchers next had the students participate in an experiment where they read an online lesson about how electricity works. For their independent variable, the researchers manipulated the way information was presented to students when they clicked on key words in their lesson. Specifically, students were randomly assigned to either receive text describing a concept (*verbal instruction*) or an illustration depicting the concept (*visual instruction*). Once the students had finished learning about electricity, they were given a final test assessing their learning.

If learning styles influence learning outcomes, then learning should be best when the style of instruction matches the style of learning (see Figure 3.3 for a reminder of this hypothesis). However, that is not at all what the researchers found. Figure 3.5 shows performance on the final test when divided up by performance on the SAT verbal component. Separating students in this way allowed the researchers to classify some students as "high verbal learners" and others as "high visual learners."

As you can see, the learning style had no effect at all. Consider the students rated as having a verbal learning style (the right side of the figure). They had better scores on the final test when given a visual presentation than when information was presented by text, the very opposite of the learning styles hypothesis. In fact, all students did better with a visual presentation. This is not a style but a regularity of memory that applies widely: Visual information is often beneficial for learning (you will learn more about this in Chapter 6 on imagery in memory). This identical pattern of data, with no indication that a match with a learning style impacts learning, occurred regardless of which measure of learning styles the researchers used.

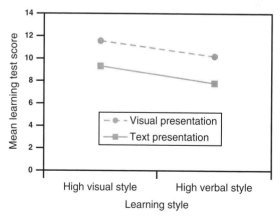

FIGURE **3.5 Learning outcomes for students rated as "high visual" or "high verbal" based on the type of instruction (adpated from Massa & Mayer, 2006).**

The conclusion from other studies investigating learning styles is much the same. In their review of the entire literature, Pashler and colleagues (2008; see also Willingham, Hughes, & Dobolyi, 2015) reported that they were unable to locate any evidence consistent with a learning styles hypothesis. Their final assessment is clear and stinging:

> The contrast between the enormous popularity of the learning-styles approach within education and the lack of credible evidence for its utility is, in our opinion, striking and disturbing. If classification of students' learning styles has practical utility, it remains to be demonstrated. (Pashler et al. 2008, p. 117)

What are the lessons from this research on learning styles? First, given the lack of evidence for learning styles, it is something you simply should not worry about in your own learning. You may have a preference for a particular method of learning, but it does not matter as much as you might think. Presenting information in multiple formats (visual and verbal) is helpful for learning but that applies to most everyone—it is not an individual style.

Second, always ask for the evidence! It is easy to find people who will endorse learning styles with the zealotry of a true believer, but that passion alone is not evidence. Instead, the best information to guide your own learning comes from a scientific approach, preferably grounded in your trusty friend, the experiment.

Putting It All Together

As you might recall from Chapter 2, the best approach to gathering information and drawing conclusions is grounded in the cycle of science (see Figure 2.2). For scientists who study learning, that often takes the form of a carefully controlled experiment that allows conclusions about whether some factor causes changes in learning. You saw this in action at the beginning of the chapter, where a carefully controlled experiment showed that learning was much better if individuals could easily call upon prior knowledge than if this knowledge was not readily available. Not all questions can be answered with an experiment, so the researcher also comes ready with an array of other tools, such as surveys, to help form a more complete understanding of memory. As you read the rest of this book, be sure to focus on the type of method that drives each of the claims made.

Tips You Can Use

1. **When evaluating a claim, determine if an experiment has been performed on the issue.** In seeking experimental evidence, you should rely most heavily on well-conducted true experiments. If an experiment has been conducted, what was manipulated? What was measured? What have these experiments shown? Do the experiments support the claims about learning?

2. **When evaluating a single study, look for confounds or other threats.** When examining only a single experiment, consider whether the methods justify the conclusions, searching for the threats mentioned in this chapter, like potential confounds. When such confounds are present (as in the claim about the Mozart effect), any conclusions are severely undermined.

3. **Seek out more than one study.** If a claim is backed by research, there should be more than a single study supporting it. For example, if examined in isolation, the original work on the Mozart effect (Rauscher, Shaw, & Ky, 1993) might mistakenly indicate that listening to classic music improves intelligence. However, inspection of the wider literature and the many follow-ups to this study shows that classical music probably has no effect on intelligence; it is simply more exciting than other, more sedate comparison conditions. The moral of the story is that a convergence of the same finding among multiple studies provides more support for a claim than an isolated finding.

4. **Do not confuse popularity with the strength of the evidence for a claim.** Simply because a claim is popular and widely accepted does not entail that this claim is true or is supported by significant evidence. For example, learning styles remains a very popular concept and is frequently endorsed by students and teachers (e.g., Howard-Jones, 2014; Morehead et al., 2016). This popularity stands in stark contrast to the scientific evidence on learning styles, which provides no support for the concept. Thus, avoid using popularity as a proxy for evidence. Instead, seek out evidence on learning from experiments and other scientific approaches to learning.

Discussion Questions

1. What distinguishes experimental versus nonexperimental approaches to research in psychology? Discuss, providing specific examples of each approach. When should each approach be used?

2. Experiments are solid grounds for understanding behavior only insofar as they are well conducted. Describe the ingredients of a true experiment and discuss potential threats to the validity of an experiment. How can these threats be effectively managed?

3. Learning styles remain a popular concept among students and educators. How have learning styles been examined scientifically? Based on scientific approaches to learning styles, what conclusions can we draw? For example, should students be concerned with whether their learning style is matched by their instructor? Why does the concept of learning styles remain so popular?

4. Suppose a friend tells you with great confidence that exercise influences learning. How would you respond? What information would you need to endorse this belief? What experimental and nonexperimental approaches would you take to test this belief?

Suggestions for Further Reading

A course in research methodology or statistics is a common feature of any curriculum in psychology. Accordingly, there are a number of books that cover scientific approaches and research methods in great detail. Ralph Rosnow and Robert Rosenthal's (2012) *Beginning Behavioral Research: A Conceptual Primer* is an excellent and accessible introduction to behavioral research. We are also partial to Barry Kantowitz, Henry Roediger, and David Elmes's (2015) *Experimental Psychology*, which superbly covers the research enterprise while providing many concrete examples for students.

Credits

Page 38: Bullstar / Shutterstock
Page 43: alexblacksea / Shutterstock
Page 45: angelo gilardelli / Shutterstock

CHAPTER 4

Metacognition

Understanding Your Own Memory

....

Learning Objectives

- Reading this chapter will help you:
  - ✦ Understand the concept of metacognition.
  - ✦ Appreciate the importance of accurate metacognition in learning.
  - ✦ Know the key steps to improving metacognition.

....

I n Chapter 1 you learned that intuitions about memory are not always accurate. Indeed, these intuitions can sometimes lead learners astray, highlighting the need for a science-based approach to serve

Understanding which topics require further study and which do not is an important part of knowing how to study.

as a guide for knowing how to effectively learn. Your path toward becoming a more effective learner starts by creating a better understanding of how your memory works. In doing so, you will become better at assessing whether you have learned something so that you can identify those topics most in need of further study. Before reading on, try Demonstration 4.1.

DEMONSTRATION 4.1

Try answering each of the questions below. After you answer each question, consider how confident you are that this answer is correct (using a scale from *0%–no way* to *100%–I'm absolutely right*).

What is the name of the largest desert on Earth?

Answer: _____ Confidence _____

Where was the potato first cultivated?

Answer: _____ Confidence _____

What is the name of the house occupied by the President of the United States?

Answer: _____ Confidence _____

What is the capital of Australia?

Answer: _____ Confidence _____

Overall, how confident are you that you answered each of the questions correctly? How confident are you that you answered at least two of the questions correctly?

In fact, three of the four questions were chosen because they are particularly tricky. These questions easily to bring to mind an answer that seems entirely correct, perhaps an answer that you are so confident about that you would bet on its accuracy. The problem is that this high confidence can occur even when you are wrong.

Consider the fourth question: *What is the capital of Australia?* Most people will quickly and confidently respond with "Sydney." It is Australia's most famous city and home to a number of well-known landmarks. To further increase your confidence in this erroneous answer, a picture

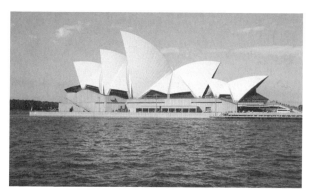

That famous opera house.

of the renowned Sydney Opera House was placed near the question! As you have probably guessed by now, Sydney is not the correct answer. But do not feel bad if you mistakenly answered "Sydney." One study (Tauber et al., 2013) asked hundreds of college students this same question, among many others. Only 1.5% of the participants answered accurately. Most provided *Sydney* as the answer and, on average, were very confident that their (wrong) answer was correct.

Now suppose that you had the opportunity to pick out the correct answer from four choices. If the correct answer was present, how sure are you that you would recognize it? Before reading on, make a judgment of the likelihood that you could pick out the correct city using the following scale: *0%–no way* to *100%–I will absolutely recognize it.*

Now try picking out the capital of Australia from among these choices:

Melbourne
Canberra
Perth
Brisbane

If you picked out Canberra then you are correct. If you did not pick out Canberra, did you also anticipate that you would not be able to pick out the correct answer? In fact, work since the 1960s (Hart, 1965) has shown that people are often very good at identifying whether they will or will not be able to recognize some bit of information they cannot recall.

To answer these questions about how confident you were in an answer, you reflected on your own knowledge and thoughts. Such thinking about your own thinking (i.e., cognition) is referred to as

Metacognition includes our understanding of what we do and do not know.

metacognition. This is a broad term (see Box 4.1) that encompasses all kinds of self-reflection about cognitive processes (Nelson, 1996). For example, among many elements, metacognition includes your knowledge of strategies that are best for learning, your understanding of whether information (like *Sydney*) coming to mind is correct, your ability to accurately predict whether information has been learned well, and your decisions about when, where, how, and for how long to study (see Dunlosky & Metcalfe, 2009; Dunlosky & Tauber, 2016).

The latter two examples are the focus of this chapter. How do you effectively predict whether you will do well on a later test and make decisions about when, where, how, and for how long to study? Many students your authors have worked with report the experience of working hard to prepare for an exam, sure that the material has been mastered, only to receive a poor grade. Often a student will say, "I studied so hard for this exam and was certain I was going to do well. I don't understand how I could have done so poorly." This dispiriting situation can be avoided by applying optimal study strategies and by creating a better understanding of what information has been learned. In other words, enhancing metacognition is part and parcel of becoming a better learner.

BOX 4.1   METACOGNITION IN THE BIG PICTURE

The term "metacognition" applies to much more than behaviors that occur while you are learning. For example, it includes your understanding of your own health, your relationships with other people, and your assessments of your competency in the workplace, among many other functions (see Dunning, Heath, & Suls, 2004). In this way, metacognition can be considered as your thinking about your own cognition applied to virtually any domain in life.

Metacognition: What Is It Good For?

Why should you care about metacognition? For example, suppose that you are well aware that you have not mastered the intricacies of the circulatory system even though an exam on this material will occur tomorrow. Your understanding of what you do and do not know (i.e., your metacognition) might be spot-on, but this knowledge itself will not magically allow you to learn the material.

Assume, though, that you are making this judgment—that the circulatory system remains a bit of a mystery—one week prior to your exam. With that knowledge in hand, you can change the situation. For example, you can set adequate time aside, ensuring that you fre-

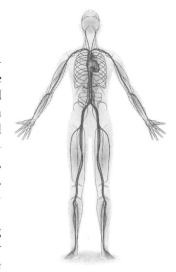

Accurate metacognition can lead to significant improvements in learning about topics such as the circulatory system.

quently spread out your studying (see Chapter 8). You can create some mini-quizzes on the material (see Chapter 9), carefully construct diagrams of the circulation of blood through the heart (see Chapter 6), and practice by trying to teach someone else about the circulatory system (see Chapter 11). In other words, starting with your assessment of what you do and do not know, you can direct your studying to master the material, creating enduring learning for the information.

In a parallel world where you have lots of time, you might do this for all information, regardless of whether you think you know it or not. However, most people have only a limited amount of time available. Thus, how can you strategically focus your time on the information that you most need to study?

This problem gets to the heart of metacognition and is addressed by considering two interrelated processes: monitoring and control (Nelson & Narens, 1990). **Monitoring** is your observation, understanding, and assessment of your own learning. For example, monitoring occurs any time you ask yourself whether you understood a question, whether you are ready for an exam, or whether you are using the best methods of studying. **Control** refers to how you use information gained from monitoring to direct your own learning. For example, if you believe that you did not fully understand Chapter 2 on the nature of science (monitoring), you might use that information and decide to reread Chapter 2 and then test yourself on important elements of the chapter (control). From this perspective, *metacognition reflects all of the processes you use to monitor and control your own learning.*

The key element here is the phrase "your own learning." You probably do not have a live-in tutor who tells you when, where, and how to study. Because most of your learning is up to you, being able to understand and effectively regulate your own learning is crucial. Fortunately, almost 50 years of research provides good reasons to care about metacognition. Here are a few:

1. **Less successful students are often unable to accurately predict their exam performance.** Many studies have asked students to make a prediction of their exam performance prior to taking an exam (e.g., Hacker, Bol, Horgan, & Rackow, 2000; Miller & Geraci, 2011). A common finding from these studies is that students who score higher on an exam are also better at predicting their performance. For example, one group of researchers (Hacker et al., 2000) had students in a psychology class predict their score prior to taking an exam. The results are shown in Figure 4.1, where students are grouped based on exam performance from the lowest

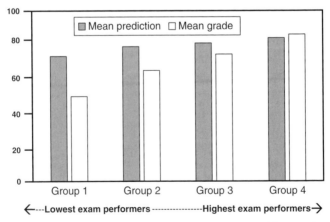

FIGURE 4.1 **Mean exam score predictions and mean grades (adpated from Hacker et al., 2000).**

performers (Group 1) to the highest performers (Group 4). Predictions (gray bars) were pretty close to actual scores on the exam (white bars) for students making better grades (see Groups 3 and 4). In contrast, predictions far exceeded actual scores for students with the lowest grades (Group 1); these students were vastly overconfident. This general pattern of overconfidence does not appear to be easy to eradicate. One study showed that students' predictions remained overconfident across 13 exams (Foster et al., 2017)! Although interesting and potentially informative, note that these are correlational data—they simply demonstrate an association between predictions and grades (see Chapter 3 for more on correlational designs). Being able to better predict your grades does not, by itself, mean that you will get good grades. It is not enough to have good monitoring (i.e., prediction) skills. That monitoring must also lead to better control (i.e., study decisions).

2. **People make decisions about studying based on monitoring.** Research on metacognition has shown that individuals use their monitoring to make decisions about how well they have learned something. They then use the information gained from monitoring to control future efforts at learning. As an example of this principle, consider work showing that people sometimes misjudge learning and then use that misjudgment to guide learning. One study (Rhodes & Castel, 2009) had participants listen to a list of words and predict, for each word, the likelihood that each word would be remembered later. Some of the words were practically shouted at the participants (loud words), whereas others were played at a conversational volume (normal words). People mistakenly believed that loud words would be more memorable than quiet words. As shown in Figure 4.2, however, despite this belief, louder words were no more better remembered than quiet items.

In another experiment assessing control processes (Rhodes & Castel, 2009; see also Metcalfe & Finn, 2008; Soderstrom & Rhodes, 2014), the researchers asked participants, for each word, to indicate whether they wanted to spend more time studying that word. When given this question, participants were almost twice as likely to ask to restudy the normal words. Why did they make this choice? They did this because they mistakenly *believed* the normal words were not learned as well as the loud words and

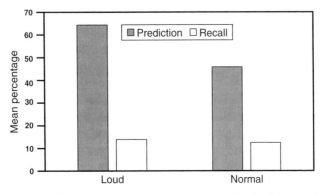

FIGURE **4.2 Mean predictions and mean recall (adpated from Rhodes & Castel, 2009).**

needed more study. In short, participants' monitoring guided their control decisions about how to study.

3. **Learning is often better when people can make their own choices.** Suppose you just read a chapter from your textbook but do not feel confident about your learning. Based on this monitoring, you decide to restudy some sections. Would your learning be better if you decided what to restudy, or if you had a friend make the choices? You might assume that control would be best if you could use your own monitoring to make choices about studying. And you would be correct. For example, students in one experiment (Kornell & Metcalfe, 2006) answered general knowledge questions like the kind given at the opening of this chapter. The students were told that they would need to know the answers for a later test and were asked to choose half of the questions to restudy one more time before the final test. One group of participants restudied the set of questions they chose. Other participants restudied each of the questions they had *not* selected, while a third group restudied a randomly selected set of questions. Performance on the final test was better when people could use their own choices to guide learning than when other sources guided the choices. This suggests that you do best when you can use your own monitoring to guide learning.

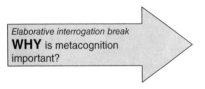

Elaborative interrogation break
WHY is metacognition important?

Ultimately, finely honed metacognition helps to effectively

control and optimize learning. Because of the relationship between monitoring and control, learning will benefit when monitoring is accurate.

Toward an Accurate Understanding of Our Learning

Consider the example that opened Chapter 1. Suppose in the next week you will be responsible for material in a variety of classes: calculus, history, political science, chemistry, and art history. How will you adequately prepare for all of these courses? One solution would be to cloister yourself off from the outside world and do nothing but study each of these subjects.

Few people would find that scenario appealing, let alone realistic. Instead, you probably need to consider each class and assess how well you know the content already. Based on that assessment, you could then plan how you will study. But the assessments will not stop there—as you study, you will need to gauge where you stand. For example, have you learned the key contributions of medieval artists? How complete is your understanding of the various forms of representative democracy? Do you know the properties of ice crystals?

The list can go on, but the broader point is that studying will be best if you can accurately assess your learning and use that information to guide further study. For instance, if you have a good grip on parliamentary versus electoral democracy, you can spend less time reviewing those principles and devote more time to information that you have not yet learned. In order to do that, you need to be able to effectively assess what you do and do not know.

How accurate is monitoring of learning? Research suggests that it is generally sound (Rhodes, 2016). For example, you were probably right to be confident that you knew the answer to the third question at the beginning of this chapter, referring to the White House. You likely also have an immediate sense that you do not know the Lithuanian words for dance (*šokis*) or potato (*bulvė*). (Bonus question: What is the chance—from 0% to 100%—that you could remember the English translation, given the Lithuanian word, if you were asked about each of these words later?)

However, in a number of cases monitoring conflicts with actual learning. You came across some instances of poor monitoring previously in this chapter. For example, one study showed that students frequently overestimate their exam performance (Hacker et al., 2000; see Figure 4.1). Another study (Rhodes & Castel, 2009; Figure 4.2) showed that people mistakenly predicted that loud words would be much more memorable than quiet words. Before reading on, try Demonstration 4.2.

You might have noticed that some of the words were quite large in size, and others were smaller. Were your ratings the same for the large and small words? Most people given this task rate the large words as much easier to remember than the small words (Rhodes & Castel, 2008), and have a general belief that large words are easier to remember (Kornell, Rhodes, Castel, & Tauber, 2011; Mueller, Dunlosky, Tauber, & Rhodes, 2014). However, the size of the word has little to do with whether you

---

DEMONSTRATION 4.2

Study each word below for about 2–4 seconds. Once you are finished studying, indicate how likely you are to remember this word on a scale from 1 (*no way!*) to 7 (*got it!*).

lake	Rating: _____
advice	Rating: _____
solution	Rating: _____
disease	Rating: _____
target	Rating: _____
temple	Rating: _____
seat	Rating: _____
shadow	Rating: _____
mantle	Rating: _____
agent	Rating: _____
stream	Rating: _____
wage	Rating: _____

Now, step away from your text and try writing down as many words as you can remember.

remember it. This makes sense: The physical characteristics of what you are trying to learn generally do not matter; it is what you do to give meaning to information that drives learning (see Chapter 5 on elaboration for much more on this idea). Regardless, the important point is that what might be called "monitoring illusions," such as the mistaken belief that the size of a word is important for learning, indicate that intuitions about learning are not always correct.

These are just a few examples, but the research literature is filled with instances of significant discrepancies between individuals' understanding of their own learning and actual learning (see e.g., Kornell & Bjork, 2009). Because monitoring plays such a vital role in how people engage in learning, it is important to reduce these kinds of errors and more accurately assess learning. Just as nearly five decades of research on metacognition indicates why you should care about it, that same bevy of research provides tips on how to improve your metacognition. The best advice on improving metacognition can be condensed to two principles: wait and test!

Delay: The Joys of Waiting

Metacognition will be at its most accurate when you can correctly distinguish between information that has already been learned and information not yet mastered. For example, imagine for a geography class that you are comfortable with Malthusian approaches to population growth but feel less confident about your knowledge of more modern perspectives. Suppose you were also quizzed at this juncture about the finer points of each set of theories. If your metacognition was accurate, you should find that you had a firm grip on Malthus but were less conversant with later developments. However, what if it turned out that despite your confidence in your understanding of Malthusian approaches, you could not tell the difference between Malthus and Milk Duds? Such poor metacognition would probably be detrimental, because you would have the illusion that you had mastered Malthus when you had not.

Poor monitoring often occurs when you pay attention to information that is not predictive of whether true learning has occurred. For example, recall the description of Kornell and Bjork's (2008) work from Chapter 1: they asked students to assess their knowledge of artists' styles if their paintings were presented all at once (blocked) or interspersed among different artists (interleaved). Participants rated blocking as

A key method of improving our monitoring of learning is to wait.

much more effective for learning than interleaving, even though interleaving was a far better way to learn each artist's style (see Figure 1.4).

One possible reason for this error in judgment is that participants were misled by seeing the same artists' paintings over and over in succession. In this kind of presentation, it *feels* in the moment like the information has been learned. That is, in the moment, what makes a Monet a Monet seems obvious, sitting right there in front of you. Students often report a similar experience when they study. For example, they might read the same section of their textbook a few times and focus on the key words. In that moment that they are rereading the section, the information *feels* very clear and easy to access. From this feeling of **fluency**—from this ease of processing and ease of access—students assume that the information must have been truly learned (cf. Kelley & Rhodes, 2002). The issue is that this in-the-moment *feeling* of fluency is not a solid index of whether you have truly learned the material. In fact, very often, such in-the-moment feelings can lead you astray in your assessments of your learning.

The key problem is this: *What you experience in the moment does not tell you about durable learning.* That is, your momentary mental experiences are often not a good indicator of whether durable, long-lasting learning has taken place (Benjamin, Bjork, & Schwartz, 1998). Having just read a key term, having just seen a Monet painting, or having just reviewed a proof does not necessarily mean that you know the concept, can identify a Monet, or understand the proof. Instead, moment-to-moment experiences can be misleading and give the mistaken impression that information has been learned.

Fortunately, there is a simple method to avoid this problem: *Get out of the moment and wait to judge your learning.* With a delay, you can get away from information that will only be available temporarily and achieve a better sense of whether the information has actually been learned. For example, how likely are you to remember the English translation to each of these Lithuanian words?

šokis?   RATING: _____
bulvė?   RATING: _____

You were asked this question a few minutes (paragraphs) ago. When it was first presented, your rating might have been guided by how much the word looked like an English word, by whether the sound of the word was similar to an English word, and so on. How did you make your rating now?

You may have noticed that now those details really had little influence on your judgment. Instead, you likely tried to recall the English word and then used your success or failure to make your judgment. This is much better information to use to understand your learning than whatever you might have focused on when you were first shown *šokis.* That is, the outcome of your quick test is diagnostic because it diagnoses the state of your long-term memory. There are many studies showing that making predictions based on information gained after a delay gives you much more diagnostic information, and thus leads to much more accurate metacognition, than predictions made using information gleaned immediately after learning (see Rhodes & Tauber, 2011, for a review).

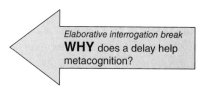

Elaborative interrogation break
WHY does a delay help metacognition?

Learning Foreign Language Vocabulary

One study (Thiede & Dunlosky, 1994; see also Scheck, Meteer, & Nelson, 2004) had participants learn almost 60 Swahili–English translations such as *dafina*–treasure. For each pair, participants made a prediction of whether the English translation could be recalled if given the Swahili word (e.g., *dafina–?*). For half of the pairs this prediction was made immediately after studying; for the other half of the pairs, participants made their prediction after a delay of at least a few minutes. Once the words had been studied and all predictions made, participants were given a test of their memory for the English translations. Delaying judgment led to much more accurate predictions about the outcome of the final test than making immediate judgments.

Learning Text

Waiting to make a judgment might be fine for learning pairs of words, but does it apply to much meatier learning? For example, does waiting to assess learning help when reading many sentences, paragraphs, or pages (what researchers call *text*)? The answer is a clear yes! Consider one study (Thiede, Anderson, & Therriault, 2003) that had participants read paragraphs of text on a diverse array of topics ranging from Norse settlements to the naval strategies of World War II. Participants were asked to write down a few keywords about each text. For example, if the text was about the *Titanic*, a participant might write *shipwreck, tragedy, iceberg*. But there was a catch that you can see in Figure 4.3, which shows the design of the experiment. Half of the participants wrote down their keywords immediately after reading the paragraph (*immediate keyword group*), whereas other participants wrote down their keywords after they had read each text (*delayed keyword group*). Next, participants predicted how well they understood each text and then took a test that asked them to remember some specific information from each text and also draw inferences.

Overall, predictions were much more accurate for the delayed keyword group compared to the immediate keyword group. This makes sense; when generating keywords immediately, it would be easier to remember a few choice terms that had been read mere seconds ago. However, at a delay, you cannot rely on what you just saw and instead will only have access to what you actually retained from the text—what "stuck," so to speak. This will be a much better basis for predictions.

But making more accurate predictions would be of little value if they did not aid learning. The second phase of the experiment shows why accurate predictions matter. After taking the first test, participants were given the option to restudy as many of the texts as they wanted. Once they had a chance to reread the selected texts they were given a second test with a new set of questions.

Figure 4.4 shows the percentage of questions correctly answered on both tests. On the first test (left side of the figure), performance was

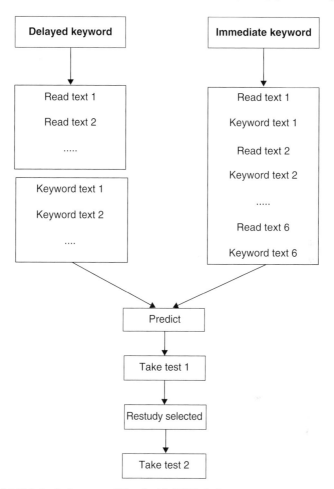

FIGURE **4.3 Thiede, Anderson, and Therriault's (2003) design.**

almost identical for both groups. However, on the second test (right side of the figure), the delayed keyword group remembered much more than the immediate keyword group. This occurred because their superior monitoring allowed individuals in the delayed keyword group to make better selections of what to study again.

The moral of this story: Delaying judgment improves monitoring and also puts you in a good position to improve learning (but see Kimball, Smith, & Muntean, 2012).

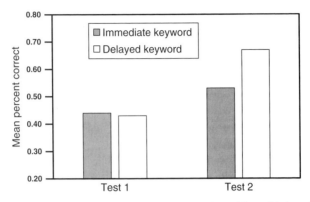

FIGURE 4.4 **Mean percentage correct on test 1 and test 2 (adapted from Thiede et al., 2003).**

Test: The Value of Testing

You might have noticed a common thread in the discussion of the benefits of delaying judgment. In each case, participants could test themselves before making their judgment. For example, the participants learning Swahili words (Thiede & Dunlosky, 1994) were given the word in Swahili and asked to make a prediction of the likelihood that they could recall the English translation, using cues like this: *dafina*–?. Similarly, the work on the delayed keyword effect (Thiede, Anderson, & Therriault, 2003) required participants to generate a list of keywords for each text prior to judging comprehension.

This pattern is no accident. Testing not only improves learning (see Chapter 9 for much more on this topic), but testing also enhances your monitoring of your own learning (King, Zechmeister, & Shaughnessy, 1980; Kornell & Rhodes, 2013). Indeed, testing appears to drive the improvements to monitoring that occur at a delay.

For example, one group of researchers (Kornell & Rhodes, 2013) had participants first learn a list of Indonesian words and the corresponding English translations (e.g., *pasar*–market). Once all of the pairs had been studied, some of the participants were given a test on each word pair (e.g., *pasar* means ?), whereas others studied the entire pair one more time. After either the test or studying the word again, participants predicted the likelihood that they could remember the English translation on a second test.

Note that a key feature of this experiment is that *all* judgments were made at a delay. If it was just the delay that improved how well participants understood their own learning, then predictions should have been equally accurate in both conditions. However, that is not at all what happened. Participants given a test had nearly perfect prediction accuracy, far better than prediction accuracy for individuals who simply studied the pair again (see also Dunlosky & Nelson, 1992).

This finding is consistent with lots of other research. For example, as discussed previously, waiting to generate a few keywords from texts makes for very accurate predictions (Thiede, Anderson, & Therriault, 2003). In further experiments (Thiede, Dunlosky, Griffin, & Wiley, 2005; see also Anderson & Thiede, 2008), the researchers showed that it is *generating* keywords at a delay that makes predictions so good. That is, simply reading a few keywords at a delay is no better for predictions than generating keywords immediately.

Why does testing at a delay help monitoring (or more broadly, meta-cognition)? For one, engaging in a test forces learners to consider not only what they are reading or thinking of in the moment, but also what is available in long-term memory. Consider this question: What is the capital of Australia? You could determine this by thinking about what you know of Australia, the information given at the beginning of this chapter, and so on. However, none of those activities allows you to directly assess what you learned quite as well as actually attempting to retrieve the answer from memory. That leads to the second feature that makes testing so good for metacognition: The result of a delayed test will indicate what memory will be like in the future. Without additional study or feedback, what can be remembered now provides a glimpse of what can be remembered in the future. Because of that feature, the act of testing not only enhances learning but also enhances metacognition. This means that testing at a delay can enable better choices about what needs further study and what has already been learned.

Elaborative interrogation break
WHY does testing help metacognition?

Two Bonus Methods of Improving Your Understanding of Your Own Learning

"Wait and test" is a solid formula for assessing your own learning and will treat you well if implemented faithfully. But that is not the end of the activities that can improve your metacognition. Here are two more methods of enhancing your understanding of your learning.

1. **Explain yourself.** How does a zipper or a cell phone work? When given questions like this, most individuals are woefully overconfident in their understanding of a complex process: They believe they have a much better grasp of the process than they actually do. One study (Rozenblit & Keil, 2002) suggests that a highly effective way to puncture this overconfidence is to have people fully explain a process (in a step-by-step fashion). A similar tip can also help you while you are studying. Rather than assume that you understand a complex process like photosynthesis, you will be a better judge of your understanding if you attempt to explain the process and then reference your answer against an expert answer. Not only will producing an explanation allow you to better see the strengths and weaknesses in your knowledge, but this act of explaining a process will also improve learning (Needham & Begg, 1991). So the next time you study, try explaining what you know to someone else and then check your explanation against an expert explanation.

2. **Understand what you need to know.** It may sound painfully obvious, but you will be better able to understand what you have and have not learned if you have a good grip on what you need to know. That is, it is difficult to achieve accurate monitoring

Explain how this works.

if you do not understand what you need to learn. For instance, consider one study (Thomas & McDaniel, 2007) that had students read texts on a variety of topics (e.g., Mount Kilimanjaro). These students were either encouraged to carefully attend to the details of the text or to consider interconnections among ideas in the text. All participants then made a prediction of how well they understood the text and were given one of two types of tests: The test either emphasized small details (e.g., the size of Kilimanjaro) or an understanding of the broader themes in the text (e.g., considering why would snow travel downhill faster on Kilimanjaro than in the Alps). Predictions were accurate when the way participants studied the material matched the type of test (e.g., participants studied for detail and were tested on detail). However, the predictions were downright terrible when there was a mismatch (e.g., participants studied for detail and were tested on themes). That is, participants' predictions were hopeless when they did not have a good grip on how they would be tested. The lesson here: Predictions will have the greatest chance of being accurate if you can match your studying to the way you will be tested (see Chapter 10 for more information on this).

Putting It All Together

Metacognition refers to a wide array of processes involved in understanding your own cognition. The classic approach is to divide metacognition into those processes responsible for assessing your learning (monitoring) and those processes involved in regulating your learning (control). This chapter focused on steps that will be most helpful in effectively understanding your own learning. The best way to achieve this understanding can be condensed into these steps:

Study→Wait→Test→Explain (Repeat as necessary).

Having effective metacognition, in and of itself, will not assure effective learning, just as knowing that you need a job and sending out a resume will not automatically get you a job and put money in your pocket. Instead, knowledge about the current state of your learning can be used to decide what to study, how to study, and how much to study. In short, effective monitoring of your own learning can help you to be strategic in your studying in a way that will help you to optimize your learning in a manageable amount of time. To truly maximize your learning, though, you must pair effective metacognition with knowledge of the best study strategies. The remainder of this book focuses on the study strategies that are more likely to lead to durable learning.

Tips You Can Use

1. **Overcome the inclination to use your in-the-moment impressions as a gauge of your learning.** It can be quite tempting to quickly review your notes, repeat the information to yourself, and feel as though you have learned well. Do not fall prey to these in-the-moment impressions. Indeed, many approaches to learning that are ineffective, such as repeating information over and over to yourself (see Chapter 5 on elaboration), give you the illusion that you are learning. Moreover, other techniques that feel more effortful may not feel in the moment that they are working. Learn to overcome these in-the-moment impressions and instead trust the science on what works.

2. **Wait and test.** How should you gauge your learning if should not rely on your in-the-moment impressions? Wait and test. Be sure to wait long enough so that the information is no longer fresh in your mind. Then test yourself and see how you do. For example, you could learn a set of concepts in the morning and then test yourself that evening or the next day (see Chapter 8 for ideal ways to spread out your learning). This approach of waiting and testing is an excellent way to gauge your learning and your progress. And it also comes with the bonus that testing is a great method of promoting enduring learning (see Chapter 9).

3. **Explain it to someone else.** Even if it is only to a pet or a stuffed animal, attempting to put a concept into your own words to explain it to someone else can serve as an excellent index of your own learning. Explaining forces you to retrieve key information, connect concepts, and logically describe ideas. For the most bang for your buck, try explaining what you are learning and check your explanation against an expert answer.

4. **Understand what you need to learn.** Monitoring will have the chance to be the most accurate when you are aware of what you need to learn. For example, suppose you have an upcoming test in a class on European history in the early twentieth century. It will be important to know whether this test will largely focus on dates, key figures,

and geography, or on concepts that drove Europe toward the Great War. Without a sense of what you need to learn, it will be difficult to compare your knowledge to the standard you are seeking.

Discussion Questions

1. Describe how monitoring and control operate during learning. For example, consider the interplay of monitoring and control as a student prepares for an exam. How does monitoring feed into control during this process? How would control affect monitoring?
2. Monitoring of your own learning will be effective to the degree that you can use diagnostic information to make judgments. What kinds of information will be diagnostic? What study strategies and steps can you take to ensure that your monitoring is based on diagnostic information?
3. The primary strategy suggested in this chapter to enhance metacognition is to wait and test. How can this approach be applied to your own learning?
4. How effective is your own monitoring? As a method of examining this, try predicting your score for any exams or quizzes you will take over the next month. Are your predictions accurate? If so, why do you believe this is the case? If not, what can you do to improve your predictions?

Suggestions for Further Reading

There are a number of excellent works on metacognition for those interested in delving more into processes related to monitoring and control of learning. *Metacognition* (2009), by two leading researchers in the area (John Dunlosky and Janet Metcalfe) is a highly readable and thorough treatment of the topic. Dunlosky and Sarah "Uma" Tauber have also edited a recent book on metacognition (*The Oxford Handbook of Metamemory*, 2016) that summarizes much of the latest scholarship. Beyond book-length treatments, there are several excellent reviews of metacognition available. Among our favorites is a recent review from Robert Bjork and colleagues (Bjork, Dunlosky, & Kornell, 2013) and a classic synopsis of metacognition from Asher Koriat (2007). Thomas Nelson (1996) also provides a highly accessible introduction to metacognition that is grounded in a broader literature from philosophy.

Credits

Page 57: Monkey Business Images / Shutterstock

Page 59: Tang Yan Song / Shutterstock

Page 64: Republished with permission of Springer, from Metacognitive illusions for auditory information: Effects on monitoring and control. Rhodes, M. G., & Castel, A. D. Psychonomic Bulletin & Review, 16, 550–554, 2009. Permission conveyed through Copyright Clearance Center, Inc.

Page 60: pathdoc / Shutterstock

Page 61: metamorworks / Shutterstock

Page 68: Raul Farfan / Shutterstock

Page 74: Denys Prykhodov / Shutterstock

....

CHAPTER 5

Can You Expand On That?

Boosting Learning and Retention by Elaborating

....

Learning Objectives
- Reading this chapter will help you:
  ◆ Understand and provide examples of elaboration.
  ◆ Distinguish between rote methods of learning and elaboration.
  ◆ Appreciate how elaboration improves learning.
  ◆ Know how to effectively apply elaboration in your own learning.

....

Look at the drawings shown in Demonstration 5.1. All of these drawings depict the head of a US penny, but only one of them is completely accurate in all of its details. Can you pick out the correct one? Before continuing, select the one you believe to be correct.

A group of college students in the United States also tried to select the correct alternative (Nickerson & Adams, 1979). Across the 36 participants, there were a variety of opinions, with eight different drawings being chosen. Fewer than half (42%) of the participants made the correct choice. In the same study, a second group of participants tried to draw both sides of a penny from memory. Ninety percent omitted the word "Liberty" (one of the elements on the head of a penny) and 50% had Abraham Lincoln facing in the wrong direction (he should be facing to the right).

DEMONSTRATION 5.1 Examine the drawings of the head of a US penny shown below.

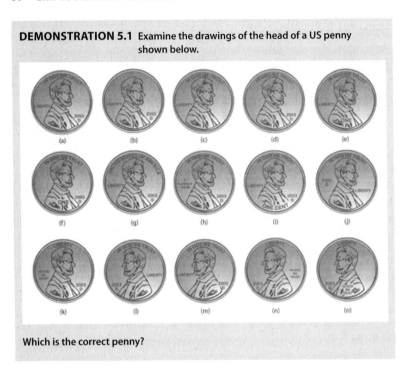

Which is the correct penny?

Consider the implications of this for a moment. The typical college student in the United States has seen the head of a penny countless times. When this research was done in the late 1970s, most financial transactions involved hard currency, so the participants in the study probably saw pennies on a daily basis. Yet memory for a penny was surprisingly poor. (The correct choice, by the way, is drawing A.)

This surprising observation is not restricted to pennies. For example, one study showed that employees in an office building had poor memory for the buttons on the elevator they used each day (Vendetti, Castel, & Holyoak, 2013; see also Castel, Vendetti, & Holyoak, 2012). Another study (Blake, Nazarian, & Castel, 2015) asked a group of 89 college students to draw the Apple logo as accurately as possible from memory. Only one of the 89 students could draw it perfectly, even though the group included a number of individuals who used Apple products on a daily basis and thus saw the logo multiple times a day. Clearly, repeated exposure to information—even at extraordinary levels—is not sufficient to produce strong learning. Other work confirms and extends this finding.

Repetition and Rote Memorization

Just as repeatedly seeing something every day (like a penny or the elevator at work) does not suffice for producing good learning and retention, repeating information to yourself—

Elaborative interrogation break
WHY does high exposure NOT ensure good memory?

engaging in what memory researchers call "rote rehearsal"—is not an effective learning strategy, especially relative to other possible methods. You already saw this in Chapter 1 when you attempted to remember word pairs using repetition versus imagery (see Demonstration 1.1 and Figure 1.1). Yet the relative ineffectiveness of repetition probably runs counter to your beliefs and intuitions. Indeed, students frequently report that repeating something over and over to themselves *is* an effective way to commit it to memory (e.g., Karpicke, Butler, & Roediger, 2009).

A now-classic study (Glenberg, Smith, & Green, 1977) shows the futility of engaging in lots of rote repetition. In this experiment, participants were given a four-digit number to remember (e.g., *1654*). After seeing the number, a word was presented (e.g., *dog*). Participants were instructed to repeat this word aloud for the stated purpose of preventing them from thinking about the number. Participants were then prompted to recall the number. Overall, there were 60 trials, with participants learning a number, rehearsing a word, and then recalling the number.

But the researchers were not actually interested in recall of the numbers. Instead, they were interested in participants' later memory for the various words that were repeated throughout the experiment. Some of these words were repeated for 2 seconds, others for 6 seconds, and still others for 18 seconds. After all of the trials and a delay of several minutes, participants were given a surprise test for those words, allowing the researchers to examine recall after varying amounts of repetition. They found that repetition did not reliably improve memory: Recall was at 11%, 7%, and 12% for the 2-, 6-, and 18-second conditions, respectively.

The type of rehearsal that was used in this study has been termed **maintenance rehearsal**. It involves the rote repetition of information (e.g., saying a word to yourself repeatedly) to maintain the information in your current thoughts. Maintenance rehearsal may temporarily keep information in mind, but it is *not* very effective for forming durable, long-lasting memories (Craik & Lockhart, 1972). Although students find the perils of maintenance rehearsal to be counterintuitive it is actually a well-established finding.

As an illustrative example, one famous study on maintenance rehearsal (Craik & Watkins, 1973) asked participants to listen to a list of words similar to those shown on the left-hand side of Figure 5.1. Prior to hearing the words, participants were given a critical letter that indicated which words should be repeated. For the example in Figure 5.1, the critical letter might be "g," indicating that participants should repeat those words (and only those words) that begin with the letter "g." The set of words was then presented one at a time using an audio tape player. Upon hearing a word that began with the critical letter, participants were instructed to say it to themselves over and over again until a new word was presented that began with the critical letter.

In this example, participants would skip over the first three words in the list because they do not begin with the critical letter. But when *gun* is presented, they would repeat *gun* to themselves. They would do this until the next critical word comes up, *gift*, at which time they would stop repeating *gun* and start repeating *gift*. The repetition of *gift* would continue as the subsequent words *train*, *picture*, and *coffee* were presented, until the new critical word, *garden*, was given. And so on throughout the list. At the end of the list, participants were prompted to report the final word that began with the critical letter. For this example, they would report *ground*.

Note that in the sample list given in Figure 5.1, some critical words were immediately followed by other critical words. *Gun*, for example, was immediately followed by *gift*. With this set up, *gun* would only be repeated during the presentation of *gun* itself. Other critical words, like *glass*, were followed by three noncritical words (words that did not start with *g*). *Glass* would be repeated during the presentation of *glass* itself, but would also be repeated during the presentation of *king*, *table*, and *artist*. By varying the number of intervening words between the critical words, the researchers varied how much maintenance rehearsal participants engaged in.

For this experiment, the researchers gave participants many different lists, and across the lists, varied the number of intervening words from 0 to 12. This would mean that some words were not rehearsed at all

Word list	
lock	doctor
boat	jacket
snake	lunch
gun	gate
gift	glass
train	king
picture	table
coffee	artist
garden	ground

Number of intervening words	
Zero	Three
gun	gift
gate	garden
ground	glass

FIGURE 5.1 List construction used in Craik and Watkins (1973).

while other words were rehearsed up to 12 times. After going through all of the lists and reporting the final critical word for each one, participants took a surprise memory test and tried to recall as many words as they could from the entire experiment. If the amount of maintenance rehearsal drove memory, then items rehearsed more often should be recalled more often.

The results shown in Figure 5.2 tell a very different story. As you can see, more maintenance rehearsal did not translate into reliably better memory: Recall was nearly identical for numerous repetitions (19% recall with 12 intervening words) and for very few repetitions (17% recall with zero intervening words). Many additional studies show that massed, rote learning produces only modest improvements in memory (e.g., Craik, Routh, & Broadbent, 1983; Stoff & Eagle, 1971).

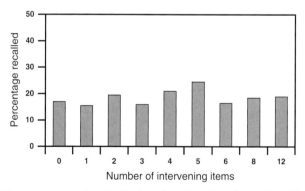

FIGURE 5.2 Percentage correct on the final recall test based on the number of intervening words or amount of maintenance rehearsal (adpated from Craik & Watkins, 1973).

Elaborative interrogation break
WHY does rote rehearsal
NOT ensure good memory?

Why is rote repetition such a poor learning strategy? Indeed, even a lot of repetition—when that repetition takes the form of blocked, rote rehearsal—does not boost retention very much. In the same way that you may have failed to recognize the correct penny in the picture at the start of this chapter, despite having seen pennies countless times throughout your life, you may also fail to remember information that you study over and over again through rote memorization.

Unfortunately, this observation runs counter to beliefs commonly held by students. Each of your authors has had the experience of speaking with students who were disappointed in an exam score, with a student earnestly explaining that he or she had studied for many hours. The implication is that the sheer amount of time spent studying should have ensured strong exam performance. There is reason to applaud any student willing to put in the time to succeed, but a focus only on the time spent studying misses the point. That is, the *quantity* of time spent studying is irrelevant if the *quality* of the time is poor. Indeed, many hours spent poring over notes and readings will count for little if the strategy used amounts to low-quality maintenance rehearsal that might only give the illusion of high-quality learning (see Box 5.1).

BOX 5.1   REPETITION AND LEARNING ILLUSIONS

Repeating something over and over to yourself helps you to maintain it in your current thoughts, but that can lead you astray in your understanding of what you will remember later on (see Chapter 4). Having the information currently accessible because you are now thinking about it makes it feel as if it will be accessible later on. But that same information, once no longer in your awareness, might actually be quite difficult to retrieve at a later point in time. How often have you found yourself thinking, "Oh I'll surely remember that," only to find that later on, you cannot? The feeling of accessibility in the moment might be partly to blame for mistaken predictions about how memorable something will be later on. A much better gauge of how well you will remember something is to set it aside and then test yourself (see Chapter 4 for more details on this strategy).

DEMONSTRATION 5.2a

For each question shown below, read the question, then read the word to its right, and say to yourself "yes" or "no" based on how the words fits with the question. Go through each question one at a time, in the order shown, until you have gone through all of the questions.

Is the word a type of animal?	duck	Yes or No?
Is the word shown in capital letters?	TREE	Yes or No?
Does the word rhyme with horn?	coat	Yes or No?
Is the word shown in capital letters?	pencil	Yes or No?
Does the word rhyme with smell?	bell	Yes or No?
Is the word a type of vehicle?	ear	Yes or No?
Does the word rhyme with shook?	book	Yes or No?
Is the word shown in capital letters?	HAIR	Yes or No?
Is the word a type of insect?	bee	Yes or No?
Is the word shown in capital letters?	film	Yes or No?
Is the word shown in capital letters?	worm	Yes or No?
Is the word a type of vegetable?	apple	Yes or No?
Does the word rhyme with small?	sofa	Yes or No?
Does the word rhyme with weight?	gate	Yes or No?
Is the word a type of building?	shoes	Yes or No?
Is the word shown in capital letters?	NOSE	Yes or No?
Does the word rhyme with blue?	truck	Yes or No?
Is the word a type of occupation?	nurse	Yes or No?

What *does* help to form lasting memories if repeating things over and over is not a sound strategy? What matters most is *how* you study, not *how long* you study. Try Demonstration 5.2a before continuing.

Quality of Processing

As you went through Demonstration 5.2a, you likely noticed that there were three types of questions given. Some questions asked you to judge whether the word was in capital letters. Others asked you to judge whether the word rhymed with another word. Still others asked you to judge whether the word belonged to a category. These questions are called **orienting questions**, because they orient you toward thinking about (processing) the words in qualitatively different ways—either by their visual appearance (i.e., judging whether words were in capital letters), sound (i.e., judging whether words rhymed with other words), or meaning (i.e., judging whether words belonged to a category). Before continuing any further, go to Demonstration 5.2b and follow the instructions.

Did your memory for the words differ depending on the type of question you initially answered about them? Take a look at how well you remembered the words you thought about in terms of their visual appearance, versus words you thought about in terms of their sound, versus words you thought about in terms of their meaning. Which did you remember best? Research shows that memory is much better when people think about the meaning of information.

Demonstration 5.2b is an adaptation of the method used in an often-cited study from memory literature (Craik & Tulving, 1975). In that study, the researchers reported 10 different experiments that varied the way that participants processed information during initial learning by using different types of orienting questions. Memory was examined with different types of tests, including free recall tests (as done here), cued recall tests (in which the orienting questions were given as memory cues), and recognition tests (in which participants were shown a word and decided whether they had seen it in the earlier question-and-answer session).

Consider one set of results taken from the study, for orienting questions that required participants to indicate whether a word was in upper or lowercase letters (case judgments), whether the word rhymed with another word (rhyme judgments), or whether it fit into a category

DEMONSTRATION 5.2b
Take out a blank piece of paper. This will serve as your answer sheet. Without looking back to the previous page in your textbook, try to write all of the words that you saw in the question-and-answer session just a few moments ago. Once you get to the point that you are struggling to think of any additional words, turn to the back of the chapter for the correct answers and see how well you did.

(category judgments). Importantly, all participants were given the same amount of time to learn each word across the different orienting conditions. If time was all that mattered for memory, there should be no difference across these conditions. However, there were substantial differences when participants were given a final, surprise recognition test. In particular, words that were processed for meaning, such as judging the category a word fit into, were much more likely to be correctly recognized (78%) than words assessed for rhyming (57%), or words that were judged as being presented in lowercase or uppercase letters (16%). This pattern of superior memory for considering the meaning of information has been observed in numerous follow-up studies.

The finding that memory varies according to the type of processing during learning is called the **levels of processing effect**. The idea is that information can be processed or studied in qualitatively different ways—in terms of visual appearance, phonemics (sound), or semantics (meaning). Thinking about information in terms of its meaning is considered a **deep** (rather than **shallow**) level of processing, and this commonly results in better memory (Craik & Lockhart, 1972).

In contrast to studies showing limited effects of the quantity of maintenance rehearsal, findings such as these demonstrate reliable effects of the type or quality of study, with semantic processing (thinking about meaning) enhancing learning and retention relative to non-semantic processing. This also leads to a key question: How can you engage in high-quality studying with meaning in mind?

Interim Summary: Taking Stock of What You've Learned

Thus far, you have learned that repeated exposure to information does not ensure that it will lead to long-lasting, durable learning. Likewise, simply reading or saying information over and over to yourself does not ensure that it will be retained well. The amount of time you study, when it takes the form of maintenance rehearsal or rote memorization, does not reliably enhance learning. More important is the quality of study. How can you enhance the quality of your studying?

Elaboration

Some types of processing (semantic) tend to enhance learning more than other types of processing (nonsemantic). But that is not the full story. Learning and memory also reflects the degree of **elaboration**—the extent to which learning is enriched by integrating information and forming associations.

Consider an experiment (Craik & Tulving, 1975) that asked participants to complete a question-and-answer session in which they saw orienting questions followed by words. Each question asked whether a presented word fit within a given sentence in a meaningful way. As an example, participants might have seen the question, *Does the word fit in the sentence: "He dropped the _____"?* This might then be followed by a presentation of the word *watch*. Having determined that *watch* completes the sentence, participants would respond *yes*. Because all questions in this experiment required such sentence-completion judgments, all involved semantic processing. What varied, though, was the complexity of the sentence frame. The sentence described is an example of a simple sentence frame. A complex, elaborate sentence frame for the word *watch* might be, *The old man hobbled across the room and picked up the valuable _____ from the mahogany table.*

Participants saw simple, medium, and complex sentence frames and were later given a surprise memory test. Some participants completed a free recall test in which they tried to recall as many of the words as they could from the earlier part of the experiment. Other participants completed a cued recall test with sentence frames given as cues to recall the previously presented words.

Figure 5.3 shows performance on the free recall test (left side) and cued recall test (right side) across the three different complexity conditions, when the words fit within the sentence frames. Memory was consistently much better, on both types of tests, with more complex sentence frames (white bars).

A common interpretation of this result is that the more complex sentence frames encourage greater elaboration—forming more associations—and therefore create a more integrated, enriched memory. Consider the sample sentences given above. There is little opportunity to form associations between the word *watch* and the elements of the simple sentence frame, *He dropped the _____*. In contrast, the complex sentence frame, *The old man hobbled across the room and picked up the valuable _____ from the mahogany table*, allows for several associations (between *watch* and *old man*, *watch* and *valuable*, *watch* and *table*, etc.), which can potentially result in a rich, integrated memory.

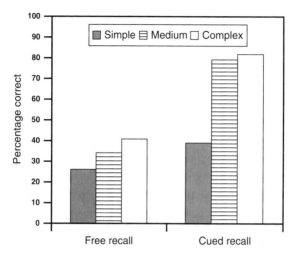

FIGURE 5.3 **Percentage correct on free and cued recall final tests for different sentence complexities (adapted from Craik & Tulving, 1975, Experiment 7).**

As a real-life example of elaboration and its benefits to memory, in 2006 the memorist Rajan Mahadevan came to speak at Colorado State University. Rajan is famous for earning a spot in the 1984 *Guinness Book of World Records* for memorizing the largest number of digits of pi at that time (31,811 of them). As part of his presentation to the crowd, he gave several live demonstrations of his exceptional ability to learn large numbers of digits in a short amount of time. After wowing the audience, Rajan described his approach to learning so much information so quickly. His primary strategy was to link different bits of information into units (chunks) that had personal meaning to him. For example, the chunk 630 might be tied to 6:30 a.m., the time he arrived at a coffee shop that morning, and the chunk 1984 might be encoded as the year that he got into the *Guinness Book of World Records*. Other numbers were learned based on meaningful phone number area codes, stretches of highway, cricket scores, and so on. Rajan noted that he has an extensive knowledge-base of meaningful numerical information, the size of a small language. Thus, Rajan's primary memorization strategy was to link what he was trying to learn to personally meaningful bits of information in his knowledge-base. This is elaboration—integrating and associating information.

How can students apply the concept of elaboration toward improving their learning and retention of course material? The research literature points to a number of possibilities.

Forming Connections to Other Information

Here is an interesting fact about a type of rabbit that is native to Canada: *During winter, the snowshoe hare turns white in color.* Having read this statement, attempt to answer the following question: *Why does the snowshoe hare turn white in winter?* Take a few moments and try to create a reasonable explanation.

The original factual statement does not provide an answer: You were told that snowshoe hares turn white, but not why they turn white. How did you answer the question? People often reason through the question based on what they already know. They might, for example, think about their existing knowledge of animals that change color. Perhaps it occurs to them that the snowshoe hare may turn white in winter to blend in with the snow, as protection from predators. But regardless of the explanation generated, trying to answer a "why" question encourages people to think about what they already know, and that links the central fact (*the snowshoe hare turns white in winter*) to their existing knowledge.

Prompting learners to respond to "why" questions is called **elaborative interrogation** because the questioning leads to elaboration—it encourages the learner to think about and therefore connect the information in

A snowshoe hare.

Answering "why" questions while reading can boost your learning.

the question with their prior knowledge. The research literature shows that engaging in elaborative interrogation often boosts learning over reading, repetition, underlining, and other commonly used methods. You no doubt noticed that throughout this book there are Elaborative Interrogation questions that ask you "why" questions. This is why—as a way to boost your learning and retention of the material!

In one study on elaborative interrogation (Woloshyn, Pressley, & Schneider, 1992), Canadian and West German college students studied facts about Canadian provinces (e.g., *Yukon is the province with the highest percentage of vehicles that are trucks*) and facts about West German states (e.g., *Hesson is the German state that grows the largest amount of wheat*). The participants had more background knowledge about facts regarding their native country than those about a different country. Participants assigned to a repetition condition were instructed to carefully read and reread each fact, with the purpose of attaining a good understanding. Others in an elaborative interrogation condition were instructed to read each fact and then answer a "why" question about that fact (*Why would that be true of Yukon?*). All participants later completed a memory test that asked them to match the facts with the provinces/states.

Figure 5.4 shows memory performance for the elaborative interrogation condition (gray bars) compared to the repetition condition (white

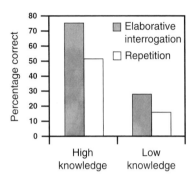

FIGURE 5.4 Percentage correct on a final matching test for elaborative interrogation vs. repetition (adapted from Woloshyn, Pressley, & Schneider, 1992).

bars) when the participants had high background knowledge (left side) and low background knowledge (right side). As you can see, retention was consistently better for elaborative interrogation and this advantage was greater when the participants had high background knowledge about the provinces/states. "Why" questioning improved memory for the facts, likely because such questioning encouraged learners to connect the facts to their prior knowledge.

The benefit of "why" questioning is not limited to facts shown in isolation. Consider the factual statement about the snowshoe hare noted previously, but now embedded within a paragraph more comparable to what you might encounter in a textbook:

> During the winter, the coat of the snowshoe hare is white in color. This change in color is the result of changes in daylight and temperature. As the weather turns colder and the days become shorter, the outer hairs of the summer coat are shed and hairs for the winter coat grow in in their place. The summer fur is gradually replaced by winter fur. (Seifert, 1993)

Here, if you were asked the "why" question, *Why does the snowshoe hare turn white in winter?*, you might try to answer the question by considering the other information in the passage and maybe other knowledge you have, too. The reader would, once again, be elaborating, but in this case by associating the central fact in the question (*the snowshoe hare turns white in winter*) to the other facts in the passage and your prior knowledge.

It is not a surprise, then, that the memory advantage for elaborative interrogation extends to facts embedded within passages like those you would find in a textbook (e.g., McDaniel & Donnelly, 1996; Ozgungor & Guthrie, 2004; Seifert 1993, 1994). In one such study (Smith, Holliday, & Austin, 2010), introductory biology students were given a passage about human digestion taken from their textbook. During a class meeting, half of the students were instructed to read the passage twice at their own pace. Other students read the same passage just once, but were prompted to answer "why is this true?" questions every 150 words or so (e.g., *Saliva must mix with food to initiate digestion. Why is this true?*). On a true/false test consisting of 105 new questions given immediately after studying, students in the elaborative interrogation group did better than those in the read-only group (76% vs. 69%, respectively).

The idea that linking to prior knowledge improves learning might sound familiar to you. Remember the vague passage about washing clothes given at the beginning of Chapter 3 (Demonstration 3.1)? Consider the results of that experiment (Bransford & Johnson, 1972) as they relate to prior knowledge. Recall that when a group of participants was told ahead of time that the passage was about washing clothes, this boosted their understanding and memory for the passage, compared to groups who were not told what the passage was about or were told after reading had been completed (see Figure 3.1). This difference occurred because being told ahead of time that the passage was about washing clothes caused participants to link the statements they were reading to their existing knowledge about washing clothes. With those links established, their knowledge could then cue their memory for the statements in the passage. When participants did not know what the passage was about, or did not discover what the passage was about until after reading was complete, they were unable to link the statements to their prior knowledge and did not get that same cuing advantage.

> Elaborative interrogation break
> **WHY** would linking to existing knowledge help you remember?

In sum, learning is enhanced when you elaborate on information by connecting that information to other things you are learning and others things you already know. "Why" questioning is an especially effective way to encourage such connections.

Connecting to prior knowledge can increase your learning.

Thinking of Examples

Another effective form of elaboration involves connecting concepts and ideas to examples. In one relevant study, college students read an essay that described a fictitious African nation (Palmere, Benton, Glover, & Ronning, 1983). This essay consisted of 32 main ideas, with each main idea presented alone or with up to three examples or details that complemented the main idea. To illustrate, the paragraph below shows one of the main ideas included in the essay, followed by three statements that support the main idea:

> Virtually all social reforms of the early twentieth century were the personal responsibility of King Manual. A state run medical service was established by King Manual in 1900. The forcible recruitment of native workers was stopped by Manual in 1915. A system of primary education was created under Manual's direction in 1920.

Eight of the 32 main ideas from the essay, selected at random, were presented alone. Another eight main ideas (also selected at random) were presented along with one example, another eight main ideas with two examples, and the final eight main ideas with three examples. The essay therefore provided participants with the opportunity to elaborate on some of the main ideas by associating those main ideas with one to three examples. Participants later tried to recall the main ideas.

The results of the experiment are shown in Figure 5.5. The bar on the far left shows the percentage of main ideas recalled when presented alone and the next three bars ($M + 1$, $M + 2$, and $M + 3$) show the percentage of main ideas recalled when the main ideas were presented

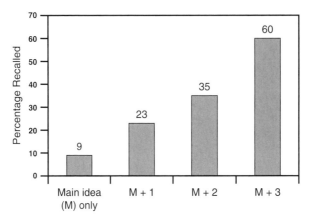

FIGURE **5.5 Percentage recalled for 0–3 examples (adapted from Palmere et al., 1983, Experiment 1).**

along with one to three examples, respectively. You can see that not only was memory better when examples were included, but the more examples the better, at least up to the three examples used here. Thus, elaborating by linking concrete examples to an idea or concept can enhance learning and memory for that idea or concept.

Relating Information to Yourself

Another way to elaborate on information is to connect the information to yourself or your own personal experiences when the content you are learning allows for such connections. Remember the study discussed earlier in the chapter, in which participants were given different types of orienting questions? In a later study, an additional condition was added—with participants instructed to think about how words related to themselves (Rogers, Kuiper, & Kirker, 1977).

Here is what happened. A set of 40 adjectives was selected, consisting of words like *shy* and *outgoing*. During an initial question-and-answer session, 10 of the adjectives were accompanied by the question, *Big letters?* (a case judgment), in order to orient participants toward thinking about the visual appearance of the word. Another 10 of the adjectives were accompanied by the question, *Rhymes with* _____? (a rhyme judgment), which oriented participants toward processing the sound of the words. Ten more adjectives were accompanied by the question, *Means the same as* _____? (a meaning judgment), which oriented participants toward processing the meaning of the words. Then in the

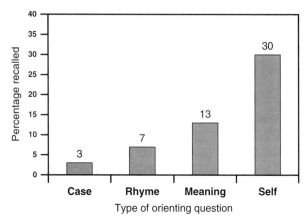

FIGURE 5.6 **Percentage recalled for different types of orienting questions (adapted from Rogers et al., 1977).**

new condition, another 10 adjectives were given along with the question, *Describes you?* (a self-judgment). After going through all of the questions in a random order and responding *yes* or *no* to each, participants took a surprise test in which they were asked to recall as many of the adjectives as possible. Figure 5.6 shows the results.

The first thing to note is that the researchers replicated earlier findings: Processing the meaning of words led to better memory than processing the appearance or sound of the words. But the self-judgment condition produced the best memory performance of all, more than double that obtained with meaning judgments. The memory advantage that occurs when you connect information to yourself is called the **self-reference effect** (see Symons & Johnson, 1997, for a review). Thus, it may help your learning and retention if you are able to relate the information to yourself in some way!

How Does Elaboration Help?

You might engage in elaboration in your own learning by linking the information you are trying to learn to what you already know, by considering concrete examples, or by tying the information to yourself. This is by no means an exhaustive list. It is also possible, for example, to connect what you are trying to learn to pictures, diagrams, and illustrations, as well as connect to mental images (see Chapter 6 for more on imagery). In all of these cases, the goal is to form associations and better integrate information with existing knowledge. Why does forming an association improve memory?

Consider an example. Suppose you are trying to learn about osmosis. In doing so, you link the concept to other information you are reading regarding semipermeable membranes. You also link the concept to what you learned in a prior lecture about diffusion. You mentally picture the diagram given in your textbook. You think about the example your instructor provided about how plant roots use osmosis to extract water from the soil. And you think of a personal experience in which you accidentally dropped raisins into your dog's water bowl and later saw that the raisins had expanded. In the end, you have created a network of connections like that shown in Figure 5.7. This should help your learning and understanding of osmosis. But why would such elaboration aid your later memory for the concept?

When you later attempt to remember the concept of osmosis, you can access that idea through the many connections you have formed. The other information you learned about semipermeable membranes may help you retrieve the information about osmosis. Your previous knowledge about diffusion may bring to mind the concept of osmosis. The diagram from your text might pop into your head and help you get to the concept. Your teacher's example or a personal experience may cue your memory. In essence, your elaboration activities have created a whole network of associations and that network of associations gives you a variety

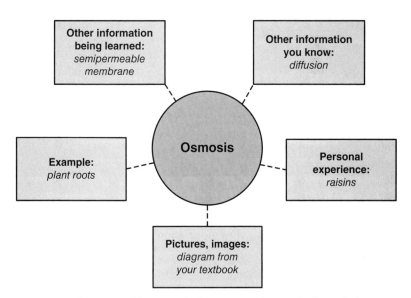

FIGURE 5.7 An illustration of the network of associations that may be formed when elaborating on the concept of osmosis.

of retrieval routes to later access the information you are seeking. The beauty is that if you are finding one route blocked (e.g., you cannot remember what your instructor said in class), you still have the possibility of remembering what you learned by going through other routes (e.g., the diagram that you can remember). Using terminology you will learn about in Chapter 10, elaboration provides you with a variety of potentially effective memory cues to help you access the memory later on.

Putting It All Together

Think back to the beginning of the chapter. Why is it that people have poor memory for a common object like a penny, despite being exposed to it countless times? The reason is that although people have seen a penny many times, they probably did not think about its features in a meaningful way or form meaningful connections during all of those exposures. That is, processing was superficial. They did not engage in elaboration.

Why is it that even extensive amounts of rote memorization have limited benefits to memory? If you simply repeat a term or concept over and over again, without attempting to give it meaning or link it to other things, then again, the processing is relatively superficial. When you merely say a concept or term to yourself over and over again, you are focusing on its sound, not its meaning or relationship to other concepts.

But even if the repetition has an element of meaning to it—such as when you repeat a word and its definition to yourself over and over again, or repeat a foreign word and its English equivalent over and over again—that is still of limited effectiveness. Why? Because your learning is redundant. New repetitions add little or nothing new to your prior learning. Much greater gains will occur in your learning, understanding, and retention of information if your study methods are of greater *depth* and *breadth*—when you not only seek a conceptual understanding of the information, but also attempt to link the information to other information and form associations. Thus, elaboration should be a cornerstone of all of your efforts to learn.

Tips You Can Use

1. **Think about the meaning of information and seek a conceptual understanding.** Do not limit yourself to processing information at a superficial level by passively viewing, hearing, reading, or simply repeating it. Rather, try to understand and give meaning to the information.
2. **Link the information to other things you are learning and things you already know.** As you try to understand and give meaning to the

information, think about how it relates to things you already know and other things you've been learning. Explicitly try to connect the new information you are trying to learn to other, meaningfully related information. This not only makes for a more richly interconnected memory, it provides you with good triggers that can later cue your memory.

3. **Ask yourself why.** Take advantage of elaborative interrogation and periodically ask yourself why questions. Take advantage of the closely related self-explanation effect by actively trying to explain information to yourself as you learn. Such activities naturally encourage you to link the information to things you already know and other things you are learning.

4. **Think of concrete examples.** As you are learning new information, try to think of concrete examples of what is being described. This may aid your initial understanding of the information, but can also generate effective cues for triggering your memory later on: Your examples may come to mind and this can then trigger your memory for the related information and concepts.

5. **Relate the information to your own life and personal experiences.** When possible, link the information to your personal life and personal experiences. Think about how the information relates to things you have personally experienced. Think about examples from your own life. Such personally relevant experiences and examples can be especially effective cues for triggering your memory later on.

Discussion Questions

1. Compare a repetition strategy to an elaboration strategy. Why is it that elaboration boosts learning and retention? Based on your explanation for why elaboration boosts learning and retention, why would repetition be so much less effective?

2. How can you apply elaborative interrogation to your own studying? What might be some limits to implementation? How could you address these limits?

3. How can you apply the self-reference effect to your own study habits? What might be some possible challenges and limitations?

4. There are a number of studies showing that when students are working on problems or reading new material, they learn and remember that material better if they explain the information to themselves as they work (e.g., Chi et al., 1989). Based on what you have read in this chapter, why does this benefit occur?

Suggestions for Further Reading

The various references highlighted in this chapter provide good reading for individuals interested in the origin and development of ideas pertaining to depth and elaboration. On some of the more specific topics discussed, Cynthia Symons and Blair Johnson (1997) offer a quantitative review of self-reference effect studies, and Fergus Craik (2002) relays some fascinating reflections on work on levels of processing. John Dunlosky and his colleagues (2013) review the elaborative interrogation literature, examining the literature from an applied perspective, with an informative discussion of issues and challenges for implementation. The same article also reviews the related literature on self-explanation, in which learners attempt to make sense of what they are learning by explaining it to themselves as they go along. Regina Wong, Michael Lawson, and John Keeves (2002) describe an intriguing study on self-explanation that was conducted in a high school geometry class.

Answers to Demonstration 5.2

Words associated with case judgments:
tree, pencil, hair, film, worm, nose
Words associated with rhyme judgments:
coat, bell, book, sofa, gate, truck
Words associated with category judgments:
duck, ear, bee, apple, shoes, nurse

Credits

Page 80: (Demonstration 5.1) Republished with permission of the American Psychological Association. Long-term memory for a common object. Nickerson, R. S., & Adams, M. J. Cognitive Psychology, 11, 287–307, 1979. Permission conveyed through Copyright Clearance Center, Inc.

Page 83: (Figure 5.2) Republished with permission of Elsevier. The role of rehearsal in short-term memory. Craik, F. I. M., & Watkins, M. J. Journal of Verbal Learning and Verbal Behavior, 12, 599–607, 1973. Permission conveyed through Copyright Clearance Center, Inc.

Page 90: FotoRequest / Shutterstock
Page 91: CandyBox Images / Shutterstock
Page 94: Africa Studio / Shutterstock

CHAPTER 6

....

Imagery
The Benefits of Imagery on Learning and Training

....

Learning Objectives
- Reading this chapter will help you:
  - Understand the benefits of imagery in learning.
  - Know how to apply imagery effectively in your own learning.
  - Appreciate the benefits of imagery for developing skills.

....

Imagine a letter D. Now rotate it 90 degrees to the left. Now place that rotated D on top of a letter J. What do you "see" in your mind's eye? Does it form a picture that you recognize, such as an umbrella?

Most people can readily form pictures in their minds that enable them to envision what something looks like even if it is not present. These images can be a very effective tool for remembering. You experienced this in Demonstration 1.1 from Chapter 1: Forming a picture in your mind that links information (in that case, pairs of unrelated words) is a great strategy for keeping that information together to aid later remembering. For instance, you might remember that the word "bird" was earlier paired with the word "lamp" because you visualized a lamp with a bird perched on top of it (see Figure 6.1).

Imagery can often be a very powerful aid to remembering. In fact, before moving on, try Demonstration 6.1.

If you tried Demonstration 6.1, you probably found that some of the words (like *snake, milk, rabbit, phone, camera, blanket, boat*) were more easily remembered than the other words like *irony, instance,* or *extent.*

FIGURE 6.1   An effective way to learn the word pair bird–lamp is to mentally imagine a bird

DEMONSTRATION 6.1

Set a countdown clock and give yourself about 90 seconds to learn the following set of words:

snake, irony, concept, instance, blanket, boat, camera, phone, aspect, extent, feet, rabbit, value, purpose, essence, milk

Next, close your book and try to recall as many of these words as you can. Return when you are finished.

Indeed, some of the words were concrete—they are easily connected to a physical representation. Other words were well known but do not really give rise to clear image. For example, it is not clear how you would imagine a highly abstract concept such as *irony* or *essence*. Research has consistently shown that memory is much better for concrete words than highly abstract words (e.g., Paivio, 1965; Tauber & Rhodes, 2012). Why would that be the case? One widely accepted idea is that concrete words allow you to create an image of what you are trying to learn. These images can later be a highly effective way of learning information. And that is what this chapter is about, the many ways that imagery can benefit learning and training.

Introducing the Method of Loci: The "Memory Palace"

The usefulness of imagery for remembering has been recognized since ancient times. Legend has it that the one of the best-known imagery techniques was developed more than 2,000 years ago in ancient Greece by the poet Simonides, who was attending a banquet to recite a poem (Yates, 1966). After reciting the poem he stepped outside to speak with someone, during which time the banquet hall suddenly collapsed, killing everyone inside. Many bodies were unrecognizable, preventing the customary burial ritual from taking place. However, Simonides was able to identify the bodies by revisiting his memory for where each individual had been sitting at the banquet table. In other words, he conjured up an image in his mind of the seating arrangement and determined whose bodies were where based on his image. However horrible this account might be, the story of Simonides is likely the origin of the term "memory palace technique," also known as the **method of loci**. Indeed, the method of loci has been effectively used by generations of orators (Yates, 1966).

In the method of loci, the learner mentally imagines (i.e., visualizes) each piece of to-be-remembered information as appearing within a well-learned set of locations. To retrieve the information later, the learner imagines moving through the well-learned set of locations and attempts to picture the information that was placed in each of the locations earlier. This technique is very effective and is still used today by many competitive or expert memorizers (Raz et al., 2009).

In his May 2012 TED talk "Feats of Memory Anyone Can Do," competitive memorizer Joshua Foer describes the method of loci and how he uses it to memorize large quantities of information (see http://www.ted.com/talks/joshua_foer_feats_of_memory_anyone_can_do). He gives the example of imagining his house for use in the method of loci to enable him to retrieve his TED talk from memory. He imagined moving through an image of his house and encountering previously imagined (or "placed") hints that reminded him of what came next in his talk. For example, in the entryway of the house, he had previously created an image of Cookie Monster on top of the horse Mr. Ed. Upon encountering this image again in his mental walk-through of his house, the image reminded Foer to introduce his friend Ed Cook. Later on, when he reached the kitchen in his mental walk-through, he encountered his previous placement of characters from the *Wizard of Oz*. This reminded him to introduce the interesting journey he began a year previously.

Although the method of loci is used by elite memorizers, it can easily be adapted for your purposes. For example, you might envision your typical walk to get from one side of your town to the other. As you imagine walking along this route, you can attach images of the information you would like to remember. The mnemonic will be most effective

FIGURE **6.2 A route to imagine.**

if you envision these images vividly interacting with aspects of your route. Consider an example using the buildings and locations depicted in Figure 6.2. Perhaps you start your walk at the bottom of the hill near the hospital and then walk by the museum. You next make your way to the grocery store and walk further up the hill to the post office before finishing your journey at the airport.

With an established route in mind, you can now "attach" information to this route to memorize. Suppose you want to remember your to-do list that consists of the following tasks: *water the plants, finish your art history paper, schedule a vet appointment for the cat, buy a new work shirt,* and *study for your chemistry test.* You could start your mental walk by picturing yourself at the hospital, imagining a torrential rainstorm dousing the trees outside. At your next stop you might imagine the many displays in the museum, with a paper under each of them, depicting the paper you need to write. Moving on to the grocery store, you could imagine riding a cart through the pet food aisle, reminding you to make an appointment for your cat. At the post office, you might imagine the machines that dispense stamps pumping out shirt after shirt. Finally, you end at the airport, imagining a plane landing on a runway with the periodic table written all over it.

Later on, when trying to recall your to-do list, you would then do your mental "walk" and revisit these images along the way to remind you of what you need to do. Your own to-do list might be much longer than

A mental "walk" using the method of loci can remind you of your to-do list.

the example used but that is the beauty of the method of loci: It is effective for even very large amounts of information. This technique may remind you a bit of the method of memorizing word pairs by forming images of the two items interacting, as in Demonstration 1.1 and shown in Figure 6.1. The method of loci might be considered a more complex extension of that method and one that can allow for more information to be remembered, in a particular order or sequence. Remembering a series of cues in a sequence can be important for tasks like delivering a speech or giving a talk without access to notes, as illustrated by Joshua Foer in his TED talk (see Box 6.1 for another method of learning information in a sequence).

The method of loci is a great illustration of the usefulness of imagery for connecting information in your mind in a way that benefits later memory. In fact, expert memorizers beyond Joshua Foer use it frequently. For example, one group of researchers studied competitors from the World Memory Championships and compared them to noncompetitive memorizers (people who do not enter competitions). The researchers found that what seemed to distinguish the competitive memorizers from the average person was that the areas of the brain known for spatial navigation and spatial memory were more active during the memory tasks among the competitive memorizers. It was as if the competitive memorizers were engaging in spatial imagery, or imagining spatial navigation, whereas the noncompetitive memorizers were not engaging these strategies (Maquire, Valentine, Wilding, & Kapur, 2003).

Not only do expert memorizers rely on imagery techniques like the method of loci, but research over the years has provided strong evidence for

---

BOX 6.1   THE PEGWORD MNEMONIC

The pegword mnemonic is another effective method for learning a sequence of information. You start by creating a series of "pegs," an easy-to-learn set of words that rhyme. The most common approach is to count to ten. For example, your pegs might be:

one–bun; two–shoe; three–tree; four–door; five–hive; six–sticks; seven–heaven; eight–gate; nine–wine; ten–hen

With these pegs memorized, you then attach what you want to learn to the pegs, creating an image that connects the information. For example, suppose you wanted to learn this list: *stapler, bottle, goat, carousel, pencil, goal, carpet, door, cannon, target*

You could take your first peg and imagine a *stapler* inside of a hot dog bun. For the second item, you might imagine large bottles walking around with shoes. For the third peg, you might image goats climbing a tree. And so forth for each item. When you later want to remember what you learned you return to the pegs. For example, *one–bun* might remind you of the stapler in the bun. *Two–shoe* would cue an image of bottles wearing shoes, and so on.

The pegword mnemonic can thus be an effective way to learn information in a specific order (e.g., Roediger, 1980).

---

its benefits. For example, one study (Bellezza & Reddy, 1978) had a group of college students imagine a series of 20 locations they would pass when walking to a familiar location on campus. Next, the participants heard a list of 20 words and were told to use the method of loci by imagining each word and then placing it along the route. For example, if the first word was *banana*, and the start of the route involved going downstairs, an individual might imagine a large banana in the middle of the stairs. Another group of college students was tested, but these individuals were only told to imagine each word as it was presented—they were never told to use the method of loci.

After hearing the full list, each group was given a blank sheet of paper and asked to write down as many words as they could remember. The results, shown in Figure 6.3, are striking. Participants using the method of loci (gray bar) remembered nearly twice as much as participants using imagery alone (white bar).

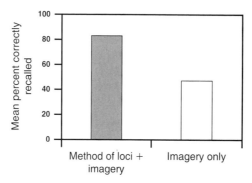

FIGURE **6.3 The mean percentage of words correctly recalled when using the method of loci or imagery only (adpated from Bellezza & Reddy, 1978).**

Why would imagery benefit memory? Some researchers have suggested that forming an image of two otherwise unrelated things interacting helps to link them in memory in a way that allows you to remember one when presented with the other (e.g., Bower & Winzez, 1970). The same ideas apply to the method of loci, as imagining your path provides strong links to what you want to remember. For example, you might fail to remember watering the plants if you were to simply ask yourself what you were supposed to do that day. However, when you retrieve your mental walk-through of the route, you retrieve the information that you associated, via imagery, with the hospital along that mental walk-through (a huge rainstorm dousing the trees).

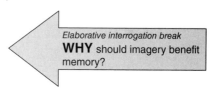

Elaborative interrogation break
WHY should imagery benefit memory?

The method of loci is not the only effective way to use imagery. What follows are several other methods of applying imagery to learning and training.

Imagery for Studying: The Keyword Mnemonic

When presented with the method of loci as a method of remembering a to-do list, you might ask yourself why it is necessary. After all, you may be one of many people who has some type of digital device for keeping track of calendars and other information. If you needed to remember a list, you could simply upload it to this device. This is a reasonable response, but there remain many situations in modern life, particularly in school and the workplace, that still require memorization. For example, when taking a foreign language course, you may need to memorize new vocabulary words in large quantities. And when you make that trip to Italy, you will want to be able to talk with locals without consulting your dictionary for every other word. Imagery may be particularly useful in these situations.

One well-studied imagery technique for memorization in school settings is the keyword mnemonic. In this method, you learn new words, such as a new vocabulary word, by first thinking of a familiar word that the new word sounds like. You then form an image that associates that familiar word with the new word that you are trying to learn. For example, the Spanish word "rodilla" means "knee." It also sounds like the word "rodeo," so you might form a mental picture of a rodeo in which the cowboy's knee is sticking out prominently (Matlin, 2005). This image allows you to associate the word "knee" with "rodeo," in turn allowing you to think of the similar-sounding Spanish word "rodilla" as meaning "knee."

As another example, to remember that the Spanish word "pato" means "duck," you might picture a duck with a pot on its head (Atkinson, 1975). However, you should carefully understand a word before using an image based on its sound. A friend of one of your authors was traveling in Mexico and felt she had committed a small faux pas at a restaurant and apologized, telling her waiter that she was "muy embarasado." In return,

The keyword technique involves using imagery to learn a new word.

she received a bewildered look from the waiter. It was then that her companion leaned in and told her that she had just informed the waiter that she was "very pregnant." So that you also avoid any misunderstandings, the sections that follow describe some ways in which the keyword mnemonic has been shown to be useful for learning in educational settings.

Foreign or New Vocabulary Learning

The examples described of applying the keyword mnemonic to learn the Spanish words "rodilla" and "pato" illustrate a great use of this method for learning foreign language vocabulary. Some researchers have gone so far as to advocate the keyword mnemonic as a foundational approach to teaching foreign languages (Atkinson, 1975; Kasper, 1993). Others have shown it to be useful for children learning complicated vocabulary words in English. For example, researchers in one study (Levin, McCormick, Miller, Berry, & Pressley, 1982) taught fourth graders complex vocabulary words. All students were first given a definition of the word. Half of the students learned the words by considering a similar-sounding word alongside an illustration depicting an appropriate use of the word. For example, to learn the word "persuade," the participants saw a cartoon with an individual persuading her friend to buy a "purse." The other half of the students were instructed to make their best effort to learn the definitions. As a test, each child was given a word and asked to remember the definition. Students in the keyword group remembered a much greater percentage of the definition (83%) than those in the control group (55%).

You can certainly use this method to learn new vocabulary, foreign language or otherwise. For instance, the keyword mnemonic could also be useful in learning vocabulary in new domains, such as biology, chemistry, or geography, to name a few.

Geographical Information

In a study with fourth- and fifth-grade students, researchers demonstrated the usefulness of the keyword mnemonic in learning states and their capitals (Levin, Shriberg, Miller, McCormick, & Levin, 1980). To apply the keyword mnemonic in this situation, students learned to associate a state name with an image of a word that it sounded like. For instance, Maryland sounds like "marry." The researchers also asked the students to associate the capital name with an image of a word that sounded similar. For example, the capital Annapolis sounds like "apple." In this situation, the students would be given an image of two apples being married in a wedding ceremony (see Figure 6.4 for an example). Students in the keyword condition were compared with other students instructed to use their own method of learning. All of the participants were later tested and asked to report the capital when given the name of a state. Those data can be found in Figure 6.5. As you can see, students using the keyword mnemonic (gray bar) had much better memory than students left to their own devices.

FIGURE 6.4 Example image used by Levin and colleagues (1980) to teach students the keyword technique. Maryland sounds like "marry" and its capital, Annapolis, sounds like "apple." The image of two apples marrying is used to form an interaction between the two.

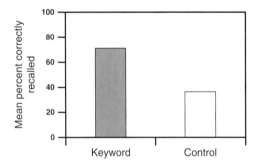

FIGURE 6.5 Percentage of capitals correctly recalled for the keyword and control groups (adapted from Levin et al., 1980).

Biographical Information

The keyword mnemonic is also an effective way to learn names. For example, one of your authors often remembers the name of a famous author of children's books, Dr. Seuss, by imagining a doctor treating the Greek god Zeus. But of course this name is already well known. How would the keyword mnemonic fare if you needed to learn entirely unfamiliar names? One study tested this idea with eighth graders (Shriberg, Levin, McCormick, & Pressley, 1982). These students were given the names of fictitious famous people and asked to learn their names and their accomplishments. For example, the famous name might be "Charlene McKune" and her accomplishment might be "taught her pet cat how to count.""McKune" sounds like the word raccoon. Therefore, the students were instructed to learn this phrase by imagining several raccoons hopping a fence in succession while a nearby cat kept count on a whiteboard. In one experiment, students in the keyword condition were over three times more likely to remember the accomplishments and names of these fictional people than students in a control condition.

Imagery for Performance Training: Imagining Doing Things Improves Performance

Have you ever imagined yourself dancing, or playing a sport? Close your eyes for a moment and imagine yourself playing tennis. Now try imagining yourself playing some other sport or engaging in an activity that you have engaged in many times before. If you are a dancer, imagine dancing. If you are a musician, imagine playing your instrument. If you are an athlete, imagine playing your sport.

Just as you can imagine navigating your bedroom to count windows, or imagining a familiar walk when using the method of loci, you can probably imagine performing actions, like playing tennis, swimming, ice skating, skiing, or even playing the piano or typing on a keyboard. Imagining performing actions can actually make you better at performing those actions later on.

One reason why imagining performing actions may enhance later performance of those actions is that there is overlap in the neural mechanisms involved in

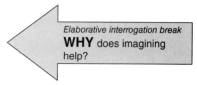

Elaborative interrogation break
WHY does imagining help?

actually performing actions and imagining performing those actions (e.g., Kosslyn, Ganis, & Thompson, 2001). That is, the same parts of the brain seem to operate in both, which may help to explain why simply imagining doing something can enhance performance when actually doing it later on.

The potential benefits of imagery on performance are so established that there is even a journal dedicated to investigating them in sport performance: the *Journal of Imagery Research in Sport and Physical Activity*.

In a blog piece titled "Imagery in Sport: Elite Athlete Examples and the PETTLEP Model," which was written for BelievePerform.com, Mary Quinton quotes some famous athletes on their use of imagery. For example, she quotes Ronaldinho, a famous (now retired) Brazilian football player, as saying:

> When I train, one of the things I concentrate on is creating a mental picture of how best deliver the ball to a teammate, preferably leaving him alone in front of the rival goalkeeper. So what I do, always before a game, always, every night and every day, is try and think up things, imagine plays, which no one else will have thought of, and to do so always bearing in mind the particular strength of each team-mate to whom I am passing the ball. When I construct those plays in my mind I take into account whether one team-mate likes to receive the ball at his feet, or ahead of him; if he is good with his head, and how he

It often helps to carefully imagine a performance.

prefers to head the ball; if he is stronger on his right or his left foot. That is my job. That is what I do. I imagine the game.

(https://believeperform.com/performance/
imagery-in-sport-elite-athlete-examples-and-the-pettlep-model.)

Have you ever carefully imagined what you will do before a performance, such as before a big game or concert? Often, if you watch elite athletes before they begin, they appear to be imagining their performance. Researchers have also considered this and have developed a procedure for implementing the use of imagery in training regimens for enhancing skilled performance. The following sections describe uses of imagery in enhancing physical performance.

The PETTLEP Procedure for Imagining Performance

Imagery is so widespread as a training technique for enhancing performance in many domains that there is an acronym for describing a well-known approach to its use: the PETTLEP Procedure (e.g., Holmes & Collins, 2001; Smith, Wright, Allsopp, & Westhead, 2007). It is especially prevalent in sports psychology, but has been increasingly used in other domains of performance as well. The PETTLEP acronym uses the first letter of seven key features of effective imagery-use during training.

Physical. All relevant physical aspects of the performance for which you are training should be imagined. If it is basketball, imagine the physical aspects of the various shots that you are trying to improve upon, including wearing your uniform in the image, imagining the ball and exactly where it is for that shot, and imagining the physical positioning of your body throughout the movements necessary for that shot.

Environment. The exact environment or context in which your performance will take place should be imagined (Chapter 10 on cues will provide some insight on why this might be important). If you are training for a big basketball game, imagine the plays in a gym with crowds cheering and the noise that you would expect at the game. Incorporate as much of the actual anticipated context as possible in your imagery. One of your authors uses the PETTLEP procedure for practicing talks while on plane trips. As part of this, your author tries to imagine the audience and the environment in which the talk will be delivered.

Task. You should realistically imagine the demands of the task at hand for which you are training. For example, which aspects of the task will be difficult? Which will require intense focus? Do not try to imagine beyond your expertise level. If you are an intermediate-level player, then imagine at that level, focusing on the techniques you are currently learning and on aspects of the task within your reach but not yet perfected. Do not try to imagine yourself at the level of an Olympian or elite performer. (For one thing, because you have not yet reached that level, you will not yet be capable of imagining the critical aspects of achieving that level of performance). Stick to imagining what is currently within your reach and in need of improvement. For example, one of your authors takes piano lessons. When unable to practice the piano, your author will engage in imagery as a substitute for piano practice (imagining playing the songs currently being practiced in lessons). When imagining practicing the piano, it is appropriate to imagine the specific techniques and pieces that are right at your current performance level. Accordingly, your author specifically imagines the intermediate-level songs currently being learned and polished in lessons but does not imagine songs in the repertoire of a concert pianist.

Timing. To make the imagery comparable to actual performance, you should ensure that the timing of your actions mimics or approximates the real timing for actual performance. However, it is also possible to imagine key aspects of your performance (on which you are trying to improve) in slow motion. For example, a beginning pianist might do this for tricky hand maneuvers on the piano, in order to gain a better mental grasp of the details of the maneuvers.

Learning. To support your training and real practice sessions, your imagery should be continually updated to reflect newly acquired skills and techniques as you advance and progress.

Emotion. Incorporate how you might feel during the real performance. However, avoid limiting emotions like intense fear. Instead, imagine positive emotions, like energy, or the great feeling of getting a round of applause or hearing a roaring crowd cheering for you.

Perspective. This has to do with whether you are imagining yourself in the first-person, or instead taking a third-person perspective (as if watching yourself on a video). Research seems to indicate that which is better may depend on the particular skill that you are seeking to improve. Some argue that tasks involving things like timing are best imagined from the first-person perspective, but tasks involving things like posture or position might best be imagined from a third-person perspective. So, when imagining practicing the piano, it might be best to take a first-person perspective, imagining yourself playing the piano and making the difficult maneuvers with your fingers and doing so with the right timing, rhythmically. But for getting your posture correct, such as sitting up straight on the bench, keeping your wrists off of the piano and your fingers curved, and so on, it may be useful to switch sometimes to the third-person perspective.

Several studies have explored elements of the PETTLEP procedure (or similar imagery techniques) and shown benefits for training and enhancing performance.

Imagery in Athletic Training

Research suggests that imagining playing a sport or engaging in an athletic training activity can lead to similar types of benefits as actual physical training (Guillot & Collet, 2008). Studies in this area have shown benefits in a wide range of athletic activities, including badminton (Callow, Hardy, & Hall, 2001), skiing performance (Callow, Roberts, & Fawkes, 2006), golf putting (Short et al., 2002), springboard dives (Reed, 2002), and soccer performance (Ramsey et al., 2010).

In one study, researchers (Reiser, Busch, & Munzert, 2011) examined the benefits of imagining strength-training exercises on actual strength. One group of participants performed a variety of arm and leg contractions (using an exercise machine with weights). Another group of participants interspersed actual arm and leg contractions with imagined arm and leg contractions. That is, sometimes these participants would lift weights and sometimes they would imagine lifting weights. Remarkably, the researchers found that the imagined arm and leg contractions that replaced actual contractions within the workout session led to the same strength benefits as a full session of real arm and leg contractions. Even more remarkably, these same strength benefits could be found when 75% of the strength repetitions were imagined instead of real. In short, there was a tangible muscle-strength benefit to imagining the strength exercises that was comparable to actually doing the strength exercises.

Another group of researchers investigated the effects of imagery-based training on field hockey (Smith, Wright, Allsopp, & Westhead, 2007). Of greatest interest, one group of participants was asked to carefully imagine playing and consider the whole scenario surrounding playing, including the clothes worn, the sounds present, and so on. These participants specifically imagined 10 penalty shots a day for six weeks. Other groups imagined only the clothes they would wear or the objects they might work with (see Figure 6.6 for examples of these elements within soccer). Their results showed that the sport-specific imagery group, that had focused their imagery on a specific technique, outperformed the other groups.

Similar evidence was also obtained with gymnasts who were learning to execute a complex full turn on the balance beam (Smith et al., 2007). The researchers compared gymnasts who actually practiced the turn with those who imagined the turn but did not physically practice (a control condition did unrelated stretching exercises). Participants performed their designated task (physical practice or imagining the technique) three times per week for six weeks. Figure 6.7 shows the score

FIGURE 6.6 Participants in one study were asked to either carefully imagine playing, imagine elements of the game (such as the uniform), or imagine the objects they would use in the game.

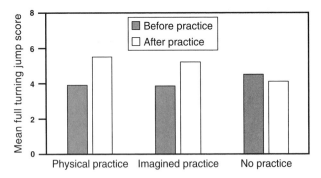

FIGURE 6.7 Gymansts' scores on the balance beam for participants who physically practiced the turn, those who imagined the turn, and a control group who did an unrelated exercise, before and after six weeks of practice (adapted from Smith et al., 2007).

given by judges who witnessed the turn before practice and then after six weeks of practice. As you can see, gymnasts who only imagined performing the maneuver improved as much as participants who physically practiced gymnastics. In other words, imagery was as good as actual practice in this case!

Imagery in Performing Arts Training

Given the known benefits to athletic performance, it should not seem like too much of a stretch that imagery may also benefit the performing arts. Some research has demonstrated the promise of using very specific forms of dance imagery to benefit dance performance (Girón, McIsaac, & Nilson, 2012). It is also known that there is overlap between neural regions involved in imagining playing a musical instrument and the neural regions involved in actually playing that musical instrument. For example, one study (Meister et al., 2004) found that asking participants to imagine playing the piano led to the same regions of the brain becoming active as when they were actually playing the piano. Based on this overlap, imagining playing a musical instrument is thought to be beneficial to musical performance. Indeed, it has even been suggested that imagining an entire ensemble will benefit coordination between one's own playing and that of others (Keller, 2012).

Imagery in the Development of Medical and Surgical Skill

Imagining actions also has potential benefits in professional domains. One group of researchers (Wright et al., 2008) examined whether incorporating an imagery training program would help nursing students master key skills. For example, nursing students were told to imagine themselves going through the process of taking a patient's blood pressure. The researchers found that students who received imagery exercises as part of their training program were better at taking blood pressure than students who trained without imagery exercises. Another study with medical students (Sanders et al., 2008) compared residents learning a new surgical skill either via imagery training or using the more common method of surgical training (where prepractice learning is done primarily from a text). Medical students who learned via imagery demonstrated better surgical skills than the medical students who only learned via textbook.

Imagery in Enhancing Performance on Cognitive Tasks

At this point, you might be thinking to yourself that imagery is only useful for tasks that are largely physical in nature, such as playing a sport or performance surgery. However, imagery can be very useful on primarily cognitive tasks. For example, one group of researchers compared participants imagining playing the video game "Need for Speed," a group actually playing the game (Wright & Smith, 2007), and a group who only engaged in imagery (imagining the stimuli, such as the joystick, rather than the actions taken during the game). Remarkably, participants who only imagined playing improved as much as participants who played the game.

More recently, some researchers studying people's ability to search for a target item in a visual array (called visual selective attention) reported that imagining the visual target beforehand improved search performance more than having an actual practice episode beforehand (Reinhart, McClenahan, & Woodman, 2015).

Imagery in Enhancing Understanding

Can imagery improve understanding? One factor that often impedes understanding is that the subject matter may be highly complex. When encountering such complexity, it often helpful to engage in "cognitive offloading" to circumvent individuals' limited capacity for processing information (Risko & Dunn, 2015). The term **cognitive offloading** refers to relying on external agents or materials to offset individuals' limited capacity for processing information at any given moment, such as using diagrams, charts, or models.

A good example of cognitive offloading as it relates to imagery is the need for so-called ball-and-stick models in advanced chemistry classes. To a point, people can usually visualize a simple molecule and imagine it rotating to bond in the key areas of another molecule. Such visualization likely assists with understanding of molecular bonding. However, as molecules become increasing complex, the human ability to accurately visualize the key processes diminishes. The problem is that the information becomes so complex that it exceeds a person's capacity for visualizing and rotating it in order to fully imagine the processes taking place. This cognitive limitation can hinder a full understanding of a process. Ball-and-stick models, such a Figure 6.8, help students to build models of complex molecules in ways that enable them to visualize what is taking place without exceeding their mental capacity for

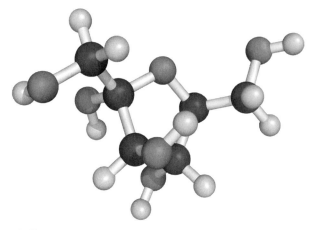

FIGURE **6.8 A ball-and-stick model of fructose.**

doing so. This is because much of the visualization itself is offloaded onto the external world, allowing for processing the critical pieces one at a time without losing the overarching visualization of the process.

Such visualizations are useful in many domains (e.g., geosciences; engineering) and are very important in the STEM (science, technology, engineering, and math) disciplines (e.g., Uttal, Miller, & Newcombe, 2013). Spatial thinking may be a critical feature of succeeding in STEM disciplines (e.g., Jee et al., 2014). Although not the only important factor, successful learning in spatially oriented fields may involve continual back and forth between one's use of external visual aids that assist with cognitive offloading for complex visuospatial material, and ones' ability to engage in mental imagery to process, think about, and elaborate on that information.

Several groups of researchers have focused on students' cognitive processing and use of maps and geospatial technologies in the very spatially oriented geosciences (e.g., Mohan, Mohan, & Uttal, 2014). Other researchers have considered students' use of drawing for increasing understanding (e.g., Ainsworth, Prain, & Tytler, 2011) and for demonstrating their current level of understanding of science concepts (e.g., Jee et al., 2014). Drawing diagrams and other visuals of your material can be useful in many respects. It incorporates elaboration, self-generation of information, testing, and other strategies from elsewhere in this book. Thus, visualization is a key component of understanding in many disciplines. For any complex subject matter, you will very likely be best served by utilizing your imagery skills along with external aids

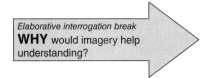

Elaborative interrogation break
WHY would imagery help understanding?

to aid you with visualization. (See chapters 7 and 11, on organization and understanding, for more information on enhancing understanding of complex concepts.)

Putting It All Together

In all, imagery confers a variety of benefits to learning. Whether it be imagining playing a sport, integrating information into an imagined route, or mastering a foreign language, applying imagery has the promise of enhancing retention. But even with those very real benefits, some perspective is in order. For example, it is unlikely that you could learn all of the key themes in Shakespeare's greatest works simply by imagining MacBeth's castle or Hamlet within the Danish countryside. However, you could profit by using imagery to learn some of Shakespeare's most famous lines, and by extension, have a greater grip on the contents for the Bard's major works. Similarly, imagining skiing will not make you a skilled skier if you do not actually get out onto the slopes and ski in order to have the actual skiing inform your next imagining, and so on. In short, although imagery can be a tool for aiding in memory retrieval and enhancing performance, it by no means should be the only the tool in your kit. This should give you some sense of how to apply imagery when it will help you the most.

Tips You Can Use

1. **Keywords for facts, names, and vocabulary.** The keyword mnemonic can be useful for memorizing words, such as for new vocabulary words, foreign vocabulary words, people's names, and even cities and their locations. The technique will work best when there is a clear connection between the word and the image you are using.

2. **Use the method of loci for sequences of information**. The method of loci is among the most powerful techniques at your disposal. It likely has many uses but stands out from the crowd when you must learn a chain or sequence of information. By this logic, it will be very useful when engaged in narration, storytelling, or public speaking.

It is also highly useful for understanding and remembering processes (e.g., the Krebs cycle).

3. **Imagining and visualization helps skilled performance.** When seeking to learn or acquire a skill a little imagining can go a long way. Try practicing by imagining yourself performing that task as if you were practicing, relying on the PETTLEP procedure discussed in this chapter. You should not replace actual practice with imagined practice but, between practice sessions, integrate some imagined practice. If you are practicing for a performance, a competition, or a test, it may even be better to imagine yourself in that setting. For example, some sports psychologists suggest imagining the sound of the crowds cheering, the smell of the field, the site and feel of your uniform on you. This helps to incorporate critical context into your imagery and can serve as a powerful cue.

4. **Use imagery to help understanding.** Complex processes, such as the circulation of blood throughout the body, are difficult to grasp through words alone. Create diagrams of processes and imagine the process you are trying to learn. For example, imagine the path blood would take from the heart through the body.

Discussion Questions

1. Imagery is clearly beneficial when learning foreign language vocabulary, geographical information, or to-do lists. How might you use imagery in learning other types of information? For example, how could you use imagery to help you learn the process of photosynthesis?

2. Considering your own learning, what do you think are the major advantages and potential disadvantages of using the keyword technique compared with the method of loci? Are there certain kinds of materials that more easily lend themselves to one technique or the other?

3. As the example with Joshua Foer illustrated, imagery can be a very powerful method of learning large amounts of information. In fact, many individuals who compete in memory competitions (yes, these do exist) report using some form of imagery as a basis for their technique. Why are these techniques so powerful?

4. Imagining your movements may confer significant benefits to performance in many skilled domains. Describe an example of how you could apply this practice to a skill you have already developed or a currently working on.

Suggestions for Further Reading

Imagery has been formally investigated by scientists for many decades. That work has yielded a number of insights and debates among those who study imagery. Stephen Kosslyn, William Thompson, and Giorgio Ganis' *The Case for Mental Imagery* (2009) is a thorough summary of the field that touches on many of the contentious debates that have driven research. Aymeric Guillot and Christian Collet's edited work, *The Neuropsychological Foundations of Mental and Motor Imagery* (2010), provides a comprehensive review of motor imagery and imagery's relation to physical action and performance. Shorter, but still comprehensive, summaries of work on imagery can be found in many cognitive psychology textbooks, including Margaret Matlin and Thomas Farmer's *Cognition* (2016), Daniel Reisberg's *Cognition: Exploring the Science of the Mind* (2015), and Michael Eysenck and Marc Brysbaert's (2018) *Fundamentals of Cognition*. Additionally, Joshua Foer writes about the use of imagery among competitive memorizers in his enthralling book, *Moonwalking with Einstein: The Art and Science of Remembering Everything* (2012).

Credits

Page 102: Tajang / Shutterstock
Page 104: Oxy-gen / Shutterstock
Page 105: Monkey Business Images / Shutterstock
Page 108: Margo Harrison / Shutterstock
Page 110: Levin, J. R., Shriberg, L. K., Miller, G. E., McCormick, C. B., & Levin, B. B. (1980). The keyword method in the classroom: How to remember the states and their capitals. The Elementary School Journal, 80(4), 185–191. With permission of authors.
Page 112: Alizada Studios / Shutterstock
Page 116: (left) A.RICARDO / Shutterstock
Page 116: (center) Studio623 / Shutterstock
Page 116: (right) topseller / Shutterstock
Page 119: ibreakstock / Shutterstock

CHAPTER 7

Organization

The Importance of Organization for Remembering

Learning Objectives
- Reading this chapter will help you:
  + Understand and provide examples of organization in learning.
  + Know how to effectively apply organization in your own learning.
  + Appreciate the benefits of organization for reducing cognitive load.
  + Explain how a good organization may reduce others' cognitive load.

Rajan Mahadevan is a famous memorist best known for having won a place in the 1981 *Guinness Book of World Records* by reciting 31,811 digits of pi without making an error. (The current world record is 100,000 digits set in 2006 by Akira Haraguchi.) How do people like Rajan achieve such world-record-breaking feats of memory?

In 2006, Rajan came to Colorado State University to speak on his phenomenal memory expertise. After wowing the audience with live demonstrations of his ability to rapidly memorize large swaths of digits, Rajan spoke about the strategies he uses. Rajan is almost effortlessly able to elaborate (see Chapter 6) on numbers in a way that is personally meaningful. For example, a simple sequence of numbers will conjure up years that are important to him, cricket scores, area codes, highway numbers, or any of a virtually countless assortment of associations that Rajan has with numbers.

Rajan's expert memory for numbers occurs in part because numbers, such as cricket scores, have great personal meaning for him.

In addition to highlighting elaboration, Rajan also spoke of the need to organize information carefully so that he could track the order in which the meaningful units of information (psychologists use the term **chunks**) had been presented. To organize the information, Rajan created what he called "supergroups." Supergroups are larger categories into which several chunks of information could be grouped together in his mind.

Rajan's use of a good organizing framework is a common feature of memory experts (Chase & Ericsson, 1982). For example, one group of researchers (Ericsson & Polson, 1988) studied the waiter JC, who could perfectly remember up to 20 orders without writing any notes. JC would take orders in clockwise fashion around a table, carefully studying the face of each customer. While doing this, he would associate each customer with elements of his or her order, such as the salad they ordered, the meat they ordered, their starch, and so forth. To later remember the orders, JC would go back to his organization, mentally traveling around the table while using each face to remember that particular person's order.

You probably do not aspire to memorize thousands of digits of pi or long lists of dinner orders, but you can learn from experts' use of organization. Imposing a good organization can be an effective and relatively simple way of learning large amounts of information, be it foreign language vocabulary, important events in history, the periodic table, or

A good organizational framework can make it easier to remember an order in a restaurant.

the key themes from *The Great Gatsby*. But a good organization also goes beyond learning large amounts of information. It helps you learn more in a shorter period of time and allows you to handle complicated information without being overwhelmed. For example, although you can read this page effortlessly, beginning readers would find the sheer volume of words nearly impossible to handle. You, however, have a deep knowledge of language and also a way to structure all of these words, processing them as components of sentences and paragraphs. This observation is backed by a great deal of research showing the benefits of a good organization for memory. Before reading on, try Demonstration 7.1.

Research on Organization and Memory

Which set of words in Demonstration 7.1 was easier to learn, the first (list 1) or the second set (list 2)? Most people doing this demonstration report that the second set is easier. Why would this be? The lists are highly similar, with each consisting of well-known words from common categories. But you may have noticed a key difference. Whereas the words from list 1 were randomly mixed together, those in list 2 were grouped by category. For instance, examples of sports were followed by examples of natural events and so forth. That is, the second list was organized whereas the first list was not. Lots of evidence points to the benefits of organization for learning.

The classic work on organization and memory (Bower, Clark, Lesgold, & Winzenz, 1969) charged participants with learning 112 words spread across four different lists. The task certainly seems daunting, but there was

DEMONSTRATION 7.1

List 1

Set a countdown clock and give yourself 30 seconds to learn the following set of words:

salt, nurse, volcano, parrot, parsley, hawk, engineer, thyme, ocean, bank, dove, canyon

Next, close your book and try to recall as many of these words as you can. Return when you are finished.

List 2

Again, set a countdown clock and give yourself 30 seconds to learn the following set of words:

soccer, tennis, rugby, snow, flood, thunder, sweater, jeans, gloves, clarinet, tuba, cello

Next, close your book and try to recall as many of these words as you can.

a catch; the words were specially chosen to be part of categories that could be divided into subcategories (i.e., there was a hierarchy). For example, some of the words were part of the category *stones* and could be further divided into the subcategories *precious stones* (e.g., *emerald, diamond*) and *masonry stones* (e.g., *limestone, granite*). One group of participants studied the words presented exactly as ordered in the hierarchy (see Figure 7.1 for an example) and another group of participants studied the words in a random order (e.g., silver, brass, ruby, copper, etc.).

Participants were later asked to recall from memory as many of the words as possible and did this in several sequences (called *trials*) where they would study the words and then take a test. Figure 7.2 shows a dramatic set of results. On every trial, participants who used a hierarchy (solid line) had much better memory for the information than participants who learned all of the information in a random order (broken line). In fact, by the second learning trial, participants in the organized condition had recalled close to 100% of the words and had perfect recall by the third and fourth trials. In contrast, participants in the random

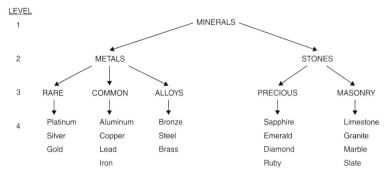

FIGURE 7.1 The hierarchy of minerals used by Bower et al., (1969).

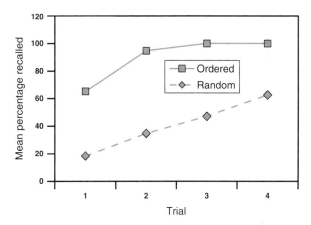

FIGURE 7.2 The mean percentage of words recalled for participants given a hierarchy or words in a random order (adapted from Bower et al., 1969).

condition were still below 40% by the second trial and were recalling only about 60% of the words by the fourth trial. Importantly, all participants were asked to learn exactly the same information; the researchers only varied whether the words were organized or random.

The bottom line? Applying an organizational structure to the material that you are trying to learn can dramatically improve learning (see also Eylon & Reif, 1984). And the categories do not have to be commonly known categories like rocks or minerals, or fruits or vegetables. Research suggests that creating your own categories on the fly works just as well. These "ad-hoc categories" (Barsalou, 1983) confer similar benefits for learning. So, try creating hierarchical categories some time!

Applying Organization in Your Own Learning

Applying an organization can be a powerful method of enhancing learning, but how might you apply organization in your own learning?

Applying a Hierarchical Structure to Flashcards

Many students suggest applying a hierarchical structure to flashcards. For example, to effectively use flashcards for learning foreign language vocabulary, you could create a card with a large, all-encompassing category label. Then, create several cards that each have a subcategory label. Next, align the actual flashcards in a column below those category labels according to their fit to the category. For instance, with the type of flashcards illustrated in Figure 7.3, you could have the broad category "living things,"

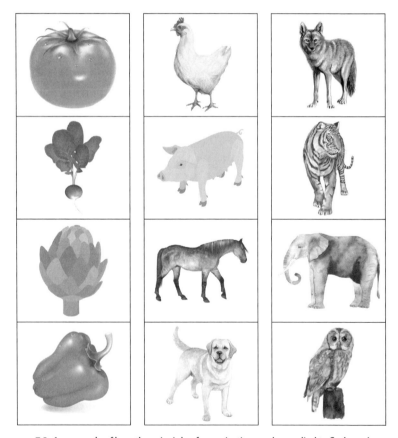

FIGURE 7.3 An example of how the principle of organization can be applied to flash card use.

then below that card, have a column of more specific subcategories: vegetables, farm animals, wild animals, and so on. Then, put the fruit cards in a stack or column below the "fruit" category label, the vegetable cards in a stack or column below the "vegetable" category label, and so on.

Devising and Diagramming Your Own Hierarchical Structure

In one of your authors' classes, students are encouraged to devise their own hierarchical structure and to diagram that in their notes. An example is depicted in Figure 7.4. The larger category of long-term memory is used at the top. It is divided into episodic memory and semantic memory, and each of these categories is further divided into subcategories discussed in class. Figure 7.5 is a hierarchical organizational diagram depicting the organization and content of this chapter, which should aid you in your further reading and retention of this chapter.

Mentally Applying Your Own Organizational Structure

In the example of Rajan Mahadevan given at the beginning of this chapter, he was mentally applying a hierarchical structure. That is, Rajan does not write down or diagram the structure that he devises. For him, the strategy is purely mental and used on the fly during competitive memorization.

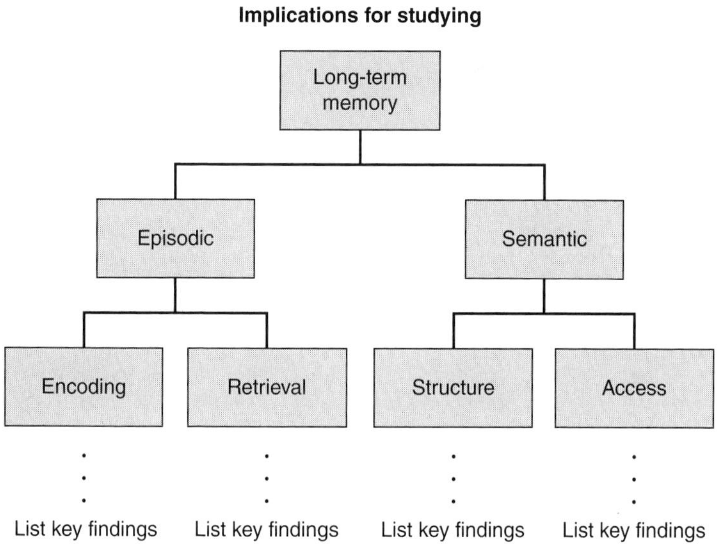

FIGURE 7.4 An example of diagramming a hierarchical structure for organizing course information in a way that makes sense to you. This is an example of material taken from a cognitive psychology course related to the topic of memory.

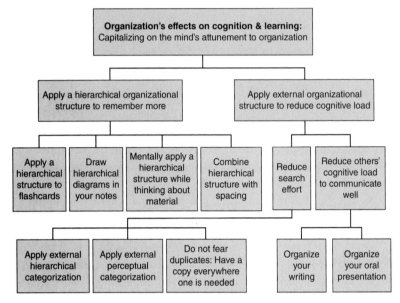

FIGURE 7.5 A hierarchical structure diagram for the content of the current chapter of this book.

You can use this strategy in many situations. Consider, for example, what is sometimes referred to as "Kim's Game," taken from a 1901 novel by Rudyard Kipling called *Kim* focusing on a character named Kim who plays a particular memory game during his training as a spy.

The game goes like this. Someone collects a number of small, random objects and puts them on a tray or table before a player. The player has about a minute to memorize the objects before they are removed. Then, the person must recall as many of the objects as possible. Try it with the set of objects presented on the next page before proceeding. Take one minute to memorize all of the objects on the tray then look away and try to recall them.

How many were you able to recall? The game is often harder than people assume. One way to approach this task is with an organizational structure, such as that depicted in Figure 7.6. Would creating a mental organization like this have helped you to remember more of the objects? Try this game for yourself with random objects and see if practicing this strategy allows you to improve. (See Box 7.1 for examples of other organizational techniques.)

Try to learn the set of objects depicted here.

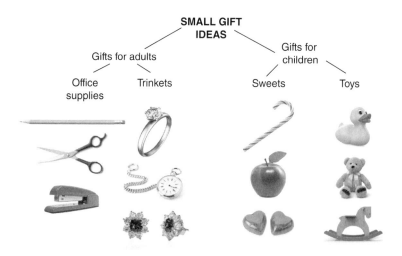

FIGURE 7.6 An example of way to apply a hierarchical structural organization to the objects presented on the "tray" on the previous page for use in Kim's Game.

> **BOX 7.1   OTHER EFFECTIVE LEARNING STRATEGIES BASED ON ORGANIZATION**
>
> In addition to creating hierarchies, there are several other effective techniques available to organize information. A popular approach is the **first letter technique**, whereby the first letter of each word you wish to learn is made into its own word or phrase. For example, how could you remember the colors of the rainbow, in order? A common method is to remember this set of letters: ROY G. BIV. That is, the colors are red, orange, yellow, green, blue, indigo, and violet. Many of your authors' students learn the steps in the cycle of science (see Figure 2.2) by focusing on the letters IDOV—induction, deduction, observation, and verification.
>
> Another organizational approach is to create a story based on what you want to learn, a method referred to as **narrative chaining**. For example, in one experiment (Bower & Clark, 1969), participants were asked to learn 12 lists, each containing 10 words. Half of the participants were instructed to create story based on the words and the other half in a control condition were given no instructions and left to their own devices. After learning each list, participants were asked to recall each, in order. On average, those who created a narrative remembered 93% of the lists; participants in the control condition recalled 13%, on average. The moral of the story—a good organization can produce dramatic gains in learning.

How Organization and Spacing can be Used Together for Effective Learning

Chapter 1 introduced the idea that mixing materials together (termed **interleaving**) can sometimes lead to better learning than blocking the same materials together (see also Chapter 8). You may be wondering if spacing and interleaving are compatible with the principles of organization outlined. For example, in Chapter 1, you learned about a study showing that interleaving different paintings by different artists was better for learning than presenting one artist's paintings together in a block (see Figures 1.3 and 1.4). Can a good hierarchical organization effectively coexist with interleaving? For example, if you

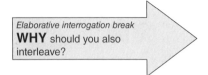

Elaborative interrogation break
WHY should you also interleave?

were managing a museum, how could you build in the benefits of inter-leaving while still having a strong organization?

You might have considered several ways to merge these concepts. For example, rather than randomly distributing paintings throughout, a museum might be organized according to artistic era with a diagram reminding visitors of this structure at the entry to each room. Within each room the paintings could be interleaved so that different artists' works were interspersed among one another. The museum would have a structured order with a clear organizational format, yet would have an interleaved learning component as well.

Organization and Cognitive Processing

The benefits of organization for learning reveal a greater truth—our minds are organized and attuned to this organization in many different ways. By understanding this structure, you can leverage the benefits of organization in learning and in other facets of your life.

Our Minds are Geared Toward Organization

While adhering to a hierarchical organizational scheme is a very useful method of remembering, the fact that this method works so well also reveals a larger principle of human cognition that relates to learning and cognitive processing more broadly. Indeed, most scientists (e.g., Baronchelli et al., 2013) believe that your mind is composed of overlapping networks organized by grouping similar information (information that has a lot in common) together.

For example, your knowledge of fruits is stored in a network representing how these ideas fit together. A simple illustration of such a network is depicted in Figure 7.7. The set of fruit circles (called *nodes*) to the left of the figure is meant to be a subset of a larger network, as depicted by the gray arrow coming from the larger network to the right of the figure. Notice that in this small subset of the larger network, the node representing the concept "fruit" has many connections to other nodes, each of which denotes a particular kind of fruit. This is a very simple example of a categorical organization within the mind that is supported by many studies showing that the structure accounts for how you recognize and process information.

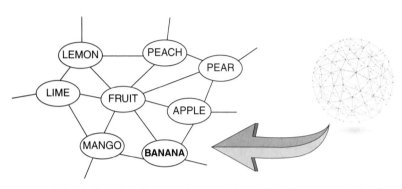

FIGURE 7.7 A simple depiction of a semantic network from within a larger network of nodes.

Thus, the mind is highly organized. This fact has significant implications for learning and cognitive processing beyond just memorization. It means that it is easier to process information that fits within the mind's existing organizational framework; in turn, information that will be easier to process may be easier to remember. This is why presenting information in a hierarchy promoted much better memory than a random presentation (Bower et al., 1969)—the hierarchy was consistent with people's existing knowledge organization. Your mind's organizational structure is also why experts remember things differently than novices when it comes to information from their domain of knowledge. Experts have more (or a different) existing mental organization than novices (e.g., Chi, Feltovich, & Glaser, 1981).

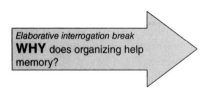

Elaborative interrogation break
WHY does organizing help memory?

Importantly, your mind's organizational structure indicates that a good organization around you can ease your **cognitive load**, or how hard you have to work mentally to process information.

Easing Cognitive Load with an Assist from Organization

All individuals are limited in their capacity for processing information. Specific limits vary from person to person, but the bottom line is that you can only have so much in mind at once. That is, you can only take on so much cognitive load at once before reaching your capacity. As an example, read the following sentences and pay attention to your ability to process them.

The doctor met with the nurse.

The doctor met with the nurse to talk about the patient.

The doctor that the nurse despised met with her to talk about the patient.

The doctor with the red hair that the nurse despised met with her to talk about the patient.

The doctor with the red hair that the nurse despised met with her to talk about the patient about to be discharged.

The first sentence was likely the easiest to process, but each sentence thereafter probably seemed progressively harder to process, culminating in a nearly incomprehensible final sentence. In this example, adding information eventually hits a processing limit where your cognitive load is simply too great. If you have ever taken a chemistry class, you may have noticed that mentally visualizing simple molecules was possible, but as the molecules became more and more complex (as in organic chemistry or biochemistry), they began to exceed your capacity for visualizing. To help escape this processing limit, chemistry professors often recommend using "ball and stick" model kits (see also Chapter 6 on imagery).

Ball and stick chemistry sets are a great example of a technique known as **cognitive offloading** (Nestojko, Finley, & Roediger, 2013; Risko & Dunn, 2015). Cognitive offloading is the idea that as information becomes too complex to process merely by thinking about it, one can "offload" some of the required resources to the external world to free up mental capacity to process what is needed in any given moment. Examples of ways in which people offload information to the external world include writing things down, drawing diagrams, and building models. Modern search engines also serve as important source of cognitive offloading (e.g., Sparrow, Liu, & Wegner, 2011).

Applying a sound organization to learning and to life can be another potent method of cognitive offloading (Levitin, 2014). Indeed, it takes mental energy to actively think about and process information and there is only so much available. This is why mental tasks are easier to perform when you can devote your full attention to them than when you try to divide our attention between tasks (as when multitasking). In fact, competitive memorizers often go to great extremes to minimize distractions when

A picture of Joshua Foer's gear for preventing distraction during memorization, from his TED talk "Feats of Memory Anyone Can Do," May 2012.

trying to learn large quantities of information, seeking to maximize the cognitive resources available for the difficult memorization task.

You might recall the journalist-turned-competitive-memorizer Joshua Foer from earlier in this book. In his TED talk, he mentioned that "distraction is the competitive memorizer's greatest enemy," and described using noise cancelling ear headphones and dark goggles with pinholes cut through them to minimize distractions while he worked at memorizing large quantities of information. Although an extreme remedy, studies have shown that a distraction as simple as having an unread email on your computer can zap mental resources (Levitin, 2014). Even when people turn off their devices and attempt to disengage, they continue thinking about what they might be missing by not having their device nearby; this consumes resources that might otherwise be devoted to studying.

How can you conserve your own cognitive resources? You can start by minimizing the effort required to locate what you need. For example, when one of your authors finds a few hours to work on writing, much of that time can be spent seeking the needed materials (e.g., notes, articles). Searching for these materials takes mental energy and detracts from the mental energy, the processing resources, needed to engage in high-quality writing.

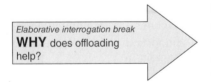

Elaborative interrogation break
WHY does offloading help?

In his book, *The Organized Mind*, Daniel Levitin notes that high-level corporate executives, political leaders, and the superwealthy often seem to have the freedom to process complex tasks at hand and make high-level decisions precisely because they have so much assistance with life's more mundane tasks, freeing up cognitive resources for the more important tasks related to leadership. For example, most people must spend time and energy thinking about grocery lists, paying bills, scheduling doctor appointments, doing laundry, mowing the lawn, responding to emails, and so on. In contrast, Levitin notes that corporate executives, political leaders, and the superwealthy often hire specialized assistants to manage these tasks. They do not spend their time worrying about getting milk from the grocery store or the next appointment on their calendar, because someone will tell them. Instead, they allocate their cognitive load to the priorities of the moment.

In contrast, being stricken by poverty can greatly elevate the cognitive demands of day-to-day living (Mani, Mullainathan, Shafir, & Zhao, 2013). For example, people with fewer financial resources must devote more cognitive resources to mundane daily tasks (e.g., cooking, cleaning, paying bills). But it is actually worse than that. The energy that goes into day-to-day decisions that financially comfortable people do not even have to make (such as whether to sacrifice milk for the children that week in order to afford to transportation to work) drains cognitive resources (Mani et al., 2013).

All of this is not to say that the deleterious effects of poverty can be overcome with mere organizational tactics, nor that you can reach CEO-level hyper-focus through such tactics. However, there are simple steps you can take to offload cognitive demands to the external world and to have more resources available for focusing on desirable cognitive tasks like learning, performing, and decision-making.

Schedule Spaced Studying Sessions With Alerts On Your Devices

Given that most people will never have a personal assistant, a personal device can be used for scheduling. Accordingly, schedule your study sessions in advance by spreading them out over time (see Chapter 8 for more on the advantages of this approach). This reduces your personal cognitive load and permits you to receive reminders about when you are supposed to study so that you can just go do it. Consider the following example. A friend of one of your authors operates a personal, private tutoring company. College students who pay for these expensive services can receive a wake-up call in the morning to get them out of bed to video-conference with the tutor and receive an organized plan for the day's study activities. The tutor continually checks in to make sure that the student is performing the scheduled tasks and remains on schedule, and may even test or quiz the student. If this sounds similar to the aforementioned personal

Scheduling devices can reduce personal cognitive load.

assistants, that's because it is. If it seems unfair to you—like it might give wealthy college students who can afford it a competitive edge in college—consider that you can do much of this yourself by capitalizing on apps that you likely have available to you on your various electronic devices. Turn your smart phone, tablet, computer or smart watch into your own personal assistant for managing your studying.

Apply Hierarchical Categorical Structure to Your Materials

Hierarchical categorization of your study materials not only helps you to retain more information, but can ease your cognitive load during studying in some respects. For example, compare the randomly arrayed tray for Kim's Game with the organization of that tray depicted in Figure 7.6. If you were to search for the bracelet, you would probably have an easier time finding it in Figure 7.6 than in the tray. It is easier to search for something among information that is organized in a way that adheres to your mind's existing knowledge organization than to search within disorganized clutter. Similarly, consider searching for a small spoon in a silverware drawer where all of the utensils were simply thrown into a big pile. It would be a maddening experience, but it is one you rarely experience. Instead, your own silverware drawer is likely organized as a tray of compartments (one for spoons, one for forks, one for knives, etc.) rather than a mixture of utensils.

Perhaps one of the most important places to apply a hierarchical categorical organization to your surroundings is your computer desktop.

One of your authors has a lab computer for student use. The computer has so many icons on the desktop that it is impossible to see the background. It is also difficult for students to find files when they need them. A categorical structure might be an ideal way to organize the files. For example, within a folder labeled "Human Memory," there might be a folder called "Working Memory." Within that folder, there might be three other folders: "Visual Working Memory," "Working Memory Capacity," and "Activated Long-Term Memory." Within each of those three folders would be research articles that fit under those particular topics.

Note that you can organize your hand-written notes similarly if you use a binder with labeled, color-coded sections for them. You can also apply a similar structure to stacks of flashcards. Keeping your study materials organized in ways that naturally fit with the structure of your knowledge-base will make it easier for you to process (as well as remember) the information. Not only does organizing by hierarchical category fit your mind's natural attunement to organizational structure, but it also decreases clutter and reduces your search time for information.

Apply Perceptual Organization and Simultaneous Presentation Structure

While categories matter when it comes to external offloading of cognitive resources through organization, it is not the only way that external organization can reduce cognitive load. Another method is to allow for immediate comparison of information by using what is called a *simultaneous display*. For example, one group of researchers (Meagher, Carvalho, Goldstone, & Nosofsky, 2017) had participants learn to classify different types of rocks. Some participants saw rocks one at a time in a random order; other participants were given the chance to see all of the rocks in a single, simultaneous display (see Figure 7.8).

Everyone later took a test in which they were shown new rocks and asked to classify the rock as igneous, metamorphic, or sedimentary. As you can see in Figure 7.9, correct classifications were more likely after simultaneous presentations.

The use of the simultaneous display format of the rocks may be analogous to the logic behind using ball-and-stick models in chemistry, or behind drawing charts and diagrams for complex processes like human metabolism. It provides an easily referenced, external guide for information that would be difficult to keep in mind all at once. How might you create simultaneous displays of information to your own

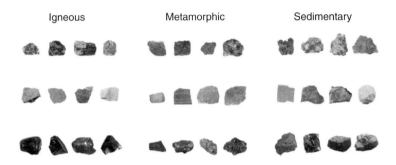

FIGURE 7.8 Simultaneous display of rock categories used by Meagher, Carvalho, Goldstone and Nosofsky (2017) in their study of simultaneous vs. sequential presentation of rocks for natural science category learning.

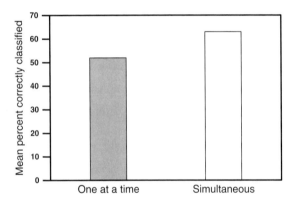

FIGURE 7.9 The mean percentage of new rocks correctly classified when rocks were studied one at a time or in a simultaenous presentation (adapted from Meagher et al., 2017).

studying and learning? For example, what if flashcards were color-coded or shaped according to likeness, and spread out on a table before you simultaneously, instead of in a stack to go through one at a time? Or, might it be useful to keep a color-coded chart or diagram up on a wall or whiteboard where you are studying? This would allow you to refer back to the simultaneous presentation of the information while you go through the rest of the information in more depth.

Reduce Search Time Through Redundancy

A less obvious strategy for cognitive offloading to the external world is to use redundancy in one's organizational scheme. Levitin (2014) advocates this, giving the example of keeping a pair of scissors in the kitchen as well as in the study to reduce time running back and forth and searching for scissors. Keeping a pair in every location where they will be needed means that the scissors will be on-hand right when and where they are needed.

A similar principle can be applied to an important area of your life: Do not fear multiple copies of documents on your computer. In order to have each file right when and where you need it, keep a copy in every hierarchy, category, or folder in which it might be relevant. For example, an article on *Great Expectations* might be stored in an "English Literature" folder as well as in a "Charles Dickens" folder. This ensures that an article is right there, where and when it is needed. Applied to your study materials, if you have a guide on how to write, you might keep a copy in every folder in which you are working on a writing assignment. If you like to use a highlighter and a red pen for making notes on your elaborations while reading, keep some in your backpack as well as on your desk, so that they are always handy.

Ease Others' Cognitive Load: Use Organization for Effective Communication

An effective organization may not only reduce your own cognitive load, but steps you take to better organizing your writing and communication can reduce others' cognitive load.

Organization in Writing

One of the key characteristics of good writing is the organization of the paper. You can appreciate this when reading a badly written paper. Badly written papers are often disorganized and can feel to the reader like sifting through clutter for the main points. Badly written papers jump from one idea to the next, or meander back and forth among different thoughts, and are difficult for the reader to process. Consider the following passage:

> Recognition memory involves the ability to recognize that something has occurred previously. Research investigating emotion in memory has resulted in an extensive body of literature spanning the last several decades with many different and often conflicting findings, as some studies show that emotion helps memory and other studies show that emotion has no effect on memory and little consensus on which is actually the case. Emotion can be positive or negative. Some people's memories are better than other's.

Did you feel a bit frustrated reading that? Why? One reason was that it jumped from one idea to the next. In short, it was disorganized, making it hard to read.

You have probably already learned about the key characteristics of good writing in your English classes and classes on writing. There is a method to the madness, so to speak, in all of those techniques that your English instructors taught you about good writing. Though perhaps not explicit in classes on writing, good writing minimizes the reader's cognitive load to maximize the reader's ability to comprehend and process what you have written. Part of this involves capitalizing on your reader's attention to organization. To do this, your own writing should have a hierarchical structure that readers can easily follow.

First, outline your writing plan before writing, using this outline to provide the scaffolding for how the paper will be organized. To be optimally effective in reducing your reader's cognitive load and maximizing communication effectiveness, use a hierarchical organization. Second, include a thesis statement for your paper, often placed as the last sentence of the first or second paragraph. Think of this as the overarching hierarchical theme to your paper—the topmost category, after your title. Given that people's minds are attuned to hierarchical organizational structures, having a thesis statement aids processing of the rest of the paper (determining where in the organizational scheme or structure the rest of the parts fit). Third, be sure to have a topic sentence for each paragraph and include these in your outline to track the overarching themes of your paper. This practice also helps the reader to mentally organize the ideas presented for easier processing while reading.

With these three principles in mind, consider a reorganized version of the sample of poor writing presented previously.

> The effects of emotion on memory are not well-understood. Whereas some studies have shown benefits of stimulus emotion on memory, others have found no effects. Although some of this mixture of findings might be attributable to individual differences among people, another factor at work might be the particular type of emotion under investigation (positive or negative) in each study. In the present study, we will investigate the hypothesis that the type of emotion (positive or negative) matters to whether emotion will affect memorability. We will test this hypothesis using a recognition memory test, in which people must decide if each test item occurred previously in the experiment or not.

Although this is not an exceptionally written paragraph, it is much more organized. There is a topic sentence. The paragraph also ends with a thesis sentence to help guide the rest of the paper. You also may have noticed that it was easier to process this paragraph than the earlier example.

Other approaches can also enhance comprehension. For example, using headings and subheadings in your writing allows the reader to connect the components of the paper to a clear hierarchical structure in his or her own mind. Consider the way that this chapter is organized. Through the use of headings and subheadings, the chapter itself can be diagrammed with a hierarchical structure diagram, as in Figure 7.5.

In forming the structure of your paper, write with your audience in mind. For instance, experts in an area will have different mental organizational structures for their knowledge than novices who are new to the area. Those structures affect how experts process and remember information, making it important to consider your audience when structuring and organizing a manuscript. If you are writing to a group of experts on the subject matter, your organization will need to be different (in order to appeal to their mind's organizational frameworks) than if you are writing to a group of novices.

Regardless of whether you are writing for experts or novices, consider the cognitive load that your writing is inducing. For example, do you remember how hard it was to process this sentence:

The doctor with the red hair that the nurse despised met with her to talk about the patient about to be discharged.

This sentence is unnecessarily long and asks the reader to process several ideas. A better practice is to construct sentences that are well within your reader's span of apprehension. In other words, do not write long sentences that may exceed your reader's cognitive load. If your reader must keep going back and rereading sentences in order to process what was written, your communication is not as effective as it could be. For example, you could divide the above long sentence into the following.

The red-haired doctor met with the nurse who despised him. They talked about the patient who was about to be discharged.

Organization in Public Speaking

The same general organizational principles that apply to effective writing also apply to effective public speaking. When giving a speech or a presentation, you should have an organizational structure to your presentation that allows the audience to easily follow your main points. You can do this with slides and visual aids. However, what if you have to essentially memorize a speech? In these cases, a good organizational structure will be critical.

In his TED talk "Feats of Memory Anyone Can Do," Joshua Foer discusses how he remembered his talk by providing himself with cues for an organizational scaffolding. He specifically used the **method of loci** detailed in Chapter 6 on imagery. During his talk, Foer mentally walked through his home, using each "place" along the mental walk-through as a cue for the next part of his talk. For example, when he got to his home's foyer in his mental walk-through, he would encounter his previously created mental image of Cookie Monster on top of the horse, Mr. Ed. This was his cue to tell the story about how he met Ed Cook, a competitive memorizer. Then, when he got to his kitchen on his mental walk-through, he encountered the characters from the *Wizard of Oz* on a yellow brick road, reminding him to tell the story of his journey.

Foer's approach illustrates a great way to cue your own memory in public speaking by using other techniques discussed in this book and to do so in a way that provides an organization to help your audience process your talk. In fact, in his talk, Joshua Foer argues that in ancient times, oration was a regular practice and attaching an organizational scaffolding to one's story or narrative was critical. It was commonly done using the memory palace method. The common English phrase "in the first place" comes from the notion that as you are speaking or telling a story, you are going to the first place in your mind's memory palace to find that information to talk about it.

Putting It All Together

You are deluged on a daily basis with information to remember—appointments, dates, assignments, names of characters from TV shows, news, and so much more. Although you have a great deal to remember, you probably find that you do not, for example, confuse an appointment to go to the dentist with your favorite character from a recent movie. You escape this confusion because your knowledge is organized. Bringing organization to bear on whatever you need to learn is similarly powerful, giving you substantial benefits when you impose organization during learning and use that organization when you need to remember the information. Further, the lessons of organization can apply throughout life, be it to a paper you are writing, a speech you need to give, or to your search for another phone charger. Reaping the benefits of organization thus have the potential to change your learning and your life.

Tips You Can Use

1. **Apply a hierarchical organization.** When trying to learn categories of information, create a hierarchical diagram of the categories and their member items. This diagram can serve as an external aid for cognitive offloading while you dig into the details of what you are learning. Organization can be extended to many other types of learning, from organizing your notes to working through flashcards. As well, hierarchies can be used effectively when writing or preparing a talk or a speech. In doing this, remember that your audience's minds will be attuned to the organizational structure you provide.
2. **Combine a hierarchical organization with interleaving.** Combine interleaving with organization to get more bang for your learning buck: Within a hierarchical categorical structure, try interleaving (mixing) the specific examples while studying.
3. **Use a simultaneous presentation diagram as a visual aid.** Keep a simultaneous presentation diagram on hand while learning and use this to track the broader points of what you are trying to learn.
4. **Minimize distractions.** Minimize distractions as much as possible while studying. Distractions drain your cognitive resources, detracting from your learning.
5. **Use calendar apps to schedule study sessions.** Calendar apps can be the next best thing to a personal assistant. Use them to schedule your spaced study sessions and have them alert you (like a personal assistant) to what you should be doing when.

Discussion Questions

1. The chapter describes how mixing materials can be combined with a good organization. How would organization relate to other topics you have learned about so far, such as metacognition, elaboration, and imagery?

2. How might you combine organization and interleaving in your own flashcard use?
3. A key theme of the chapter is that learning will be enhanced when your all of your cognitive resources can be brought to bear on learning. Besides drawing diagrams and organizing your flashcards, how else might you engage in cognitive offloading in your own learning?
4. Suppose you were charged with giving a speech on the benefits of elaboration (the focus of Chapter 5) one week from now to group of high school students. How would you craft that speech following the principles of organization outlined in this chapter?

Suggestions for Further Reading

Bat-Sheva Eylon and F. Rief (1984) have an excellent treatment of how organization can benefit learning and is highly recommended. Lawrence Barsalou's (1983) work on ad hoc categories provides a nice illustration of how categorical structures can be applied on the fly even to information for which the structure does not seem obvious. Although not the focus of this chapter, a compelling line of work indicates that individuals are very good at prioritizing their learning; Alan Castel is a leading authority in this area and his work is well worth reading (see, e.g., Castel, 2007). For a broad focus on the benefits of mental organization, we recommend reading Steven Levitin's excellent book *The Organized Mind: Thinking Straight in the Age of Information Overload* (2014). Finally, for a more entertaining read on the origins of the memory game Kim's Game, you might consider reading Rudyard Kipling's 1901 novel *Kim*.

Credits

Page 124: Lance Bellers / Shutterstock
Page 125: wavebreakmedia / Shutterstock
Page 127: Republished with permission of Elsevier. Hierarchical retrieval schemes of recall of categorized word lists. Bower, G. H., Clark, M., Lesgold, A., & Winzenz, D. Journal of Verbal Learning and Verbal Behavior, 8, 323–343, 1969. Permission conveyed through Copyright Clearance Center, Inc.
Page 128: First column (top to bottom): Olivkairishka / Shutterstock, Andriy Lipkan / Shutterstock, Rinat Sultanov / Shutterstock, Oleksii Natykach / Shutterstock; Second column: viktoriya_art / Shutterstock,

Rvector / Shutterstock, Valentyna Chukhyebova / Shutterstock, Dneprstock / Shutterstock; Third column: Panaiotidi / Shutterstock, mymaja8 / Shutterstock, Kat_Branch / Shutterstock, AnSuArt / Shutterstock

Page 131: Pencil: Vitaly Zorkin / Shutterstock; Scissors: old-cowboy / Shutterstock; stapler: Kaytoo / Shutterstock; earrings: Fruit Cocktail Creative; watch: Alexander Hoffmann / Shutterstock; ring: bioraven / Shutterstock; hearts: Andersphoto / Shutterstock; candy cane: StudioSmart / Shutterstock; apple: Preto Perola / Shutterstock; rocking horse: Anton Vasylenko / Shutterstock; duck: Nerthuz / Shutterstock; teddy bear: Anteromite / Shutterstock

Page 134: Baronchelli, A., Ferrer-i-Cancho, R., Pastor-Satorras, R., Chater, N., & Christiansen, M. H. (2013). Networks in cognitive science. Trends in Cognitive Sciences, 17, 348–360. Reprinted with permission of John Wiley and Sons, all rights reserved.

Page 138: Rawpixel.com / Shutterstock

Page 140: (Figure 7.8) Reprinted from The Lancet, Vol. number, Author(s), Title of article, Pages No., Copyright (Year), with permission from Elsevier.

CHAPTER 8

Give It a Break!

Spacing Your Study and Practice

....

Learning Objectives
- Reading this chapter will help you:
  - Distinguish between massed and spaced methods of learning.
  - Appreciate the benefits of spacing and the drawbacks of cramming in learning.
  - Distinguish between blocked and interleaved methods of learning.
  - Know how to effectively apply spacing and interleaving in your own learning.

....

Suppose you are planning a trip to Costa Rica and want to learn and remember Spanish phrases like "Where is the restroom?" Or perhaps you are taking a math class and need to remember the equations for computing the volume of a sphere, a cone, and a cylinder. Or maybe you are studying for the written portion of your driver's examination and are trying to remember the meaning of obscure signs that you have never seen before. And also suppose that you are planning to review this information multiple times. Would you be better off going over each bit of information again and again, consecutively, until you are convinced that you have mastered it? Or would you be better off if you review the information, then move on to other things, with the plan of coming back later? Likewise, suppose you are preparing for an exam that covers four chapters of your textbook. Would you be better off if you review one chapter each night for four nights or if you review all of the chapters to some extent each night?

Spacing can help you learn information, such as the words on road signs in Costa Rica.

All of these examples converge on a fundamental question: When you go to study something repeatedly, should the repetitions occur in succession (i.e., be **massed**) or should the repetitions be spread out over time (i.e., be **spaced**)? In scenarios such as these, students commonly choose to mass rather than space their studying (e.g., Hartwig & Dunlosky, 2012). They may also feel that massing their studying is working well. But the science of learning says that spacing is best: Learning tends to be much more durable and long-lasting when you spread out your study efforts. Take a minute to complete Demonstration 8.1 before you continue reading.

In Demonstration 8.1, you were shown Swahili–English word pairs for study (see Nelson & Dunlosky, 1994). Each pair was repeated three times, but in some cases, the repetitions occurred consecutively (they were massed). In other cases, the repetitions were spread out in the list (they were spaced). As you were reading through the pairs and trying to commit them to memory, what was your sense about how learning was progressing? Did you notice a difference in how quickly and easily you seemed to go through the massed items, like *rafiki*–friend and *chakula*–food, versus the spaced items, like *tabibu*–doctor and *fagio*–broom?

People commonly report that it feels as though learning is quicker and easier when information is presented in a massed fashion. When you encountered *rafiki*–friend that second and third time, it was fresh on your mind because you encountered it a moment earlier. As a result, your sense may have been that you had it down pretty well. In contrast,

DEMONSTRATION 8.1

Set a countdown clock and give yourself 2 minutes to read each of the following Swahili-English word pairs in preparation for a test.

ziwa–lake	farasi–horse	tabibu–doctor
theluji–snow	farasi–horse	chakula–food
tabibu–doctor	tabibu–doctor	chakula–food
rafiki–friend	ziwa–lake	chakula–food
rafiki–friend	fagio–broom	ziwa–lake
rafiki–friend	chura–frog	zulia–carpet
fagio–broom	chura–frog	fagio–broom
zulia–carpet	chura–frog	pipa–barrel
theluji–snow	theluji–snow	pipa–barrel
farasi–horse	zulia–carpet	pipa–barrel

Now, without looking at the above list on the page, try to write down the English word from each pair from memory.

zulia-_____   rafiki-_____

chakula-_____   tabibu-_____

chura-_____   fagio-_____

farasi-_____   pipa-_____

ziwa-_____   theluji-_____

when you encountered *tabibu*–doctor for the second and third time, it was not as fresh on your mind because your most recent experiences were with other pairs. A little bit of forgetting had taken place in the short time since *tabibu*–doctor appeared earlier. You may go a little slower and feel that learning is not as easy. But, as described in Chapter 1, your feeling in the moment while you are learning is not always a good indicator of what will be accessible later on. In this case, although learning may feel quicker and easier with massed studying than spaced studying, a wealth of research shows that spaced studying produces more durable learning. This phenomenon is called the **spacing effect**.

The Science of Spaced Study and Practice

The first systematic research on spaced study was described by Hermann Ebbinghaus in his famous book *Memory: A Contribution to Experimental Psychology,* published in 1885. Using himself as the sole participant,

Ebbinghaus found that when learning a short list of 12 syllables, what took him 68 consecutive repetitions of the list on the same day took just 38 repetitions when spread out over three days. That is 44% less study time to achieve the same amount of learning, just by breaking up his studying!

In more recent research (Sobel, Cepeda, & Kapler, 2011), fifth grade students were taught relatively rare vocabulary words (e.g., *tacit, gregarious*). Learning occurred in the classroom using an interactive tutorial in which the teacher led students in reading and recalling the definitions of the words, as well as reading sample sentences and creating novel sentences using the words. The students completed the tutorial a second time, but one group did so just one minute after the first completion, whereas a second group did so one week after the first completion. Five weeks later, all students tried to recall the definitions. Overall, students did not remember much, which is not surprising given that five weeks passed before the final test, with no additional practice. But the key finding was that recall was nearly three times greater when the lessons occurred one week apart (20.8%) than when they occurred consecutively (7.5%).

This benefit of spaced learning have been well established by hundreds of studies. Comprehensive reviews of the literature (e.g., Delaney, Verkoeijen, & Spirgel, 2010; Donovan & Radosevich, 1999; Janiszewski, Noel, & Sawyer, 2003) show spacing advantages across a wide variety of materials, including definitions, foreign-language vocabulary, facts, pictures, passages of text, and lectures; across many topic areas, including math, history, biology, and music; and in both laboratory studies and classroom studies. In one meta-analysis (Cepeda, Pashler, Vul, & Wixted, 2006) that included 271 comparisons of massed versus spaced study for learning, 259 of the comparisons showed an advantage for spacing. The spacing advantage held when the final assessment came less than a minute after learning all the way up to several weeks after learning. The clear implication of this research is spacing your learning has clear advantages over massing.

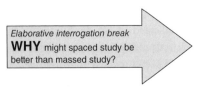

Elaborative interrogation break
WHY might spaced study be better than massed study?

So Study More Frequently?

At this point, you may be thinking, "I should break up my studying and spread it out. But does this mean I should study a greater *amount*?" The message is a bit different than that. Even if you spend the same amount of time studying, but spread that time out, you will see gains in learning.

Indeed, in most studies on spacing, researchers carefully control for study time, so that the amount of study time is the same for the massed and spaced conditions. As an example, one experiment varied the distribution of learning in a way similar to Demonstration 8.1 (see Dempster, 1987, Experiment 3). Participants studied English vocabulary words and definitions using a massed schedule or a spaced schedule. Each word and definition appeared three times, for 7 seconds each time, but the repetitions occurred consecutively in the massed condition, or with other items inserted between the repetitions in the spaced condition. Based on that design, participants in all conditions studied each word and definition for about 21 seconds. If only the total amount of study time was important, then participants' learning should have been the same regardless of whether that studying was massed or spaced.

The results contradicted this hypothesis. Participants recalled 52% of the definitions in the spaced condition compared to 35% in the massed condition. Spaced learning improved retention by nearly 50%, even with the amount of study time held constant! The lesson here is that by spacing learning, you get much more bang for your buck in the same amount of time.

Space Within a Session? Across Sessions?

You may have noticed that some of the studies discussed previously investigated spaced versus massed learning in the same study sessions (Dempster, 1987), whereas others examined massing versus spacing of the sessions themselves (see Ebbinghaus, 1885; Sobel et al., 2011). Does this matter? Consider a study using flashcards.

Do you use flashcards to help you learn course material? Quite a few students do, with about 40 to 60% of students saying they use them at least some of the time (Karpicke, Butler, & Roediger, 2009; Morehead, Rhodes, & DeLozier, 2016). Flashcards can be very effective for enhancing learning and retention when used well (see Chapter 9 on testing). One study investigated learning with (electronic) flashcards and examined how the spacing of practice affected that learning (Kornell, 2009).

Participants in this study attempted to learn pairs of synonyms, such as *feckless: ineffective* in a simulated flashcard task. Participants would see the first word of the pair, followed by a blank (*feckless: _____*). When ready, participants would then press a button to reveal the synonym, the equivalent of flipping over the flashcard.

Synonyms were repeated four times but, in a *high spacing condition,* the repetitions were set up so that 20 other synonym pairs occurred before a pair was repeated. In a *low spacing condition,* only five other synonym pairs occurred before a pair was repeated. All synonyms were learned in a spaced fashion, so this study examined different degrees of spacing (rather than massing versus spacing). In addition, all learning occurred within a single session, so the study focused on the effects of **within-session spacing** (for an illustration of this type of spacing, see Panel A of Figure 8.1).

After learning, participants estimated the percentage of the words they would be able to remember from each condition. A day later they completed a recall test. The results are shown in Panel A of Figure 8.2. If you look at the two bars on the left, you can see that participants believed they would remember more of the items in the low spacing condition (gray bar) than the high spacing condition (white bar). But if you look at the two bars on the right, they actually remembered more items from

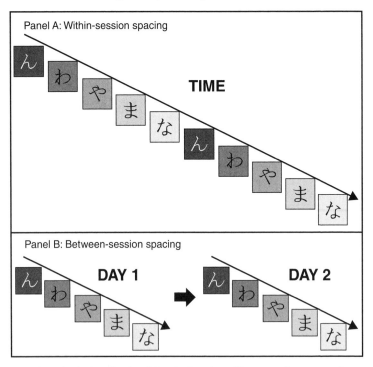

FIGURE **8.1** Hypothetical studies involving the learning of Japanese characters using a within-session spacing schedule (Panel A) and a between-session spacing schedule (Panel B).

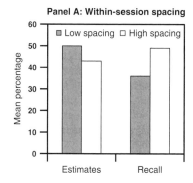 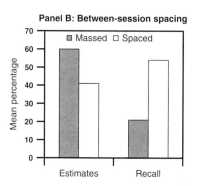

FIGURE 8.2 Participants' estimates and recall for a study of within-session spacing (Panel A) and for a study of between-session spacing (Panel B). Adapted from Kornell (2009).

the high spacing condition. Thus, there was a benefit of greater spacing, even when that spacing occurred within a single learning session.

In the same study (Kornell, 2009), the researcher included another experiment using the same task and materials, but with **between-session spacing** (for an illustration of this type of spacing, see Panel B of Figure 8.1). In a spaced condition, synonyms were studied eight times spread out over four study sessions that occurred over four days. In a massed condition, the eight study opportunities occurred during a single study session on a single day. Participants provided estimates of their learning for each condition, then took a test about 24 hours later.

The results are shown in Panel B of Figure 8.2. As you can see, participants believed that massing study within a single session would lead to better memory than spacing study across sessions. Yet the spacing advantage was huge, with performance over 150% (!) better in the condition that included between-session spacing. Overall, this work shows in a single study what has been shown in many separate studies: You get learning benefits when you distribute study and practice within sessions *and* across sessions.

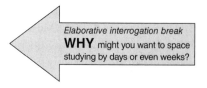

Elaborative interrogation break
WHY might you want to space studying by days or even weeks?

How Much Spacing?

The research reviewed so far indicates that a greater degree of spacing can boost retention. For example, words repeated every 20 trials were more likely to be remembered than words repeated every five trials. Experiments that have closely examined this have focused on the amount of time between each presentation, termed the *lag*. These studies indicate that not only is spaced learning better than massed learning, but more extensive spacing (longer lags) is better than less extensive spacing (shorter lags). The finding that longer lags tend to produce better learning than shorter lags is called the **lag effect**. But the question remains: What is the right lag?

Some striking findings indicate that very long lags can be highly beneficial. One researcher (Bahrick, 1979) had participants learn English–Spanish vocabulary across six learning sessions, and those learning sessions either took place back-to-back on the same day (0 day lag), one session per day for six days (1 day lag), or every 30 days (30 day lag). On a final test given one month after the last learning session, memory was best for the 30-day lag, followed by the one-day lag, then the zero-day lag. The superiority of the 30-day lag remained when participants were tested eight years later (Bahrick & Phelps, 1987).

Does this mean that you should seek the longest lag possible? As it turns out, no. On the one hand, you do not want the lag between learning episodes to be so short that additional study or practice is effortless. When additional study is effortless, little new learning takes place. Instead, you want there to be enough time between study episodes that you will experience some forgetting and the additional study or practice is at least somewhat effortful. It is this effort that seems to reinforce learning. By extension, as lag increases, there will typically be more forgetting from one learning episode to the next. Restudy will therefore be more effortful and will more strongly reinforce the original learning. Logically, though, this will only work up to a point. You should not, for example, wait a decade between spaced study opportunities. A decade is an extreme example, but the point is that if the lag is too long, forgetting may be so complete that learning essentially starts over from scratch. Thus, there is an optimal lag that lies between short lags (in which learning seems effortless) and very long lags (in which the prior learning has been largely lost).

What is that optimal lag? Early research (e.g., Bahrick, 1979) suggested that as the lag between learning episodes increased, retention improved. It turns out that it is not so simple. There is an optimal degree of spacing that produces the best retention, and beyond that point, performance begins to decline. To complicate matters further, this optimal degree of spacing differs depending on how long the information needs to be retained.

BOX 8.1   DOES SLEEP PLAY A ROLE IN SPACING BENEFITS?

We now know that sleep benefits memory (Born, Rasch, & Gais, 2006). Researchers have established that sleep plays an important role in memory **consolidation**, the transition of memory from a temporary state to a more permanent state in the brain (e.g., Rudoy, Voss, Westerberg, & Paller, 2009). How might this contribute to the benefits of spacing?

If spacing occurs over days or weeks, sleep is also occurring in between the spaced sessions. It stands to reason, then, that the occurrence of sleep between study sessions may help to solidify memories. Sure enough, research suggests that sleep does play a role in spacing effects in which sleep intervenes between sessions (Bell, Kawadri, Simone, & Wisehart, 2014).

The bottom line? Get some sleep between your spaced study sessions for an added boost to retention, and plan far enough in advance to benefit from many instances of sleep in between your study sessions!

To illustrate, one study (Cepeda et al., 2008) had participants learn obscure facts such as, "What European nation consumes the most spicy Mexican food?" (The answer is Norway.) There were two learning sessions followed by a final test. The researchers simultaneously varied the lag between learning sessions (0 to 105 days) and the delay until the final test (7 to 350 days). The optimal lag was shorter for relatively short delays, but longer for relatively long delays (see Figure 8.3). Other estimates show that at short test delays of minutes, the optimal lag is about the same as the length of the delay. At longer test delays on the order of many days, the optimal lag is closer to 10% of the length of the delay (Cepeda et al., 2009).

But as a practical matter, if you are trying to retain material for a week, the optimal lag seems to be on the order of days. If you want to retain material over the duration of an entire semester-long course and into future courses, spacing on the order of weeks seems to be

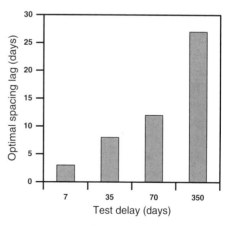

FIGURE 8.3 Estimated optimal lags for different test delays (adapted from Cepeda et al., 2008).

best. Keep in mind, though, that these are *optimal* lags. You will typically see some improvement in retention when you space rather than mass study, even when the lag is short and even when spacing occurs within a single session.

Interim Summary: Taking Stock of What You've Learned

It is clearly beneficial to space out your studying and practice. This is not an issue of investing more time, but a benefit you gain when you break up and spread out your study time. Spacing helps whether you distribute your studying within a learning session or between sessions and more extensive spacing is better, up to a point. How do these recommendations stack up against one of the most commonly reported study habits of students: cramming?

Cramming

By now it has probably occurred to you that the science of learning argues against cramming as an effective way to learn and study. You may, nonetheless, have had the experience of cramming for a quiz or exam and doing just fine. Why would that happen?

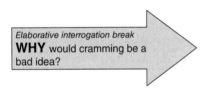

Elaborative interrogation break
WHY would cramming be a bad idea?

When speaking of cramming, students are typically referring to a situation in which they study a large amount of material in a single session shortly before an exam. For example, suppose you have a big midterm coming up in your biology class. If you did all of your studying the day before the test in a four-hour session, you would be cramming. Cramming therefore takes the form of massing with respect to study sessions and runs counter to the principles of spacing. As an example of how cramming compares to spacing, consider the study with electronic flashcards (Kornell, 2009).

In Experiment 2 of that study, participants saw synonyms eight times each. Figure 8.4 represents final test performance for the different learning scenarios encountered by participants. All of the gray bars on the left are for massed conditions, in which the synonyms were studied eight times in a single session, with that massed study session occurring four, three, two, or one day prior to the final test, respectively.

The last of the massed sessions (labeled "1 day prior") represents a situation like cramming, with all studying occurring in a single session the day prior to the test. The bar on the far right (labeled "spaced study session"), in contrast, shows final test performance for a spaced condition in which the participants studied the synonyms a total of eight times spread out over the four days prior to the test. As you can see, participants' recall was almost 40 higher for the spaced condition than for the cramming session! Again, this was not the result of studying *more*, but a result of studying in a *more distributed* fashion.

Despite this advantage for spacing, student cramming remains a common practice. For example, in two recent surveys, over half of college students reported that they most often study in a single session before a test (Hartwig & Dunlosky, 2012; Morehead et al., 2016), although they may sometimes have the intention to space their study (Blaisman, Dunlosky, & Rawson, 2017). In addition, students commonly offer anecdotes in which they crammed for an exam and did just fine. One of your authors recalls cramming for a physics test for several hours straight, immediately before going to bed. To his dismay, he then dreamt about physics, and in those dreams, reformulated the physics equations he had been studying! Luckily, he was able to quickly review the equations in the morning, and to his surprise, salvaged a B on the

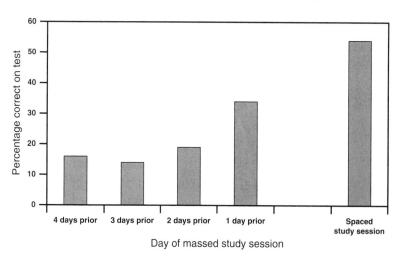

FIGURE 8.4 Percentage correct on the final test for the massed and spaced study sessions (adapted from Kornell, 2009).

I REALLY CRAMMED LAST NIGHT.

Cramming is an ineffective way of promoting long-term learning.

exam. But there are a couple of important points to keep in mind about this.

First, in nearly all real-world cramming scenarios, there is actually some amount of spaced learning involved. For example, even if your intense studying occurred in a single session right before an exam, it is usually the case that some learning occurred during lectures, some when going through your textbook, and some when practicing or reviewing your notes. You probably engaged in within-session spacing during your cramming session, too. Thus, any success experienced might partially reflect a degree of spaced learning. Had you spaced out your study sessions, too, you would have learned and remembered the material even better.

Second, in the same way that many students can offer anecdotes in which they did just fine after cramming, many students can also offer anecdotes in which that same material seemed to be forgotten very quickly. The same author who skated by with a B on that physics exam later had a difficult time learning and understanding some of the new material in the course because it built on the old material that he no longer remembered. When it came time to prepare for the cumulative final, he discovered that it took a great deal of time and effort to relearn the old material once again. The point is that cramming may sometimes be sufficient for getting you through an exam that occurs shortly after studying, but it is less effective than spacing when it comes to durable learning.

In short, just because you sometimes do well on an exam after a cramming session, do not be tempted to conclude that cramming works. It's fool's gold. At best, cramming only works in the limited sense that it may get you a passing grade on a test that will be given very soon. The science of learning shows that you have every reason to expect better performance on that same test with spaced learning. But even more importantly, spaced study and practice will support the kind of long-lasting learning that is needed and expected in your coursework and more general educational pursuits.

What About Problem-Solving?

To this point, the studies discussed have focused on learning verbal information, like foreign-language vocabulary and definitions. You may be wondering whether the same principles apply to learning in the context of solving problems, like you might find in a math or physics class. Intuitively, you might expect that if you are learning to solve two simultaneous equations with two unknowns, it would be best to work through a series of sample problems one after another until you feel you have it down. Or, if you are learning to apply Newton's second law ($F = ma$), it might be best to keep working on relevant problems until you feel you have completely mastered them. The available evidence shows, though, that it is better for long-term retention of knowledge if you space out solving your practice problems (see Chapter 11 for more information on this).

For example, one study examined students' learning of mathematical permutation problems, comparing a massed condition (in which students completed a set of ten problems in a single session) to a spaced condition (in which students completed five of the problems in one session, then the other five in a second session that occurred one week later). On a test given four weeks later, performance in the spaced condition was double that of the massed condition (Rohrer & Taylor, 2006)!

And Skill-Learning?

What about learning skills? You have probably heard that if you want to improve your free-throw shooting in basketball, you need to step up to the free-throw line and shoot free throws again and again, one after another. Establish "muscle memory," you are told. Or, if you want to improve your rendition of Beethoven's "Für Elise" on the piano, you need to play it over and over again until you get it down. But is this the best way to learn? Before reading on, try Demonstration 8.2.

If you are like most people, it may have felt easier and like you were improving more quickly with massed practice. This is just like what you often hear from a basketball player who is massing practice of free throws. But as you learned in Chapter 1, what seems to be working in the moment is not necessarily what is best for retention. When it comes to establishing a skill like shooting a free throw or tossing a crumpled up piece of paper, which is best, massed practice or spaced practice?

DEMONSTRATION 8.2

Be forewarned, if you have friends or family around you, they are going to think you are goofing off rather than studying! But you can tell them you are doing your homework.

Find an empty glass or cup and place it a few feet away from you. Now crumple up a piece of paper. You're going to try to toss the paper into the cup. Yes, we're serious. You are going to do it two different ways, though. For the first several attempts, toss the paper, then after you gather it, do something else for a half-minute or minute, like browse on your computer or watch TV, before you try again. After you've done that, practice a new way. Take several more attempts, but this time, toss the paper again and again, one shot right after another. What do you think? Which felt easier to you? Did it feel like you were getting better with one method more than the other?

Learning to play the piano is an example of skill learning that benefits from a spaced practice schedule.

A large body of research on the massed versus spaced learning of skills reveals a pattern similar to learning of vocabulary, math, foreign languages, and so on. In the same way that repeated study of foreign language words and definitions may feel easier when the repetitions occur consecutively, skill-learning may feel easier (and initial improvement may even occur more quickly) when practice is massed. But retention of those skills is typically superior in the case of spaced practice.

As an example, one study examined how well surgical residents could perform a type of microsurgery when that surgery occurred about a month after they were trained (Moulton et al., 2006). The study compared a group of residents who completed four training sessions in the same day (the standard, massed practice approach to surgical training) to a group of residents who completed the same four training sessions one week apart. Across several different measures, the residents who received spaced training were significantly better on the final surgical test. Parallel findings have been reported for many other skills in athletics, music, and performance (Donovan & Radosevich, 1999; Lee & Genovese, 1988).

Is it Good or Bad to Mix Things Up?

What if you are trying to learn two or more subtopics or types of problems at the same time? Would it be better to cluster together the learning of each subtopic or type of problem, or intermix the learning of the multiple types? For example, if you were learning how to compute the volume of a cube and the volume of a sphere, would it be better to study and work on a set of problems pertaining to the volume of a cube, and then separately study and work on a set of problems pertaining to the volume of a sphere? Or should you study and work on both types of problems together, intermixed?

In a study that asked exactly this question, college students were taught how to compute the volumes of four geometric solids: wedges, spherical cones, spheroids, and half cones (see Rohrer & Taylor, 2007). All of the students were given tutorials on how to find the volume of each type of solid, along with 16 practice problems, four for each solid. Students in a *blocked practice condition* first read the tutorial on finding the volume of one particular solid, immediately followed by the four practice problems with that type of solid. They then received the tutorial and practice problems for another type of solid, and so on. Students in an *interleaved condition* first read all four of the tutorials, then received the 16 practice problems in an intermixed order. A final test was then given one week after learning. The results from the practice and test sessions are shown in Figure 8.5. As you can see, during practice (left side of the figure), performance was better in the blocked condition (gray bars) than in the interleaved condition (white bars). But on the final test, performance in the interleaving condition was about three times better than the blocking condition! This advantage for "mixing it up" is called the **interleaving effect**.

Note that you already saw an example of the interleaving effect in Chapter 1, in the study where participants learned to classify paintings by different artists (Kornell & Bjork, 2008; see Figure 1.4). Recall that in one condition, participants studied paintings blocked according to

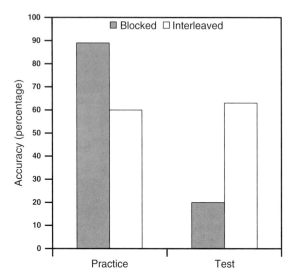

FIGURE 8.5 Practice and test accuracy for blocked versus interleaved practice (adapted from Rohrer & Taylor, 2007).

artist, but in a second condition, the paintings from the different artists were interleaved. After learning, participants completed a test in which they saw new paintings and had to identify the artist who created each one. At the end of the experiment, participants were also asked whether they thought learning was helped by blocking or intermixing. Performance was much better in the interleaved condition (61%) than the blocked condition (35%), yet 78% of the participants believed blocked presentation was as good as or better than interleaving.

Consider, though, the design of these interleaving experiments in light of what you know about spacing. Although each of the individual volume problems given in one study (Rohrer & Taylor, 2007) were different, presentation order was massed according to the type of problem (i.e., the volume formula needed) in the blocked condition. In the interleaved condition, the different types of problems were given in an intermixed order, which had the effect of spacing out the problems of a particular type. Likewise, although each of the individual paintings (Kornell & Bjork, 2008) shown in the study were different, they were massed by artist in one condition, but were intermixed (and therefore spaced) in the other condition. Is the interleaving advantage just due to spacing with respect to the type of problem or grouping? Or is there an additional benefit that has to do with the intermixing? These studies cannot answer the question, because the problems and paintings in the interleaved conditions were spaced *and* intermixed at the same time.

Additional research was therefore conducted to disentangle the potential effects of spacing and intermixing. In one study (Taylor & Rohrer, 2010), elementary school children solved four different types of mathematics problems. The problems were either blocked or interleaved. In the blocked condition, though, the participants completed unrelated "filler" tasks in between the individual problems, so that these problems were spaced out to about the same extent as in the interleaved condition. Therefore, the problems were spaced (in time) in both the blocked and interleaved conditions. With spacing equated, interleaving (77%) still produced much better performance than blocking (38%) on a test given one day later. Thus the interleaving effect is not just due to spacing, but must also be due to intermixing problem types (see also Birnbaum, Kornell, Bjork, & Bjork, 2013).

What is it about intermixing that helps learning? A common interpretation is that intermixing helps learners *discriminate* between similar concepts (Kang & Pashler, 2012). It is easy to confuse the formulas for computing the volume of different geometric objects. It is also easy to confuse different artists' painting styles. Intermixing can help people learn the difference between the different types of problems and paintings. This would aid them in choosing the appropriate formula on later test problems or in identifying the appropriate artist on a later test. Accordingly, the benefits of interleaving are likely to be greatest when mixing together similar content that requires some effort to discriminate. For example, it may be helpful to interleave your learning of various artists' painting styles for an art history course, but mixing art history and organic chemistry would provide little additional benefit beyond what would be gained by spacing alone (Hausman & Kornell, 2014).

In short, research indicates that interleaving similar types of problems and subgroupings of information can be helpful for learning, allowing you to take advantage of the spacing effect. But it can also help you discriminate between the potentially confusable things that you are learning.

Putting It All Together

The benefits of spacing for learning have been known since Ebbinghaus's pioneering study of memory in the late 1800s. Further work has refined Ebbinghuas's conclusions and shown that the benefits of spreading out studying can be found in learning vocabulary, paragraphs of text, mathematics, a variety of skills, and virtually any other type of information you might choose to learn. Moreover, mixing together similar topics has the added benefit of spacing learning and promoting your ability to distinguish between similar concepts. The substantial and widespread benefits of spacing are often somewhat surprising. Indeed, many students favor an intense, single session of studying. But you now know what the science of learning shows: Spreading your studying out over time makes for longer-lasting learning.

Tips You Can Use

1. **Do not cram!** Do not fall prey to the mistaken belief that cramming does the job. You will get more bang for your buck with spacing than cramming, given the same amount of study time. You will also retain the information to a greater extent beyond the exam, leaving you better prepared for later assessments and better prepared to learn new information that builds off of your acquired knowledge. In short, if you space your learning now, you will likely save time and effort in the long run.

2. **Plan ahead.** A spaced practice schedule that includes multiple sessions spread out over several days requires that you plan ahead. If you procrastinate and fail to plan ahead, you will suddenly discover that it is the day before the exam and no longer possible to space out your studying over multiple days. You will be forfeiting a valuable opportunity to enhance learning and retention, one that does not require you to study more or for longer, but only requires you to plan better. An effective way to strategically manage your time is to formally schedule spaced study sessions for yourself. Many people carry an electronic device like a phone or smartwatch, which has a calendar application or something similar. Use that technology to set up spaced study schedules, complete with reminders.

3. **Space your practice at multiple levels.** Distribute your study across days. Distribute your study across multiple sessions during the day. Distribute your learning of a particular bit of information across episodes within a learning session. Space your practice at all of these different levels and make it part of your regular study routine. In addition to scheduling spaced study sessions, you can also think about the things you are learning while you are commuting to campus or jogging on a treadmill at the gym. You can take advantage of electronic flashcard applications, as well,

and quiz yourself regularly, whenever you happen to have a few minutes available. There are even some flashcard applications that vary spacing according to how recently you have studied the material or how well you seem to know it, in attempt to create more optimal spacing.

4. **Mix it up.** As part of your spaced-learning strategy, mix it up. Avoid the single-minded approach of studying the same subtopic over and over again successively, or practicing the same type of problem over and over again successively. Instead, interleave your study of subtopics and subgroupings of information, and interleave your practice of different types of problems, especially when the things you are learning are potentially confusable. In doing so you will not only be spacing your learning, but you will also gain a better understanding of the differences between the things you are learning, leading to better discrimination and less confusion.

5. **Sleep!** Get enough sleep and get some sleep between study sessions. Spacing your studying across multiple days or weeks usually means that you are getting some sleep in between study sessions. This can provide an additional boost to your learning over and above the benefits of spacing itself, because sleep helps memory consolidation, the transition that memories go through in becoming more permanently stored in the brain (see Box 8.1).

Discussion Questions

1. Flashcards can be effective for learning and studying when used appropriately. Based on the principles discussed in this chapter, what would be effective ways of using flashcards?

2. Think about cramming. What are some potential negatives of leaving most or all of your studying to a single session shortly before a quiz or exam, as alluded to in this chapter, and otherwise? Do you think there are positives of doing at least some reviewing shortly before the assessment? Why do you think that students persist in cramming? What can you do as a student to combat this bad habit?

3. Your authors are often asked if it is effective to interleave studying of material from completely different courses. From what you have learned about spacing and interleaving effects, how would you answer this question?

4. Think about you daily life habits with regard to diet, exercise, activities, and so on. How do these daily habits interplay with what is discussed

in this chapter? What can you do differently to facilitate better study habits that are grounded in spaced learning?

Suggestions for Further Reading

There are a number of excellent reviews of the voluminous literature on the spacing and lag effects for those who wish to dig into those topics more deeply. Nicholas Cepeda and colleagues. (2006) provide the most comprehensive quantitative review of spacing as applied to the learning of verbal materials (but see Chris Janiszewski, Hayden Noel, & Alan Sawyer, 2003, as well). John Donovan and David Radosevich (1999) also examine how spaced practice impacts the learning of skills. Peter Delaney, Peter Verkoeijen, and Arie Spirgel (2010) provide an excellent theoretical treatment of the topic, and John Dunlosky and colleagues (2013) review both spaced and interleaved practice from an applied perspective, with excellent discussion of issues and challenges for implementation. For some recent work specific to the topic of interleaving, we recommend a very interesting paper by Doug Rohrer, Robert Dedrick, and Sandra Stershic (2015), examining long-term learning of mathematics in a middle school classroom following interleaved practice.

Credits

Page 150: CREATISTA / Shutterstock
Page 160: Ralph Hagen / Cartoon Stock.
Page 162: Noam Armonn / Shutterstock

CHAPTER 9
....

Learning to Love Testing

....

Learning Objectives
- Reading this chapter will help you:
  - ✦ Understand the many benefits of testing for learning.
  - ✦ Appreciate different explanations for the benefits of testing.
  - ✦ Know how to effectively apply testing in your own learning.

....

What do you think of when you hear the word "test"? Do your palms get a little sweaty? Does your breath shorten? Are you haunted by memories of bad test experiences? It is certainly not difficult to find people who hold an aversion to testing. For example, a student once told one of your authors that she would rather spend her time petting scorpions than taking a test. Each of your authors makes frequent use of testing in their own classes and, when announcing this policy on the first day of a course, often get pained looks from students. However, this chapter should convince you that the benefits of testing are more like the warm glow of petting a friendly puppy than a dalliance with a scorpion. Indeed, your authors find that by the end of a semester the transformation from scorpion to puppy has usually occurred, with students wanting more testing in all of their courses (cf. Agarwal, D'Antonio, Roediger, McDermott, & McDaniel, 2014).

Why does testing conjure up such negative images? One possibility is that testing is often viewed only as a method of evaluation, determining whether learning has been adequate. For example, when 146 college instructors were asked why they might recommend testing to their students, the majority (68%) indicated that testing permitted students to determine how well they had learned a concept (Morehead, Rhodes, & DeLozier, 2016). Students similarly regard testing largely as a method of checking knowledge (Hartwig & Dunlosky, 2012; Kornell & Bjork, 2007; Morehead et al., 2016). Coupled with the fact that tests are often the primary (or sole) basis for students' grade in a course, it is understandable that thoughts of testing can evoke some degree of anxiety in students.

The problem with this view is that it misses the most important reason of all to test. Namely, *testing is a powerful method of learning.* More formally, retrieving (remembering) information results in better learning than restudying (e.g., rereading) that information, a finding referred to as the **testing effect**. In the pantheon of strategies you might use for learning, testing is a veritable Zeus, producing durable, long-lasting learning that is largely unmatched by most other approaches (Dunlosky et al., 2013). To name but a few of the benefits:

- Testing increases retention and does so over long periods of time.
- Testing aids your ability to understand information.
- Testing reduces forgetting.
- Testing helps you to better understand and monitor your own learning.

This chapter describes the benefits of testing in detail in the hope that testing will become a regular part of your studying regimen. As it turns out, there has been evidence for the benefits of testing for a long time. Before moving on, try Demonstration 9.1a.

DEMONSTRATION 9.1a

Take out a sheet of paper and number it 1 through 8.

Directions. For this demonstration you are going to see a short list of words. Start by giving yourself about 12 seconds to learn these words:

party	*kitchen*	*children*
week	*face*	*dust*
nature	*animal*	

You are now finished with this part of the demonstration!

Testing Enhances Memory: Did We Know This All Along?

The advantages of testing have been documented for a least a century (e.g., Gates, 1917; Spitzer, 1939), but testing has only slowly been accepted as an effective partner in learning. One early study examined the benefits of testing in an experiment with all of the sixth graders (3,605 to be exact) from 91 elementary schools in Iowa. Each of the students read a 600-word passage about bamboo. They were also given 25 test questions on the passage (see Box 9.1 for a sample of the passage and materials used). Importantly, the researcher varied when participants were given a test and how often.

Students were divided into 10 groups and tested on different schedules; the benefits of testing can be illustrated by focusing on four of those groups. Group 1 read the passage and then took an immediate test on the passage. This was followed by tests given the next day (one day later)

BOX 9.1   MATERIALS FROM SPITZER'S (1939) EXPERIMENT

Passage

Near Savannah, Georgia, is the Plant Introduction Garden of the United States Department of Agriculture. In one section of this garden are the bamboos. These plants are members of the grass family. They resemble their relatives, corn and wheat, in structure of stem, which is rounded, divided into joints, and more or less hollow. Bamboos also resemble pines and spruces by having tall, straight trunks and cone shaped heads or crowns, and by being evergreens.

Test Questions

1. Who maintains an experimental garden near Savannah, Georgia? ( ) The Bamboo Growers Association ( ) The US Government ( ) The US Custom Office ( ) The florists of Savannah ( ) The State of Georgia.
2. To which family of plants do bamboos belong? ( ) trees ( ) ferns ( ) grasses ( ) mosses ( ) fungi.
3. Which two trees do the bamboos resemble most? ( ) royal and date palms ( ) willow and tamarack ( ) white oak and burch ( ) walnut and hickory ( ) pine and spruce.

and 21 days later, allowing the researcher to assess whether a test given shortly after learning helps memory on a final test given after three weeks. Likewise, Group 2 had an immediate test and then took two more tests, one after seven days and one after 63 days, allowing the researcher to assess forgetting that took place nine weeks later. Groups 6 and 8 took only a single test, after 21 and 63 days, respectively. These groups served as a control comparison, allowing the researcher to assess how much forgetting would occur three or nine weeks after learning, but without any previous tests.

The data for this study can be found in Figure 9.1. As you can see, students taking a previous test had very little forgetting. For example, students in Group 1 (solid line) experienced only a small drop from their immediate test (53% correct) to a final test given three weeks later (49% correct). In contrast, students in Group 6 (open circle), given only a single test three weeks after learning, remembered much less (26%). Students in Group 2 (broken line) also showed the benefit of a previous test, with only a 10 percentage-point drop from the immediate test (53% correct) to the final test (43% correct). Those given only a single test after nine weeks (Group 8, open square) remembered only a quarter of the passage (26%).

Based on these data, the researcher recommended that "Immediate recall in the form of a test is an effective method of aiding the retention of learning and should, therefore, be employed more frequently"

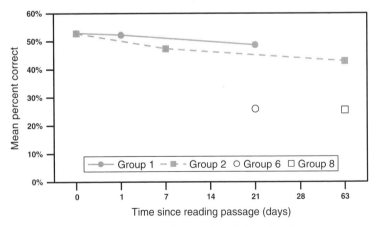

FIGURE 9.1 **Mean percentage correct by the time since first reading the passage (adapted from Spitzer, 1939).**

DEMONSTRATION 9.1b

Take out the sheet of paper that you numbered 1 through 8.

Directions. You'll now see the words from the earlier list in Demonstration 9.1a. If the word is in in complete form, just copy it down. If the word is incomplete, think of the full words and write that down.

face	*dust*	*week*
p_____	*nature*	k_____
a_____	ch_____	

You are now finished with this part of the demonstration!

(Spitzer, 1939, p. 655). These calls went largely unheeded (see Roediger & Karpicke, 2006b). Research has come a long way since that time and now includes conditions that truly allow testing to be compared to other strategies. Before moving on, try Demonstration 9.1b.

Testing the Benefits of Testing

In order to argue that testing is one of the best learning strategies available, it should be clear that testing out-performs other potential strategies. For example, imagine that you just read a chapter from your textbook and come back after a break, ready to review the material. Would learning be better if you reread the chapter or should you test yourself?

To answer that question, you would need to gather information from experiments using the proper design. In particular, one alternative explanation for any benefit of testing is that a test serves as something akin to a rereading opportunity. For example, in the study (Spitzer, 1939) described previously with sixth graders in Iowa, all students only took tests. It might not be that testing per se actually helped learning, but that seeing test questions (see Box 9.1) simply exposed participants to the information again. By this view, it is not retrieving information that helps learning, but viewing that information again that drove improvements.

In order to compare these competing explanations, the ideal experiment should make it so that participants' exposure to information, be it through testing or studying, is the same. All that should differ is whether participants must retrieve the information or simply restudy (reread) that information. Figure 9.2 diagrams the design of an ideal

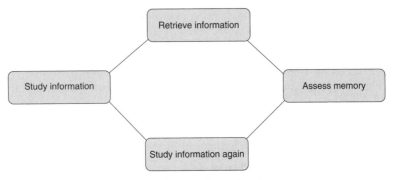

FIGURE 9.2 Ideal design for investigating the effects of testing.

experiment. Using this design, participants learn some kind of information. During the next phase, that information is either restudied again or participants retrieve information during a test. Finally, all participants are given some type of final assessment of memory.

This design can be implemented either between- or within-subjects (see Chapter 3 for details on these features of experiments). For example, the same participants might restudy some information and do a practice test on other information (within-subjects), or different participants might restudy or test on information (between-subjects). Using designs such as these, hundreds of studies have demonstrated the many benefits of testing.

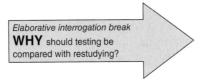

Elaborative interrogation break
WHY should testing be compared with restudying?

A World of Testing Benefits

The benefits of testing are almost too numerous to mention. Indeed, one review outlined at least 10 major benefits that can be attributed to testing (Roediger, Putnam, & Smith, 2011). What follows are four of the most prominent benefits of testing.

Testing Enhances Retention of Information

The clearest benefit of testing is that it enhances your ability to engage in durable learning of information. That is, testing increases the chance you will learn information and that this learning will persist over time. For example, one famous study (Roediger & Karpicke,

2006b) had students read several short passages about different topics like the sun or sea otters. For some passages, right after the initial reading, the participants were asked to read the passage one more time. Because they studied it twice, they can be labeled the *study-study* group. For other passages, right after reading, the passage was taken away and participants were asked to write down as much as they could remember. Because this group studied the passage once and then took a test, they can be labeled the *study–test* group. After all of these activities, the researchers then had everyone take a final test to assess learning for the passage. Some participant took this test only five minutes after studying/testing on the passages. Others came back and took the final test two days or one week later, allowing the researchers to examine learning over time. The researchers measured how many ideas participants could remember from the initial passage.

Figure 9.3 shows the results of this study. Two patterns stand out. First, lots of studying in a short space of time seemed to confer a slight advantage when the final test was given after five minutes. Second, testing led to much better long-term retention of the information. Specifically, an initial test led to better memory when the final test was given two days or one week later. Many studies have shown this pattern, suggesting that the benefits of testing are most apparent when the final assessment occurs more than few minutes after initial learning (see Kornell,

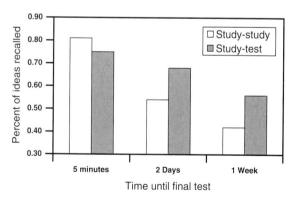

FIGURE 9.3 The percentage of idea units correctly recalled following multiple study opportunities (study–study) or initial study followed by a test (study–test). Adapted from Roediger and Karpicke (2006b).

Bjork, & Garcia, 2011; Rowland, 2014, for reviews; but see Adesope, Trevisan, & Sundararajan, 2017).

The bottom line is that when it comes to durable, long-lasting learning, testing gives you much more bang for your buck. That is, your time will be spent much more efficiently when you practice retrieving information rather than simply reading that information over and over. As an illustrative example, in one experiment (Karpicke & Roediger, 2008), participants learned Swahili words and their English translations (e.g., *pomba*–beer) in cycles. The participants continuously learned the words and took a test (*pomba*–?), only to repeat the procedure until all of the translations could be correctly recalled once. But there was a catch. For some participants, when a translation was correctly recalled the first time, it was not tested again and continuously restudied in subsequent cycles. Thus, participants in this group had multiple study opportunities. For other participants, when a translation was correctly recalled the first time, it was never studied again and only tested in subsequent cycles. Thus, these participants had multiple testing opportunities. Everyone then came back and took a final test one week after the initial learning phase. On average, those who had many testing opportunities correctly remembered approximately 80% of the translations. Participants who had many study opportunities remembered approximately 36% of the translations. Thus, lots of testing is much better for learning than lots of restudying (but see Soderstrom, Kerr, & Bjork, 2016, for an analysis of spacing benefits in this experiment). To finish up your own demonstration of the benefits of testing, try Demonstration 9.1c. Did you also see a benefit for information that was tested versus information that was just read one more time?

The research literature is filled with findings showing benefits of testing for a variety of materials. Two recent reviews of the literature confirm this (Rowland, 2014; Adesope et al., 2017). For example, one review of 159 different studies and thousands of subjects in experiments

DEMONSTRATION 9.1c
Flip over the sheet of paper you were using and try to remember as many words from the original list as you can.

showed that participants were about 2.5 times more likely to remember tested information on a final assessment compared with studying alone (Rowland, 2014). Phrased differently, given the same amount of time learning the material, engaging in testing makes you over twice as likely to remember that information.

Testing Enhances Understanding

Suppose you were charged with learning the differences between families of birds (e.g., jays, thrashers, finches) such that when provided an example of a bird, you could correctly name the family. Are you better off studying each family or being tested on the families? Given the focus of the chapter, you probably voted for testing. Indeed, testing appears to improve your learning of concepts, such as classifying a new bird into the correct family.

One group of researchers (Jacoby, Wahlheim, & Coane, 2010) investigated exactly this possibility. Some participants in their experiment repeatedly studied pictures of birds from different families. Other participants studied the birds and then were repeatedly tested; for their test, they were given an example of a bird and recalled the correct family. All participants later took a new test that, in part, asked them to classify birds never seen before into the correct family. Participants who engaged in lots of previous testing were more accurate at classifying new birds.

Testing also seems to help when you must make a leap to identify new applications of a concept (see Chapter 11 on understanding for much more on this topic). For example, one researcher (Butler, 2010) had participants read passages about topics such as bats. Following some of the passages, participants were given the chance to reread the passage. In other conditions, they answered questions about the passage (e.g., "What major role do bats play in ecosystems?").

Elaborative interrogation break
WHY would testing enhance understanding?

On the final test, several questions asked participants to draw an inference between what they learned and a new application that was never stated in the passage. For example, they might be asked to consider how bat wings could inform the design of new aircraft. The results showed that participants were better able to make the leap to the correct inference after testing than rereading. There is still much work to be done on the effect of testing on understanding, but the existing data (see also Rohrer, Taylor, & Sholar, 2010) indicate that testing may be an excellent way to enhance understanding.

Testing Diminishes Forgetting

Go back and take a look at Figure 9.1 and compare learning for the two groups of students (circles) given a final test three weeks after initial learning. You will notice that students who took a prior test remembered nearly twice as much (53%) as students who did not have a prior test (26%). That is, a prior test reduced how much information participants forgot. The same pattern of a prior testing reducing forgetting is also apparent if you examine students who had their final test nine weeks after initial learning (squares in Figure 9.1).

Other work has also shown that testing protects against forgetting. For example, one group of researchers (Szpunar, McDermott, & Roediger, 2008) capitalized on a method that induces significant forgetting. A well-known finding is that prior information will interfere with new information, causing you to forget (e.g., Underwood, 1957), a phenomenon termed **proactive interference**. For example, suppose you recently moved and were asked by a friend for your new home address.

Testing can reduce forgetting.

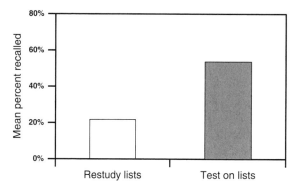

FIGURE **9.4 The mean percentage correctly remembered on the final list for participants who restudied vs. tested on prior lists (adapted from Szpunar et al., 2008).**

You might find this difficult because existing knowledge of your old, better known address would interfere with your ability to remember your new address. That is, this previously learned information (your old address) might interfere with your ability to learn new information (your new address).

The researchers in this study used a different method to introduce proactive interference. Namely, they had participants study five different lists of words, one after the other. Proactive interference will increase across lists as more information builds up. For that reason, the researchers focused on participants' ability to remember the fifth and final list, because that list should suffer the most from proactive interference given that it was preceded by four other lists. Participants in their study either took a test after each list was presented or were asked to study the list one more time before moving on to the next list.

Memory for the final list is presented in Figure 9.4. As you can see, participants who took a test while learning (gray bar) remembered more than participants who only restudied the lists (white bar). That is, testing protected learning from other information that might get in the way of an individual's path to a memory.

Testing Enhances Monitoring of Learning

By now you are probably convinced of the many benefits of testing for your learning. Recognizing the benefits of testing is important, because research has shown that there is often a disconnect between people's intuitions about the effects of testing and the actual evidence on it (e.g., Karpicke & Roediger, 2008; see also Kornell & Son, 2009). Fortunately, engaging in testing is an excellent way of sharpening your ability to understand what you have and have not learned (e.g., Kornell & Rhodes, 2013; Tullis, Finley, & Benjamin, 2013; see also Soderstrom & Bjork, 2014).

For example, in one study (Miller & Geraci, 2016), participants learned pairs of Lithuanian-English translations (e.g., *kreida*–chalk). Immediately following this study phase, participants predicted how many of the words they would remember on a subsequent test. All of the participants overestimated how much they would remember. Next, the researchers gave half of the participants a mini-test experience, allowing them to try to recall four of the pairs they had studied. Following this mini-test, participants were given another chance to predict their performance before taking the final test. Participants given the mini-test were now dead-on in their prediction of how much they would remember on the final test (a comparison group not given a test remained overconfident after making a second prediction). This accuracy in prediction dovetails with other work showing that practice testing makes you much better at identifying what material has or has not been learned (Kornell & Rhodes, 2013; see also Chapter 4 on metacognition).

Interim Summary: Understanding the Benefits of Testing

Testing enhances your ability to learn information, puts you in a better position to make logical leaps and draw inferences, slows the progress of forgetting, and enhances your understanding of your own learning. This is certainly not an exhaustive list of the myriad benefits of testing. For example, testing may serve to better organize your knowledge (Zaromb & Roediger, 2010), increase your preparedness to learn new information (Izawa, 1970), and may even prevent your mind from wandering off during class (Szpunar, 2017; Szpunar, Khan, & Schacter, 2013).

Why does testing confer such widespread benefits to learning? There is no consensus in the research literature, but two major ideas stand out. One possibility is that testing is a highly effective form of elaboration (see Chapter 5) that allows you to better make connections between what you are learning and other information in memory (Carpenter, 2009). For example, consider the finding described earlier showing that testing increased the chance that participants made an inference from learning about bats to applying knowledge of bats to aircraft design (Butler, 2010). Testing may have encouraged participants to focus not only on the mechanics of bat flight, but also further forged links to existing knowledge of how other animals fly and technology developed by humans for flight. This elaboration would make it easier to remember the tested information because the learner created multiple connections that would allow a route back to what was learned. The connections created might also have spurred additional thinking about bats and propulsion.

An alternative account is that testing provides a powerful and unique link to get back to a memory (Karpicke, Lehman, & Aue, 2014). For example, consider work on using testing to reduce interference from prior learning (i.e., proactive interference). You might recall the study showing that taking practice tests make it less likely for other information to interfere with learning and cause forgetting (Szpunar, McDermott, & Roediger, 2008; see Figure 9.4). One way to think about this finding is that the extra testing made it easier for participants to create a mental path back to their learning and to escape the influence of other information that could block that path (see Chapter 10 on cues for much more on this idea). Regardless of the reason for the benefits of testing, demonstrations of its effectiveness are legion (Adesope et al., 2017).

A Guide to Effectively Using Testing

How can you most effectively engage in your own testing? There are two major considerations to keep in mind when engaging in testing that will provide you with the greatest benefits.

Produce During Testing

Testing appears to confer benefits across different ways of testing yourself. For example, there are clear benefits from open-book tests (Agarwal, Karpicke, Kang, Roediger, & McDermott, 2008), and tests where the learner is charged with simply thinking of the answer rather than writing that answer down (Lehman & Karpicke, 2016; but see Tauber et al., 2018). But as a rule, testing will usually be most effective when the learner produces information rather than recognizes information (McDaniel, Roediger, & McDermott, 2007).

Producing information during testing benefits learning more than recognizing information.

Consider work by Carpenter and DeLosh (2006). They had participants learn lists of words and then practice with different kinds of tests. On some practice tests, participants were given a list of the words they studied, in combination with some words never seen. Participants' task on this *recognition test* was to circle the items they remembered studying. For other lists, participants attempted *free recall*, writing down as many of the words as they could remember. After the lists were studied and the practice tests done, all participants were given a final test and asked to either write down everything they could remember (free recall) or identify (recognize) words they had studied (see Figure 9.5).

Of greatest interest is whether one type of practice test results in the best performance. Figure 9.6 shows the data and indicates that practicing a free recall test (gray bars) led to better memory than a practice recognition test (white bars), no matter how memory was finally assessed.

This finding is not accidental. For example, a review of over 150 different studies (Rowland, 2014) indicated that free recall tests and cued

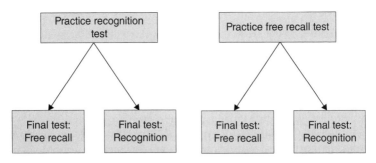

FIGURE 9.5 An illustration of Carpenter and DeLosh's (2006) procedure.

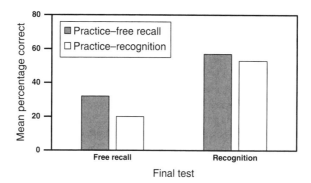

FIGURE 9.6 **Mean percentage remembered following practice free recall and recognition tests for a final free recall or recognition test (adapted from Carpenter & DeLosh, 2006).**

recall tests, where you must produce information after being given a hint, led to bigger learning benefits than practice recognition tests. This is not to say that multiple-choice tests are not helpful. Indeed, a good multiple-choice test that makes you carefully choose between potential alternatives can be highly effective (Bjork, Little, & Storm, 2014; Little, Bjork, & Bjork, & Angello, 2012). Thus, although a best practice is to produce information during testing, you can also benefit from challenging multiple-choice tests that require deep thought to choose between alternatives (see also Adesope et al., 2017).

Space Your Testing

Testing is one of the best learning strategies available to you. But there is another strategy that ranks up there with testing in terms of effectiveness and ease of use: spacing. The combination of the two is simply dynamite for learning.

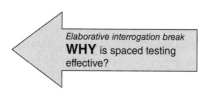

Elaborative interrogation break
WHY is spaced testing effective?

One method of marrying spacing and testing is to spread out learning over time, just as described in Chapter 8. Then, within those spaced sessions, employ many testing opportunities. Learning is highly durable when you engage in multiple testing opportunities for the same information, spread out over days, weeks, and even months, an approach termed **successive relearning**. In some of the earliest work on this method (Bahrick, 1979), individuals who repeatedly practiced recalling Spanish vocabulary on a weekly or monthly basis still showed outstanding memory for that vocabulary years later (Bahrick & Phelps, 1987).

Consider a fascinating study of successive relearning conducted in an introductory psychology class (Rawson, Dunlosky, & Sciartelli, 2013). Students in this class were charged with learning a variety of concepts and were randomly assigned to learn that information with lots of studying (*study condition*) or lots of testing (*testing condition*).

In the *study condition*, participants were shown a set of key concepts from class. For example, they might be shown a concept such as, "Classical conditioning involves learning to make a reflex response to a stimulus other than the original, natural stimulus that normally produces the reflex." Participants saw this concept five times in a single session, mixed in with other concepts from class. They returned two days later and studied these concepts once again, with each concept shown multiple times. This general approach (study a set of concepts, return to study the concepts again) continued throughout the course, with most sessions involving restudy of concepts already seen in the course and new concepts.

Participants in a *testing condition* also learned concepts from class repeatedly over the course of the semester. However, rather than simply studying the concepts, they were given a test. For example, they might be asked, "What is classical conditioning?" The participant would type in an answer and then receive feedback on whether the answer was correct. Importantly, participants could not finish a session until they had recalled the concept correctly three times. Thus, the learning session was a series of tests on multiple concepts for the course, requiring that each concept be recalled three times correctly before the session was over. Just as in the studying condition, participants came back two days later, but instead of studying they practiced testing on the concepts, again being held to the standard that each concept must be recalled three times correctly. This general procedure continued throughout the course, with new concepts mixed into each session.

The procedure is somewhat complex, so it might help to take a step back. Each group was repeatedly exposed to key concepts from their course over an entire semester. The primary difference was that one group repeatedly read concepts (*study condition*) and the other group was repeatedly tested (*test condition*) on the course information.

Students' performance on their multiple-choice course exam provides an indication of the effectiveness of repeated testing. The researchers recorded students' performance for items that were practiced during the experiment (*practiced items*). Other items were not practiced in the experiment, permitting a comparison to a baseline (*baseline items*); for these items, participants learned the information as they normally would in class. Participants who repeatedly tested scored over a letter grade better on practiced items (84%) compared to baseline (72%) items. Repeated study conferred a much smaller advantage for practiced relative to baseline items (78% vs. 73%).

Did repeated testing lead to more durable learning than studying? The researchers investigated this by having participants return nearly a month later for a final cued-recall test, where they were asked to describe key concepts from the course (e.g., "What is classical conditioning"?). The results of that test are shown in Figure 9.7. Participants' memory for the concepts was much better following repeated testing (left side of the graph) than repeated studying (right side of the graph). Other studies have similarly reported that the advantages of repeated testing are long lasting (e.g., Rawson, Vaughn, Walsh, & Dunlosky, 2018).

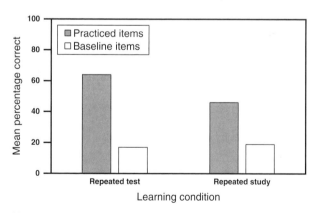

FIGURE **9.7** Mean percentage correct on a cued recall test for participants who repeatedly tested or repeatedly studied for practiced concepts and for concepts that were not practiced (adapted from Rawson et al. 2013).

How can you leverage this information about repeated testing in your own studying? There are several principles to keep in mind.

1. **Space your studying (see Chapter 8) and your testing.** Testing will be most effective when it is done in short sessions spread out over days, weeks, and even months.

2. **Spaced testing will be most effective if you overlap new information and old information during studying.** For example, suppose you are taking a history class that will cover the progression of the American Revolutionary War. A first study session might be devoted to the origins of the war, including testing on such key milestones as the Stamp Act, and the Boston Tea Party. A few days later, a second study session would include tests on those prior concepts and then introduce new concepts, such as major events in the first year of the war (e.g., Lexington and Concord, Battle of Bunker Hill). A third study session would include all of the prior milestones and introduce new ones (Paine's "Common Sense" pamphlet, Washington crossing the Delaware) and so forth. Thus, your testing would involve constantly interweaving new and old concepts.

3. **Seek repeated correct retrievals of the same information in each study session.** A general rule of thumb would be to seek at least two or three correct retrievals of each concept in each study session. Once you have learned the information well, retrieving previously learned information should actually take very little time (Rawson et al., 2013).

An example of a week's schedule of repeated testing is shown in Box 9.2. As you will note, each day involves testing on prior concepts but also includes new concepts. Your own schedule will likely involve more information and longer periods of time, but Box 9.2 illustrates how repeated testing can be accomplished. You can also leverage technologies available to you to better implement repeated testing. For example, putting test questions into a calendar application could provide you with test questions delivered as alerts. Figure 9.8 shows just such an application used by one of your authors to learn Mandarin.

BOX 9.2   AN EXAMPLE SCHEDULE USING SUCCESSIVE RELEARNING

Day 1	Day 2	Day 3	Day 4	Day 5	Day 6	Day 7
"What is the importance of the Stamp Act and Boston Tea Party"? x3		"What is the importance of the Stamp Act and Boston Tea Party"? x3		"What is the importance of the Stamp Act and Boston Tea Party"? x3		"What is the importance of the Stamp Act and Boston Tea Party"? x3
		"How did Lexington and Concord and the Battle of Bunker Hill influence the war?" x3		"How did Lexington and Concord and the Battle of Bunker Hill influence the war?" x3		"How did Lexington and Concord and the Battle of Bunker Hill influence the war?" x3
				"What is 'Common Sense'? Why was the crossing of the Delaware important? x3		"What is 'Common Sense'?" Why was the crossing of the Delaware important? x3
						"How did the British occupation of Philadelphia and encampment at Valley Forge influence the war? x3

FIGURE **9.8** An example of setting a calendar to schedule testing sessions.

Putting It All Together

Early work on human learning documented the benefits of testing. For example, based on data collected nearly 80 years ago, one researcher (Spitzer, 1939) recommended that practice testing should be used more often in the classroom. Hundreds of studies and many thousands of participants later, this recommendation still rings true and has been refined by a variety of work illustrating the many benefits of testing.

Given these many benefits, the ideal class should include a number of low-stakes testing opportunities for students that permit them ample opportunity to practice retrieving key information. This recommendation is being taken up more frequently by educators (e.g., Hopkins et al., 2016) who have identified the value of testing as a method of learning rather than only viewing it as a means of evaluation. Whether or not regular testing is instituted in your classes, practice testing should become a prominent part of your repertoire of study skills.

Tips You Can Use

1. **Test and test repeatedly.** Testing is at its most powerful when there are multiple opportunities to test, spread out over time. Indeed, some of the largest benefits of testing occur when students test themselves on the same information and seek multiple, successful retrievals of that information. Thus, testing should be integrated into any spaced study schedule, and that schedule should include many opportunities to practice retrieving the same information over time.
2. **Produce during your tests.** A well-constructed multiple-choice test can serve as an excellent basis for practice testing. Unfortunately, well-constructed multiple-choice tests are hard to come by and very

difficult to create if you are left to your own devices to construct the test. For that reason, when in doubt, force yourself to produce information during tests, either by recalling without the help of cues or with few cues to lean on.

3. **Practice testing should align with final testing.** As you practice testing, you should have an eye on the type of information you will ultimately be responsible for. For instance, if your final test will emphasize isolated facts, your practice testing should force you to recall facts. Likewise, if your final test will emphasize the relationships broad concepts, your practice testing should be based on those concepts.

4. **Remember: testing is a better use of time than restudying.** The concept bears repeating: Testing will give you greater value for your time than studying (e.g., reading) alone. Take advantage of this property of testing to use your time wisely and well. For example, the next time you want to review a chapter from your book, try testing yourself on the key concepts rather than rereading.

5. **Make testing your go-to method of evaluating learning.** Testing not only improves learning, but comes with the additional benefit that it help you determine what needs more study. This method of evaluation works best when it is instituted after a delay. So take a break and then come back to test and experience the double-barreled benefits of better learning and better insight into your own learning.

Discussion Questions

1. Early research on learning indicated that testing might have significant value in education. Why was testing not adopted more widely as an educational practice? Why did testing largely remain regarded as a method of evaluation?

2. The chapter outlines four major benefits of testing for learning. How could you realize these benefits in your own learning? How could a learning curriculum be designed to realize these benefits?

3. What are the two possible reasons that testing improves learning? Do you believe one account is more plausible than the other?

4. One best practice in learning is to engage in multiple testing opportunities spaced out over time. Why would testing be so effective when done over spaced intervals? How could this be explained both by accounts of testing and accounts of spacing?

Suggestions for Further Reading

There are a number of outstanding reviews of testing that are well worth the time of the interested reader. Among our favorites is a broad review of the direct and indirect benefits of testing from Henry Roediger, Adam Putnam, and Megan Smith (2011). Henry Roediger and Jeff Karpicke (2006a), while not integrating the most recent research in testing, offer a deep historical review of early efforts to examine testing. The testing effect is the subject two recent meta-analyses (see Adesope et al., 2017 and Christopher Rowland, 2014), with the latter sticking more closely to laboratory research on testing. There is also a large literature on testing within the classroom (see e.g., Robin Hopkins and colleagues 2016; Mark McDaniel et al., 2007; 2011; 2013). We particularly recommend an opinion piece from Pooja Agarwal, Patrice Bain, and Roger Chamberlain (2012), who include the perspectives of a teacher, principal, and scientist on the merits of implementing testing in the classroom. On the larger subject of testing within education, Aaron Benjamin and Harold Pashler's (2015) view that opposition to standardized testing ignores the educational benefits of testing is well worth considering.

Credits

Page 172: Public Domain, no credit needed
Page 178: Syda Productions / Shutterstock
Page 182: Phovoir / Shutterstock

CHAPTER 10

Cues You Can Use

How to Jog Your Memory

....

Learning Objectives
- Reading this chapter will help you:
  - ✦ Understand why cues matter in learning.
  - ✦ Identify the different types of cues that might support learning.
  - ✦ Explain the four key components of an effective cue.
  - ✦ Know how to effectively use cues in your own learning.

....

Have you ever smelled something that took you right back to the past? One of your authors can remember such an experience. The smell of a particular perfume took her right back to a moment in high school, complete with vivid memories of the clothes she wore back then, the friends she had, and even who she was dating. Other information, such as hearing an old song or looking at a yearbook, can also take you right back to an earlier period of your life that you have not thought about in a

The scent of a certain perfume can trigger memories.

> **BOX 10.1   THE OPENING STANZA OF "THE STAR SPANGLED BANNER"**
> Oh, say can you see by the dawn's early light
> What so proudly we hailed at the twilight's last gleaming;
> Whose broad stripes and bright stars thru the perilous fight,
> O'er the ramparts we watched were so gallantly streaming.
> And the rocket's red glare, the bombs bursting in air.
> Gave proof through the night that our flag was still there.
> Oh, say does that star-spangled banner yet wave?
> O'er the land of the free and the home of the brave!

long time. Does this mean that memories residing in your mind can be triggered, so to speak? What can you do to help trigger memories of information that you have already learned and are having trouble remembering?

The Power of Cues

Before reading further, try singing "The Star-Spangled Banner" (see Box 10.1). But there is a catch: Begin right after the lyrics "we watched." (This demonstration works best if you sing aloud!)

You might have found yourself first making your way through the song, starting from the beginning, before you could pick up from "we watched" to the next set of lyrics ("were so gallantly streaming"). Why would you need to go back to the beginning of the song? One idea is that the song is well-learned, but has been learned in a specific order. Thus, to get to "we watched" you need to start with "Oh say can you see," which leads you to "by the dawn's early light," which in turn brings to mind "What so proudly we hailed" and so forth. This example shows that you can often remember more if there is a good hint, or **cue**, to guide you back to what you have learned.

But this does not just apply to songs. For example, what is the name of the capital of the Czech Republic? If the answer does not come to mind, try responding based on this cue: *Pr____*. If that does not work, try this cue: *Pra ___*. By now but you might have guessed that the answer is *Prague*. Even if you did not immediately get the correct answer, you have probably heard of Prague. However, it was only when given the right cue (like the first two or three letters of the answer) that you were able to recall this memory.

Why Do Cues Matter?

Why would a cue be important for remembering something you have already learned? Clearly, a good hint is valuable when you have learned some bit of information but cannot quite access the memory (as when the cue *Pra* helped you remember *Prague*). In that instance, a strong cue can help you remember information that you might not otherwise be able to retrieve (Tulving & Pearlstone, 1966). But the value of cues goes beyond the utility of a hint when you are having trouble retrieving information. The value of cues speaks to the very nature of memory in at least two ways.

When Information is Forgotten, It Is Often Still There

In 2006, the famous memorist Rajan Mahadevan (who earned a place in the 1984 *Guiness Book of World Records* for reciting the initial 31,811 digits of pi) gave a presentation at Colorado State University about his experience as a competitive memorizer. Included was a live demonstration of his phenomenal memorization capabilities, in which he memorized and then recited large strings of digits for a crowd, such as the grid of digits shown below. At one point, Rajan appeared stuck. After a long pause, with the audience in a hush, Rajan finally remembered the digits. Afterward he stated, "Persistence is the hallmark of expertise!" to the audience's laughter. Then he explained: "What I did was, I knew the first number was 8, so I started counting, 801, 802 . . . until I got to 833 and thought ah! 833!"

What does Rajan's experience illustrate about forgetting? For one, it shows that forgetting sometimes occurs when you are unable to access (retrieve) information you have previously learned. For example, what was the name of your seventh grade math teacher? This is a bit of information you surely know, but is often difficult to remember. That is, you may be experiencing **retrieval failure**, which occurs when information

0	9	5	5	2	0	0
2	1	2	7	1	2	6
2	5	5	3	3	4	0
2	2	1	0	5	9	1
3	9	9	7	2	3	4
7	9	6	0	5	0	7
0	0	9	7	2	9	2

A representation of a grid of numbers that Rajan Mahadevan quickly memorized for an audience at Colorado State University.

has been learned but cannot be remembered in the moment (Tulving & Pearlstone, 1966). A strong cue is one way to defeat retrieval failure. For example, if given the first two letters of your teacher's last name, you would probably stand a good chance of remembering the name.

In Rajan's case, he started with what little bit he *could* access, working to generate cues that might trigger the memory. For him, this meant counting from 801. Because numbers have deep meaning to him, counting by starting with what he knew (8), allowed him to sift through possibilities until he recognized the correct number as meaningful from his elaborative encoding (833). He knew that the memory still existed; he also knew the cuing himself would allow access to the memory.

Rajan's experience shows not only that cues help jog memory, but also that more information is present in memory at any given time than you can necessarily access at that time. Indeed, one reason you experience retrieval failure is that other information competes for access, getting in the way of what you are trying to remember (Kuhl & Wagner, 2009). A good cue is an excellent way to defeat this competition.

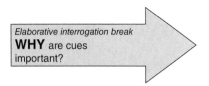

Elaborative interrogation break
WHY are cues important?

Learning Does Not Occur in Isolation

Every experience that you have becomes interwoven in memory with other information and experiences. Any time you are learning, you are not only delving into the topic at hand but also learning a much richer array of information. This will usually include other information that comes to mind during learning, the physical environment where you are learning (the room, the table you are sitting at, the people surrounding you), and your own mental or physical state (e.g., your caffeine level).

For example, imagine that you are sitting in a biology lecture on the differences between mitosis and meiosis. In this case, you are not only learning something about cell division and reproduction, but you are also learning other information, often without even realizing it. Consider just a few possibilities:

- Your lecture likely took place in a classroom.
- You may have used a specific notebook or laptop for note-taking.

- You may have been seated near other students.
- Your instructor may have had a slight cold that changed her voice that day.
- You might have been feeling particularly excited to hear about cell division.
- You may made connections to prior knowledge about sexual reproduction.
- You drew vivid diagrams of the key processes.

Thus, even this simple example illustrates the many different links that could be learned in just one lecture.

The upshot is that any information that has been associated with what you have learned can potentially serve as cues to later access the information from your memory. For example, you might recall the lecture by carefully thinking back to the room, remembering your instructor's voice that day, or imagining the diagrams you drew. From this perspective, cues are effective handles that allow you to grab memories from the vast baggage claim of memory. Every bit of context associated with your original learning episode can later serve as cues for accessing other elements of that memory later on.

A World of Cues

The cues or hints that allow you to access prior learning come in endless varieties, ranging from what comes to mind at any given moment to what is around you in your surroundings, and everything in between. Although there are a large variety of cues that can influence memory, several types of cues have received the most attention from researchers. Before moving on, try Demonstration 10.1. Start with the procedure described in Demonstration 10.1a, then turn the page and complete the procedure described in Demonstration 10.1b.

Informational Cues

The information you are learning and any information associated with your learning can be an effective cue. For example, Chapter 2 described the cycle of science. The cycle of science begins by considering existing data, identifying general premises that can be tested (*induction*), and then proceeding to hypotheses about very specific outcomes (*deduction*). What is the next step? If you cannot remember, try thinking

DEMONSTRATION 10.1a
Study each word below (underlined) and its accompanying phrase. The phrase will help you think about the word.

1. A day of the week   Thursday
2. A government leader   king
3. A type of bird   cardinal
4. A vegetable   cabbage
5. Associated with heat   stove
6. A round object   ball
7. A girl's name   Susan
8. A type of footwear   boots
9. A manmade structure   bridge
10. A weapon   cannon
11. A sweet food   banana
12. An indication of possession   mine
13. A tool   wrench
14. Found next to a highway   motel
15. A type of sports equipment   racket

Next. Spend 30 seconds counting backward by fours from the number 353. We'll get you started: 349, 345 . . .
   Once you are done counting backward, turn to the next page.

back to the diagram of the cycle of science (Figure 2.2). Or, consider the sample experiment on feedback that illustrated the cycle of science.

Each of these hints is a cue that could help you remember that third step. Cues of this sort can be powerful, and there is some evidence that cues that take you back to the original learning can be the most powerful. (By the way, *observation* is the third step.)

This principle is exemplified by Demonstration 10.1 (taken from Thieman, 1984; see also Light & Carter-Sobell, 1970; Tulving & Thomson, 1973). In the original experiment using this method, participants studied words associated with a short phrase. When the participant was tested, a phrase then appeared for the participant to use to remember the studied word.

In some cases, the phrases used at study and test were the same. For example, in the demonstration you completed, you studied "A day

DEMONSTRATION 10.1b

Now we would like you to remember as many words as you can that you studied. For each item you will be given a cue; sometimes it will be the same cue you studied but in other cases it will be different. It will always be related to word you're looking for.

1. A girl's name
2. A sweet food
3. A card game
4. A day of the week
5. A kitchen appliance
6. A type of noise
7. A weapon
8. A member of royalty
9. A clergyman
10. A tool
11. Needed in snow
12. A social event
13. A vegetable
14. A vacation rest stop
15. Associated with coal

You can find the answers at the end of the chapter.

of the week—Thursday" and received the same phrase for the test. For other items, you studied one phrase (e.g., "A government leader—king") but were given a somewhat different phrase at test (e.g., "A member of royalty"). In other cases, the meaning of the phrase was entirely different from what you studied ("A type of bird—cardinal") to your test ("A clergyman"). Thus, on the test there was always a cue, and it was either identical, very similar, or completely different from what you studied.

The results of an experiment using this procedure are shown in Figure 10.1. As you can see, there was only a slight drop in memory performance when a similar cue was used instead of the same cue. However, when the cue conveyed a completely different sense of what was learned, people remembered much less than when the same or a similar cue was used. Thus, cues are especially effective if they get you thinking along the lines of original learning.

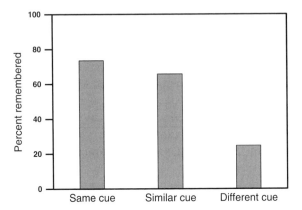

FIGURE **10.1** The mean percentage of words recalled with identical, similar, and different cues (adapted from Thieman, 1984).

Cues from Mental/Physiological State

Just as the information previously associated with learning can be a cue, your mental and physical state can also serve as a cue to memory. This might include how you are feeling at the time that you study (e.g., sad, happy, excited), the presence of substances (e.g., caffeine) in your body, or even your current aerobic state (e.g., having just exercised).

Miles and Hardman (1998) report an interesting study on the latter type of cue—aerobic state. They had participants hop on an exercise bike and learn a list of words. Sometimes they would engage in vigorous exercise, pedaling hard until their heart was beating about 200 times per minute (exercise condition), or other times the participant would sit calmly in the seat and learn the words (rest condition). A few minutes later participants took a test, either while exercising or at rest. Thus, the experimental design involved four different combinations of learning and testing conditions (see Figure 10.2):

1. Learning while exercising and testing while exercising (study exercise–test exercise).
2. Learning while exercising and testing while at rest (study exercise–test rest).
3. Learning at rest and testing while at rest (study rest–test exercise).
4. Learning while at rest and testing while exercising (study rest–test rest).

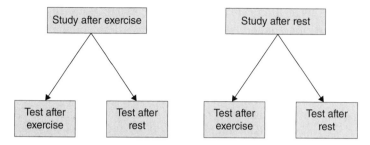

FIGURE **10.2 A diagram of Miles and Hardman's (1998) procedure.**

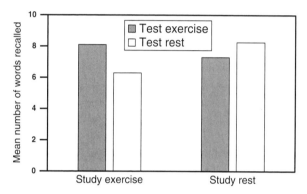

FIGURE **10.3 Mean percentage of words recalled when study and test were at rest or during exercise (adapted from Miles & Hardman, 1998).**

The results are shown in Figure 10.3. Consider the two conditions involving participants who exercised while learning (left side). Memory was best when the test was also accompanied by exercise (gray bar), compared with testing while resting (white bar). The same pattern, although in a milder form, occurred when participants studied while at rest. Similar results, with memory being best when the test and study state match, have been reported with alcohol and other substances (e.g., Goodwin et al., 1969) and with mood (Teasdale & Russell, 1983).

The Physical Environment as a Cue

Does this experience ring a bell? You are sitting in your room and have the sudden urge to head to the fridge for a drink. But upon arriving at the fridge you have completely forgotten why you were there in the first place. There are many potential explanations for your forgetting, but one possibility is that the place where you attempted to retrieve your memory (the kitchen) was very different from the place where you originally "learned" that you wanted something to drink (your room). Because the two contexts are not very similar, you could not remember what you wanted. In fact, using virtual reality, a group of researchers (Radvansky, Krawietz, & Tamplin, 2011), reported that forgetting was more likely after people walked through doorways. One reason is that (virtually) walking into a new room was a big change in context. Surrounded by this new context, there were fewer effective cues available to help participants remember the room they just came from.

This example suggests that the physical environment can be a cue for memory. One of the most famous studies (Godden & Baddeley, 1975) of this idea had divers learn a list of words while sitting on a beach, and then under about 20 feet of water. Participants were then asked to recall as much as they could remember of the list, either in the same environment as the learning phase or in a different environment. For example, participants sometimes learned the words on the beach and took a test on the beach (same environment); at other times they learned the words on the beach and were tested underwater (different environment).

The results of this experiment are shown in Figure 10.4. The key finding is that memory was best when retrieval took place in the same environment as learning. Consider instances when participants learned words on the beach (gray bars). In those cases, memory was much better if they were tested in the same environment (on the beach) than in a different environment (underwater). The pattern is the same when participants learned underwater, with memory much better when tested underwater than on dry land.

One famous study had participants learn a set of words on land and underwater.

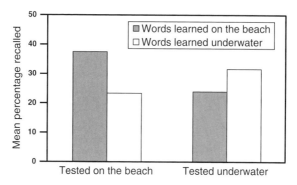

FIGURE 10.4 **Mean percentage recalled when study and test were on a beach or underwater (Godden & Baddeley, 1975).**

Later work (Smith, 1979) showed that even *imagining* a prior context could produce the same effects as actually being in a physical context. In this study, participants learned a list of 80 words in a distinctive basement room. They returned 24 hours later and were asked to write down as much as they could remember. One group of participants were tested in the same room (same context), another was tested in a different room (different context), and a third group was tested in a different room but asked to imagine details of the original learning room before taking the test (different context-image). Participants who tested in the same context remembered quite a bit more than participants tested in a different context. However, participants who imagined the original learning context had nearly identical performance to those in the same context. Applied to your own exam taking, this suggests that imagining being in the context in which you originally learned the information could help you retrieve information from memory.

Context in Context: A Principle and a Caveat

You might have noticed a trend in the research discussed so far. In each case, the best learning occurred when the cue present during studying matched the cue at testing. For example, the study with divers (Godden & Baddeley, 1975) showed that if you are going to learn underwater your best bet is also to test underwater. Likewise, if you are going to study on an exercise bike (Miles & Hardman, 1998) or learn about birds like a cardinal (Thieman, 1984), memory will be best if you can have the same context for a test as you had in the study phase.

Students learning about these benefits of matching the study and test context often ask this question: Should I study in the same classroom where I will be tested? That is, if a matching context is best for learning, would studying be most effective if it matched the test?

The short answer to this question is simple: No! You do not need to worry about studying in the same context where you will be tested. The longer answer to the question illustrates how to best use cues in your studying. But first consider at a very interesting field experiment (Saufley, Otaka, Bavaresco, 1985).

Researchers in this study tracked students who took an exam in either their usual classroom or in a different classroom. If retrieving in the same place where a large portion of learning occurs is all that matters, then students testing in the same classroom should have higher exam scores than students testing in a different classroom. But that is not at all what the researchers found. In fact, across seven courses and thousands of students, there was no difference in exam performance for being in the same versus a different classroom. To take just one example, 221 students in an introductory biology course took their exam in the same room where class met, and 250 students took their exam in a different classroom. Those in the same room scored an average of 76.74 on the exam and those in a different room scored an average of 77.50.

There are probably several explanations for these results. For one, much of learning happens outside of class (such as studying in your own room), so the particular classroom context might not be all that important. The average student has also probably seen hundreds of classrooms, many of which are quite similar to one another. Over time, these rooms might blend together and work poorly as a cue for specific information learned in a specific classroom.

These explanations paint part of the picture, but consider one other element. Presumably, a classroom would be associated with all of the information that had been learned in that course. For the biology course highlighted in the example, students were taking a midterm, so they had learned about half of the course material. Accordingly, the classroom would be associated with all of the lectures, in-class activities, and discussions that had occurred up to that point. Having been associated with hours of material, would the classroom be effective for zeroing in on one particular piece of information that you are trying to remember in response to a test question? No, it would not.

Instead, *cues are effective when they are uniquely associated with a memory.* Put differently, the more information associated with any one cue the less effective that cue will be (Watkins & Watkins, 1975).

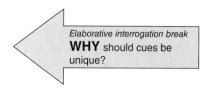

Elaborative interrogation break
WHY should cues be unique?

For example, suppose a friend tells you she is thinking of a president of the United States. Who does she have in mind? This is a terrible question. As of this writing there have been 45 presidents, and the question she asked is a cue to all of them. Instead, a better cue might be "I'm thinking of the third president of the United States, the author of the Declaration of Independence." This is a better cue not just because this is a famous president (Thomas Jefferson), but because that cue alone is uniquely connected to the information she is asking for. With this idea in mind, several principles stand out as best way to use cues for your studying.

The Best Cues for Studying Are . . .

There are several ingredients to a good cue, but the following four properties of cues stand out as the most powerful.

Unique Cues

The case has already been made but it bears repeating—the best cues for studying uniquely specify the memory. That is, the key is not whether a studied context matches a testing context (Nairne, 2002), but whether the cue provides a unique, distinct, and not easily confusable path back to a memory.

Recall that one of the primary reasons you forget is that other information gets in the way and competes for access to the memory you want. For example, suppose you are trying to remember a character from *Sesame Street* and keep getting stuck on the names of other famous children's characters (Dora the Explorer, Big Bird) rather than the character you are seeking. Indeed, using the cue "famous children's show character" will not be effective because that could bring to mind many characters. A better cue might "lives in a trash can," because that cue is tied to only one character (Oscar the Grouch).

Thus, the most effective cue for retrieving a specific piece of information from memory is one uniquely tied to just that memory and not many others. When cues only tie to one memory, there are few other memories jostling for access. Consider the power of unique smells highlighted at the start of this chapter. The smell of a unique perfume may suddenly take you back to a specific time of your life. But the same thing does not happen you smell something more common, like strawberries or peppermint gum. Why? Competition among memories. Strawberries and peppermint gum are common smells and do not trigger any one particular memory very easily, making it less predictable which memory or thought will come to mind when smelling them. In contrast, a smell that is uniquely tied to one particular memory is likely to call to mind that particular memory.

One group of researchers (Aggleton & Waskett, 1999) tested this idea by quizzing people about their memory for a visit to the Jorvik Viking Centre in York, England. Visitors to the Jorvik Centre experience a blend of Viking smells that are unique to the museum. The researchers gave people questionnaires to probe their memory for a prior museum visit that occurred years earlier. One group of participants first answered questions after receiving a set of common smells. They then took the questionnaire again after receiving that unique blend of Viking smells as a cue. When given the unique Viking blend, participants correctly remembered about 19% more details than when given common smells.

Common smells may not be effectives cues to trigger memories.

The Jorvik Viking Centre in York, England uses an unique blend of smells that can be a strong cue to memories for a visit (see Aggleton & Waskett, 1999).

Just as a unique smell can trigger a memory, so can a unique phrase. For example, participants in one study (Moscovitch & Craik, 1976) learned a list of words by answering a question about each word. Sometimes the question would focus on the rhyming qualities of the word (does this word rhyme with *hot*?), the category it belonged to (is this an example of a boat?), or whether the word fit well in a sentence. As you might remember from Chapter 5, this is really a manipulation of elaboration. Importantly, participants either saw the same questions repeated for many words (called the *shared* condition because the same question was shared with multiple words) or received a different question for each word (called the *unique condition* because each question was unique to that one word). Later on, participants were given the question as a cue and asked to remember the word that went that question.

The results of the experiment are shown in Figure 10.5. First, as described in Chapter 5, the more participants elaborated on words, the more they remembered, exemplified by the fact that thinking about a category or whether a word fit in a sentence resulted in better memory than thinking about what a word sounded like. Second, unique cues (solid line) resulted in much better memory than cues shared with multiple words (broken line). So, despite what your mom or dad told you, sharing is bad, as least when it comes to cues for memory.

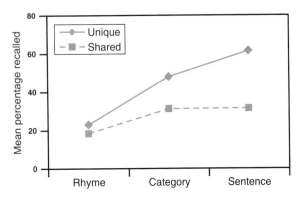

FIGURE 10.5 **Mean percentage of words recalled for unique and shared cues (adapted from Moscovitch & Craik, 1976).**

How can you apply this to your own learning? Try to create mental cues that *uniquely tie to the newly learned information*, yet will be easy for you to think of come test time. These unique mental cues might be concrete examples of the idea or concept, personal experiences you thought of that are in some way related to the information, or those diagrams you drew during learning.

Cues from Variable Learning Contexts

Just like having too much information attached to one cue hinders learning, having too much information attached to one context is also bad for learning. That is, contexts are more helpful when they are varied rather than the same or similar (another good reason *not* to study in the same classroom that you will be tested in).

One group of researchers (Smith, Glenberg, & Bjork, 1978) tested by this having participants first learn a list of 40 words in a distinctive room. Three hours later participants studied the same list of 40 words again, but with a catch: They either studied in the same room used for the first session or in a different building. Later, all of the participants were given a surprise test and asked to write down as many of the studied words as they could remember. (This test was done in a neutral context that participants had not been previously exposed to.) Thus, the researchers tested whether participants were in the *same context* or a *different context* across study sessions. Participants in the same context remembered about 40% of the words, whereas those who experienced different contexts remembered about 61% of the words.

Why did different contexts help remembering? The different contexts likely provided additional connections to the learning material that could be used as a retrieval cue. That is, multiple potential "routes" to the desired information might be created by learning it in different contexts. For example, suppose you and a friend need to learn about plasmas for chemistry class and decide you each need about four hours to study. You decide that will you study for two hours on Monday and two hours on Wednesday, whereas your friend decides to study for four hours on Wednesday. Based on what you know about spacing (Chapter 8), you should anticipate that studying in two blocks of time will result in better learning than studying everything in a single block of time.

Indeed, by studying in two separate blocks, you have created two distinct mental contexts for the material. At each point in time when studying you might have considered different aspects of the material being learned, done your studying in conjunction with different classes, been in a different mood, or studied in a different place. Introducing these changes in your studying will provide a richer set of connections as you try to remember the finer details of plasmas. The bottom line is to make sure that you not only space out your studying, but also try to mix up the contexts while you learn. In this case, variety is not only the spice of life, but also the spice of learning.

Cues from the Thought Processes Engaged During Learning

Imagine that you are in an astronomy class, about to take a test on the sun. To prepare for the test, you worked hard to understand how fusion reactions power the sun's energy and support life on Earth. However, on the exam, the questions (the cues) ask for different information, such as specifics about the size of the sun, the length of time it takes for the sun's radiation to make it to Earth, and so forth. That is, you studied based on a high-level understanding of complex processes, but your exam focused on isolated facts.

This would be an unsettling situation, because the type of thought processes you engaged in during learning would not match well with the type of thought processes needed to succeed on the test, leaving you badly unprepared. And it highlights another principle of what makes a good cue: The processes evoked by the cue should match the processes you used during learning (Morris, Bransford, & Franks, 1977).

One study (Thomas & McDaniel, 2007) tested this by first having participants read six short texts about a range of topics such as spiders, sharks, or the Himalayan mountain Kanchenjunga. For half of the texts, the researchers wanted participants to take a very detailed approach. To encourage this, they deleted letters from words in each sentence and instructed participants to fill in the missing letters as they read. For the other texts, the researchers wanted participants to grasp the broader concepts of the text. To encourage this conceptual approach, participants were given paragraphs as single sentences on laminated slips of paper, ordered randomly. Participants were charged with arranging the sentences so that the paragraph made sense.

Once all of the texts were read, the participants were given a test. Some of the questions emphasized specific details from the text. For example, participants were asked, "The walls of ice in Kanchenjunga range from _____ feet high." (The answer is 600 to 1,000 ft.) On other questions, a key concept was emphasized. For that type of question, participants might be asked "The downward speed of snow is much faster in Kanchenjunga than in the Alps because _____." (This occurs because there is more snowfall.) Thus, some of the questions matched the method of studying (e.g., studying in detail and receiving questions on details), whereas other questions diverged from studying (e.g., studying for detail but asking about concepts).

Figure 10.6 shows a big cost when the type of studying does not match the test cue. Take the case of studying conceptually (right side of Figure 10.6). That is an excellent strategy when cues on the test call for conceptual knowledge (white bar), but fares badly when the test emphasizes detailed knowledge (gray bar). Similarly, studying in detail (left side of Figure 10.6) is great when being asked facts (gray bar), but is a poor strategy when the question requires deeper, conceptual understanding (white bar). The moral of the story is clear: The way you study should match the way you expect to retrieve information later on.

Cues You Generate During Studying

One of the most effective sets of cues will be those you generate while studying. In fact, this is a central component of many of the study techniques discussed. Consider the method of loci (Chapter 6). The image of a familiar route serves as an easily retrievable, mentally generated cue for accessing the novel information attached to that cue via imagery.

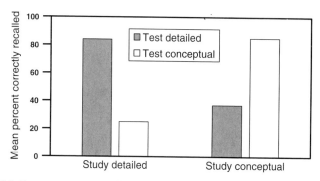

FIGURE 10.6 **Mean percentage recalled when study and test were detailed versus conceptual (adapted from Thomas & McDaniel, 2007).**

Research suggests that the best cues will be durable and not tied to what you were doing or thinking at the time you created the cue. For example, suppose you wanted to learn that Beethoven was the composer of "Für Elise." It would not be effective to create a cue such as "I feel hungry now and I'm always hungry for Beethoven." Hunger is not a unique state and you may be in a completely different state, with a full stomach, by the time you need to retrieve.

A better cue might be something like "Dun Dun Dun Dun!" or "Symphony No. 5." This cue is uniquely linked to the memory and should remain durable over time. For example, whether you are hungry or full has nothing to do with the cue. Thus, your best bet is to generate cues that represent distinct properties of what you are trying to learn (Mäntylä & Nilsson, 1988).

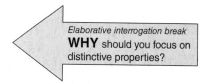

Elaborative interrogation break
WHY should you focus on distinctive properties?

Putting It All Together

Cues and contexts are complicated. Some of the most dramatic results in all of experimental psychology have been observed by mixing and matching the context of studying with the context of a test. For example, divers (Godden & Baddeley, 1975) recalled about 40% less if they learned information underwater but retrieved it on dry land. However, others have reported no impact of physical context cues based on where students take exams (Saufley, Otaka, & Bavaresco, 1985).

There are principled reasons for these differences across studies, but as a practical matter, you should not worry about where your exam takes place. Much more important is whether your studying yields unique, durable cues that distinguish information you want to remember from other information. Vivid, distinct examples often make a fine cue. Indeed, one of your authors remembers the key principles of market economies by recalling a joke told by an economics professor ("You could teach a parrot to be an economist; all she would need to say is 'supply and demand'"). To this day, he cannot think about those principles without imagining a parrot. Whatever methods you use, keeping your cues unique will enhance learning.

Tips You Can Use

1. **Devise unique mental cues.** The most effective cues are those that are uniquely tied to the information that you are seeking to retrieve from memory. While studying, try to mentally generate cues that you can later use, making them uniquely tied to the information at hand.

2. **Vary your study contexts.** Each time you study, change it up so that your memories are tied to lots of potential cues (to maximize the likelihood of thinking of a cue that will access the desired memory when needed). One way to do this is to change when and where you study, providing different contexts and cues associated with each study episode. This is also another good reason to space out your studying.

3. **Try the method of loci.** As noted in Chapter 6, the method of loci is a powerful and effective strategy for learning a sequence of information. By its very nature of tying unique images to information that needs to be remembered, it fulfills many of the requirements of a good cue.

4. **When really stuck, try taking a break.** Thinking of the wrong information can sometimes prevent you from remembering the right information. The wrong information may dominate your thoughts and compete with the right information that might otherwise come to mind. Taking a break by shifting your thoughts to something completely unrelated can clear your mind, allowing you to approach the problem fresh on the next attempt. This may increase the likelihood of accessing the right information next time.

Discussion Questions

1. Having a retrieval context match an encoding context appears to help learning in some instances, but provides little, or limited, benefits in other instances. How would you explain this discrepancy? What do these mixed results say about how to conduct your own studying?
2. How can you best create distinctive cues for learning? That is, how can you create unique and distinguishable cues that can support your own learning?
3. How can each of the three varieties of cues discussed in this chapter (informational, state, physical) be applied to your own learning?
4. Cues tend to be useful to the degree that they match the way you have learned information. How does you ensure that this match exists? Is there a method of studying that would be useful if you were unsure of how you will be tested?

Suggestions for Further Reading

There is a variety of interesting research and debate on how strategies for studying and the cues present at retrieval influence memory. Steven Smith and Edward Vela (2001) provide a comprehensive summary of research on physical context and argue that it does benefit memory, although that benefit is limited. Eric Eich (1989) has an excellent chapter on physical and mental context effects and advances several ideas on when context will or will not matter. Henry Roediger and Melissa Guynn (1996) have a superb chapter on retrieval that covers contexts, among several topics related to retrieval. Others have convincingly argued that the focus should be on the degree to which cues are unique or diagnostic of prior learning episodes. James Nairne (2002) and Winston Goh and Sharon Lu (2012) are strong examples of this perspective.

Answers to Demonstration 10.1

Same cues:
1 = Susan; 4 = Thursday; 7 = cannon; 10 = wrench; 13 = cabbage
Similar cues:
2 = banana; 5 = stove; 8 = king; 11 = boots; 14 = motel
Different cues:
3 = bridge; 6 = racket; 9 = cardinal; 12 = ball; 15 = mine

Credits

Page 191: Leon Rafael / Shutterstock
Page 200: totophotos / Shutterstock
Page 204: knipsdesign / Shutterstock
Page 205: Wozzie / Shutterstock

CHAPTER 11

Learning Is More Than Remembering

Understanding, Discovery, and Innovation

....

Learning Objectives
- Reading this chapter will help you:
  - Appreciate the nature of understanding.
  - Explain how memory supports understanding.
  - Identify methods that promote understanding.
  - Know how to effectively draw analogies that support understanding.

....

*D*o not put all of your eggs in one basket.
You have probably seen and heard this saying many times. Do you know what it means? Can you think of an example from your life that reflects this saying? If you can do all of these things, this suggests that you understand the meaning of this saying. You have grasped it and you have a deep enough understanding of what it means to convey it to others. That is exactly what this chapter is about: understanding.

Thus far, most of this book has addressed the issue of better retaining information in memory. Indeed, what people often mean by "learning" is acquiring a new fact or piece of information and then hanging on to it over time. However, there is clearly much more to learning than just remembering facts and bits of information. Every time you discover something new or figure out a way to be innovative, you have learned something. A new connection was made, an "aha!" moment occurred, a light bulb went off in your head. When you arrive at a new approach, a new idea, or a new understanding—something clicked.

Do you know the meaning of the saying, *do not put all of your eggs in one basket?*

When presenting the state-of-the-art research on learning and memory to instructors, your authors are often asked: "How do we enhance *understanding* among our students?" Understanding is one of the most important facets of learning. The term *understanding* denotes apprehension or the notion of really grasping something or "getting it"—much like your ability to understand the saying presented at the beginning of this chapter. Chances are, you understood the saying. You grasped it. You got it. But what if you were trying to help someone else to understand its meaning? Perhaps the person has never seen or heard the phrase before. How would you help this person understand what it means? This is somewhat analogous to what instructors try to achieve with their students.

Effective learning may help you to create new ideas.

Your goal when learning is likely not to learn an isolated piece of information, but to come to an understanding within a broader framework. This might involve learning how something works, like the bonding of atoms to form a molecule, the aerodynamics that enable flight, or the economic forces of supply and demand.

In other cases, the goal is learning how something came to be, like the evolution of humans, the origins of the universe, or the precursors of the French Revolution. Although achieving understanding may be difficult at times—and it is difficult to predict or control the precise moment when you will finally understand something—research suggests that there are ways to increase the likelihood that understanding will eventually occur for you. Increasing the likelihood of understanding not only applies to learning new things that others can teach you, but also to discovering or inventing new things for the first time, or developing an innovative new solution to a problem.

Insight

Insight is the term used by scientists to describe the moment of understanding—when everything starts to click. Have you ever been daunted by a problem when suddenly the solution strikes without warning? For example, one of your authors recalls being perplexed by how to hang pictures with nails but with no hammer available. After fretting over the problem for some time, he suddenly realized that he could use the sole of a boot to strike nails into a wall. This realization of a solution to a previously intractable problem is an example of insight.

Many associate insight with the "aha!" moment that scientists or inventors sometimes experience when they suddenly realize the solution to a problem or figure out how something works. But the same type of experience can occur in any learning situation when you suddenly understand a complex idea like the process of natural selection. Indeed, this moment of understanding may be very similar to the moment someone solves a challenging problem or discovers a brand new invention. It can be an exhilarating, emotional reaction, along the lines of "Oh! Now I get it!" Researchers have long studied the moment of insight. Does it come on gradually or suddenly? Can you predict its onset? Can it be facilitated? Understanding the process that leads to the "aha!" moment may increase the likelihood of insight happening in your own learning.

How Mechanisms of Memory Affect Understanding

Although learning is more than remembering, the basic principles of memory's everyday operation drive understanding. For example, if you understood the saying *Do not put all of your eggs in one basket*, this is because relevant information was accessed from your knowledge-base upon reading it, allowing for immediate grasp of its meaning. But what about when you are presented with something that does not cue the relevant knowledge needed to grasp it?

The first thing to realize is that no new insight or realization magically materializes. Every new insight or discovery came from something already known. The "newness" of a seemingly novel insight or idea usually lies in the new way that connections were made among already known bits of information. This means that existing memories are always involved. In short, every new insight builds on what is already in your mind—in your knowledge-base.

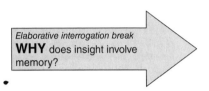

Elaborative interrogation break
WHY does insight involve memory?

Although it is very difficult to predict the moment when you will grasp something new, you can capitalize on what is known about memory to increase the likelihood that the moment of understanding will eventually hit. What factors block understanding?

It turns out that normal mechanisms involved in remembering can place you in a rut when trying to understand something new or trying to solve a new problem. You might recall from Chapter 10 on cues that the best cues uniquely specify a memory—they are not shared with lots of other memories. For that reason, a classroom is a poor cue to get to a specific memory, because a classroom is typically associated with lots of other memories, such as the many hours you spend in class. It is hard to predict which memories will rise to the surface, so to speak, in response to a bad cue. You may inadvertently end up conjuring up the wrong memories. In turn, the wrong memories might compete with and get in the way of more useful information, preventing you from accessing the right memories. A unique cue decreases competition from the wrong memories, increasing the chance that the memory you are seeking comes to mind. In fact, a strong unique cue is effective precisely because it can keep other memories from competing for your attention.

This is a great way to make sure you get to the right memory, but there is a downside. A unique cue or a retrieved memory can sometimes be so good at eliminating the competition that you miss out on some of the information you need. This means that you might fail to have a novel insight or grasp a concept precisely because you are thinking of the wrong information at the moment and it is blocking the right information.

Everyone has probably had an experience along these lines when trying to recall a name. One of your authors recently experienced this when trying to think of a researcher's name that started with "K." Your author was trying to think of the researcher "Kraus" in order to look up an article, but could not think of the name because of having just read something by a researcher named Katz. Thus, the name Kraus would not come to mind because the name Katz kept dominating awareness. It was as if the more recently thought-of name was getting in the way of (researchers use the term *interfering* with) access to the sought-after name.

Your understanding can be hurt not only when the wrong information gets in the way of your path to the right information, but also when you have the wrong mindset or frame of mind. This is because the wrong knowledge is active. For example, you have probably worked with number puzzles in which you try to determine the pattern for the order of a set of numbers. Why are the numbers below arranged in this order (taken from Matlin & Farmer, 2016)?

8, 5, 4, 9, 1, 7, 6, 3, 2, 0

Were you able to solve the problem? Most people find the problem very difficult to solve, but there is actually a very simple solution—you just need to change your mindset. As a hint to change your mindset, try thinking about each of the numbers as words.

Did you get the solution now? You may have discovered that the numbers are in alphabetical order. When given this problem, most people assume that the answer involves a mathematical solution. That incorrect mindset makes a solution nearly impossible. It is only when you approach the problem from a completely different mindset, considering how the words are spelled, rather than their mathematical relationship, that the solution presents itself.

Escaping the Grip of the Wrong Mindset

Check out the three words below. Can you think of a single word that links all three?

cottage
swiss
cake

You may have discovered the answer: *cheese*. Items like these are referred to as remote associates, because discovering the link occurs when you can identify the common word that is not present (it is remote).

Now try finding the common link from the three words below. You will note that next to each word is another word in italics that may or may not help you find the link:

tank *water*
hill *ant*
secret *hideout*

Now try stepping away for a minute and examining the three words on the left again. Did that help you find the answer (*top*)?

One group of researchers (Vul & Pashler, 2007) used exactly this procedure to show the kinds of problems that arise when you have the wrong hint or mindset. Participants in their study saw remote associates just like these. One group of participants saw the associates without the misleading hints (tank, hill, secret), while another group received the same associates but with the misleading hint included. Finally, a third group was given the misleading hints but received a five-minute break away from solving the problems before trying again. The researchers measured how often participants were able to solve the problems. Those data are shown in Figure 11.1. As you can see, the misleading hint hindered participants' ability to solve the problem compared with getting no hint at all. However, a short break seemed to wipe away the harmful effects of a bad hint.

There are two lessons from this experiment. First, having the wrong mindset, as when participants were given the misleading hint, hurts

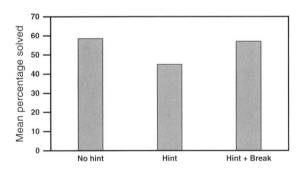

FIGURE 11.1 **Mean percentage of problems solved for participants with no hint, a misleading hint, or a misleading hint with a break (adapted from Vul & Pashler, 2007).**

your ability to discover the best solution. Second, you can sometimes free yourself from the wrong mindset by taking a break.

Indeed, when stuck on a problem, setting the problem aside can increase the likelihood of discovering its solution (Beeftink, Van Eerde, Rutte, 2008; Kounios & Beeman, 2015). So if you find yourself working hard but at an impasse, take a break from working on the problem. Importantly, take a break that involves thinking about something else for a while. This can mean going on a walk, playing a musical instrument, or working on another task. On your next attempt to solve the problem, you will have a fresh perspective that may open you to solutions that you were unable to think of on the last attempt.

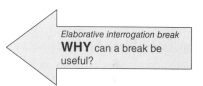

Elaborative interrogation break
WHY can a break be useful?

The Importance of Spaced Attempts

The idea to take breaks harkens back to a key study strategy discussed in Chapter 8 on spacing. It turns out that spacing is a very useful approach for more than just remembering things—it is an excellent strategy for working toward understanding difficult new material and for trying to solve novel problems. For example, as just noted, spaced attempts promote a fresh perspective on a problem each time you come back to work on it. In this way, spacing can release you from the clutches of the wrong information. Spacing also confers at least two other benefits that improve understanding.

Spacing Prepares Your Mind for Insight

Repeated, spaced attempts at solving a problem or understanding a difficult concept can increase the chance that you will notice good cues that can help you retrieve the relevant information that you need to solve a problem. That is, merely having attempted to solve a problem on previous occasions can increase the chance that you will later detect the cues that are relevant to eventually reaching the solution (Kounios & Beeman, 2015). Detecting the right cues, even when these cues are subtle, can facilitate insight (Bowden, 1997). You are more likely to notice subtle cues when you are "primed" for their detection by having the problem consistently on your mind (Kounios & Beeman, 2015). Indeed, people are more likely to remember problems that they failed to solve than problems that they successfully solved (Baddeley, 1963; Seifert & Patalano, 1991). In this way, problems that are not solved often stick in your mind, perhaps preparing you to be more attuned to potential cues that could help solve them later (Kounios & Beeman, 2015). For spacing to work, be sure to put in sufficient time before taking a break (Sio & Ormerod, 2009). In other words, you should not just glance at the problem or read it, but spend time in genuine, effortful attempts at understanding. This helps to prepare your mind for success on later attempts and allows you to reap the benefits of prior failure.

Including Sleep In Your Spacing Promotes Insight

Getting episodes of sleep in between study sessions can do wonders for your learning. Sleep plays a major role in making memories stable (a process called **consolidation**) and is likely an important contributing factor in the effects of between-session spacing on learning (Bell, Kawadri, Simone, & Wiseheart, 2014). In addition to memory benefits, sleep also actively prepares your mind to detect solutions to tough problems and to enhance understanding. For example, one group of researchers (Wagner, Gais, Haider, Verleger, & Born, 2004) gave participants problem sets to solve called number reduction tasks. The sets had a very subtle solution that required participants to notice hidden patterns across problems. Once that hidden pattern is discovered, the solution becomes very easy and fast. The authors of this study gave

Sleep can enhance learning and promote insight.

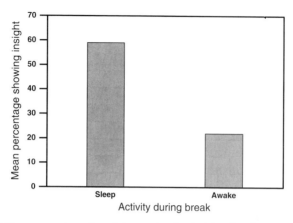

FIGURE 11.2 **Mean percentage of participants showing insight after sleeping vs. being awake (adapted from Wagner et al., 2004).**

participants training on the sets and then had them come back to work on the problems after eight hours. Some of the participants slept during this break and others stayed awake. Figure 11.2 shows their results. While nearly 60% of participants who slept discovered the hidden structure, only 20% of those who stayed awake detected the structure.

Thus, getting episodes of sleep between each new attempt at understanding or solving a problem builds a trajectory toward eventual insight. So make sure to sleep between your spaced attempts! You get to enjoy the benefits of resting, while your brain does some of the work while you sleep.

Innovation and Escaping the Wrong Mindset

One of your authors recently attended a talk on imagination by the philosopher Amy Kind. The talk considered how far imagination can extend from one's existing knowledge and experience. To illustrate her point, Dr. Kind asked some intriguing questions. For example, can a person who is considering having children really imagine what it is like to be a parent without ever having been one? Can a person who has never tasted a durian imagine what it is like to smell and taste one? (A durian is a very distinctive Asian fruit that usually leads to strong reactions from people; some hate it and find it obnoxious and others like it, but no one can quite describe it for anyone who has never smelled or tasted one).

A durian is a distinctive Asian fruit. Can someone who has never eaten a durian imagine what it would be like to taste one?

It was an interesting thought exercise on how imagination is tied to our existing knowledge and experience. Recently, an acquaintance of one of your authors who works at NASA searching for alien life mentioned that they are combing through massive collections of data in their efforts. A big problem is that they do not know exactly what they are looking for. That is, it is difficult to conceive of what life elsewhere might actually entail, and so there are not good theories or hypotheses aiding the analysis of the abundance of data.

Similarly, consider some of the ideas from this July 23, 2015 *Mental Floss* article called "1966's Insane Wedding Gowns of the Future." The author describes videos of what designers in 1966 imagined wedding gowns would look like in the future. Looking at the gowns now, in 2019, they look remarkably odd and of the 1960s in their styles. This is a great example of being tethered to existing knowledge and experience, even when trying to envision the future. Imagination can only take you so far beyond your existing representations! Consider also old episodes of *Star Trek* and how computers on the spaceship were envisioned at that time, compared to modern-day movies about space travel. Someday, people will be able to look at the movie *Passengers* and see the influence of the second decade of the twenty-first century in the thinking (the touch screen technologies are very similar to modern-day smartphone apps).

In short, when it comes to imagination and mental leaps beyond your current knowledge, you are largely tethered to what is already in your knowledge-base. For your moment-to-moment efforts to solve problems, there are some concrete steps that can help. You can take a break and change context to temporarily escape from the wrong

Wedding gowns of the future developed in the 1960s (from Keyser, 2015).

mindset. However, your ability to take giant mental leaps will be limited by how far you can stretch the tethers of your existing knowledge and experience. One way to do that is to find a good analogy.

Giant Mental Leaps: The Role of Analogy

The geneticist and Nobel Prize-winner Barbara McClintock is famous for having made many gigantic innovative leaps in her career (Kounios & Beeman, 2015). How is it possible to make gigantic mental leaps while still working within your existing knowledge-base and experience? The route to achieving great mental leaps appears to be based on analogy (Gentner, 2002; Green, 2016; Holyoak & Thagard, 1995; 1997).

An **analogy** refers to the relationship between two similar situations. Take this example: *night is to day as happy is to sad.* In this case, the similarity between the two situations described is that both referred to opposites; *night* is the opposite of *day* and *happy* is the opposite of *sad.* Often, an analogy is based on similarities that are not immediately obvious but are reflected in the underlying relationship between two elements. For example, the saying mentioned at the start of this chapter, *Don't put all of your eggs in one basket,* is not usually used to tell you how to distribute your eggs (although, when it comes to eggs, this is good advice). Instead, it refers to a deeper meaning about not putting all of your resources in one place, such as putting all of your hopes into one job application, all of your money into one investment, and so on.

Similarly, you could say that electrons revolve around the nucleus of an atom analogously to the way that planets revolve around the sun.

The ability to make these types of analogical connections between situations, termed **analogical reasoning**, can contribute to insight, understanding, and innovation. Several historical anecdotes highlight the value of a good analogy. Perhaps the most widely known is the story of Archimedes from the third century B.C. Archimedes was tasked with determining if the king's crown had been made of pure gold or if

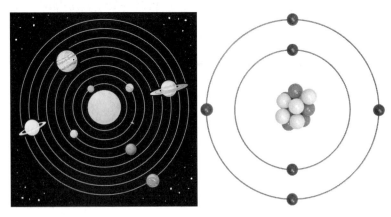

Planets revolving around the sun are analagous to electrons revolving around the nucleus of an atom.

another, cheaper metal had been melted in with the gold. He worked tirelessly trying to devise a way to make this determination. Eventually, he set the problem aside and went to do something else. Later on, while sliding into his bathtub, he noticed how the water rose as he sank into the tub. He suddenly realized the solution to his problem. If he submerged the crown in water, he could measure how much water the crown displaced. This would allow him to determine if the crown was pure gold. Legend has it that in a fit of excitement over the realization of his discovery, Archimedes leapt from his bathtub and ran down the streets naked screaming "Eureka! Eureka! I've got it!" (This is the origin of the phrase, *the Eureka effect.*)

Note the role of analogy here in Archimedes's discovery. Somehow, he made the connection between water rising as he sank into his bathtub and how the water would rise if he submerged the crown in it, and realized how he could use that information to solve his problem of establishing the purity of the crown.

The story of Sir Isaac Newton is another anecdotal example of a role of analogy in the achievement of insight. It is said that Newton's universal law of gravitation was inspired when he watched an apple fall from a tree. Supposedly, this prompted him to think about the force or pull on the apple, which in turn led him to extend this thought to the potential role of gravitational force in planetary motion. The story is so widely held that a descendent of the original apple tree whose fallen apple inspired Newton continues to be displayed and maintained at the Botanic Gardens in Cambridge with a plaque that reads:

Sir Isaac Newton's Apple

This apple tree is a descendant by vegetative propogation of a tree which grew in the garden of Woolsthorpe Manor, near Grantham, and which is reputed to be the tree from which fell the apple that helped Newton to formulate his theory of gravitation. The original tree is said to have died about 1815–1820. The variety is "Flower of Kent."

Another descendent of the tree was donated to the Massachusetts Institute of Technology (MIT) years ago as well.

Although these anecdotes are certainly interesting, they are not direct, empirical evidence for a role of analogy in the achievement of understanding, or giant mental leaps and breakthroughs. In a classic study, a group of researchers (Gick & Holyoak, 1980) examined the role

DEMONSTRATION 11.1   THE RADIATION PROBLEM

Suppose you are a doctor faced with a patient who has a malignant tumor in his stomach. It is impossible to operate on the patient, but unless the tumor is destroyed the patient will die. There is a kind of ray that can be used to destroy the tumor. If the rays reach the tumor all at once at a sufficiently high intensity, the tumor will be destroyed. Unfortunately, at this intensity the healthy tissue that the rays pass through on the way to the tumor will also be destroyed. At lower intensities the rays are harmless to healthy tissue, but they will not affect the tumor. What type of procedure might be used to destroy the tumor with the rays without destroying the healthy tissue?

of analogy in promoting insight by having participants try to solve a problem known as the radiation problem (Duncker, 1945). Before going further, read Demonstration 11.1 and try solving the problem.

Did you come up with the solution? If not, you are not alone. Only about 8% of college students in the study could come up with a solution on their own. Would having an analogy to draw from, similar to Archimedes sinking into his bath, help? Try Demonstration 11.2, which includes an analogous problem, and see if you notice any similarities to the radiation problem.

DEMONSTRATION 11.2   THE ATTACK-DISPERSION PROBLEM

A small country was controlled by a dictator. The dictator ruled the country from a strong fortress. The fortress was situated in the middle of the country, surrounded by farms and villages. Many roads radiated outward from the fortress like spokes on a wheel. A general raised a large army and vowed to capture the fortress and free the country of the dictator. The general knew that if his entire army could attack the fortress at once it could be captured. The general's troops were gathered at the head of one of the roads leading to the fortress, ready to attack. However, a spy brought the general a disturbing report. The ruthless dictator had planted mines on each of the roads. The mines were set so that small bodies of men could pass over them safely because the dictator needed to move troops and workers to and from the fortress. However, any large force would detonate the mines. Not only would this blow up the road and make it impassable, but the dictator would then destroy many villages in retaliation.

Did you notice similarities between the two problems? Now, what if you were presented with the solution to the attack-dispersion problem? Do you think that having the solution to this analogous problem would help you solve the radiation problem? Go ahead and read the solution to the attack-dispersion problem below.

Solution to the Attack-Dispersion Problem

The general, however, knew just what to do. He divided his army up into small groups and dispatched each group to the head of a different road. When all was ready he gave the signal, and each group marched down a different road. Each group continued down its road to the fortress, so that the entire army finally arrived together at the fortress at the same time. In this way, the general was able to capture the fortress and thus overthrow the dictator.

Did reading the solution to the attack-dispersion problem inspire you to solve the radiation problem? In one experiment, although only 8% of participants solved the radiation problem without an explicit analogy, 76% solved the problem when given the attack-dispersion story and its solution beforehand (see Figure 11.3). But this happened only if they were told that the attack-dispersion story might provide some useful hints (more on this later).

Data such as this provide compelling evidence that having an analogy from which to draw connections can prompt insight. These findings

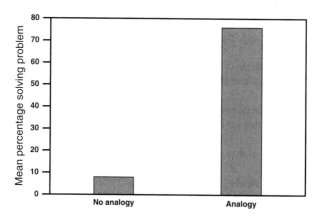

FIGURE 11.3 Mean percentage of participants solving the radiation problem (adapted from Gick & Holyoak, 1980).

Princeton physicist Paul Chaiken (left) drew an analogy from a drum of M&Ms to solve a centuries-old physics problem.

support the ideas indicated anecdotally in the stories of Archimedes and his bath and of Sir Isaac Newton and the apple. Examples of the role of analogy in insight and discovery can be found even in stories of modern-day discoveries.

Consider, for instance, the Princeton physicist Paul Chaikin and his love for M&Ms. As a prank, some of his students put a 55-gallon drum of M&Ms in his office. Looking at the huge drum of M&Ms prompted Chaikin to consider how well the M&Ms seemed to pack tightly into the drum. This, in turn, led to his insight that the elliptical shape of the M&M might actually be the shape that allows particles to randomly pack together tightly. In carrying out studies to test this hypothesis, Chaikin and his colleagues found support for the idea, helping to solve a centuries-old problem in physics regarding how particles randomly pack themselves together ("M&M's obsession leads to physics discovery", 2004).

Chaikin and colleagues' analogy from M&Ms is consistent with a more general idea that analogies play a central role in scientific progress (Gentner, 2002; Hesse, 1966). For example, one group of researchers (Dunbar, 2001; see also Dunbar & Blanchette, 2001) observed this process in action by visiting a number of research labs to examine scientists' and students' thinking processes live, so to speak—while new discoveries were taking place. As they observed a lab's interactions, the researchers would code something as an analogy if it involved using another knowledge-base to either explain a concept or to modify an existing concept or idea. They found that analogies were used

Elaborative interrogation break
WHY does analogy lead to great leaps?

frequently and were often used most effectively by expert scientists. Thus, whether it is a scientist making a new discovery or a student is coming to an understanding by acquiring of new knowledge, analogy plays a central role.

Note that analogy can explain how it is that people can make mental leaps beyond their current grasp or understanding while still being tethered to what is already in their knowledge-base and repertoire of past experiences. That said, successful analogical reasoning requires retrieval of the relevant background knowledge in order to detect the analogy between that prior knowledge and the current problem or situation at hand. It turns out that retrieving the right background knowledge for an analogy is very difficult. For example, in the radiation problem in Demonstration 11.1, about 25% of the participants still missed the solution even when reading the analogous attack-dispersion problem. This can be solved to some degree by giving a very clear hint. For example, 92% of participants solved the problem when explicitly told that the attack-dispersion problem provides useful information to solve the radiation problem.

Thus, providing a clear hint, or being explicit about the fact that something is intended to serve as an analogy, can help people to engage in and potentially benefit from analogical reasoning. This is a good reason to go to your instructor and ask for an analogy when you are struggling to understand something.

When solving a novel problem, there may be no one who can provide you with an analogy because a solution has never been discovered before. In this type of situation, the importance of spaced attempts applies. Keep coming to the problem with a fresh mindset, keep increasing your mind's preparedness to detect relevant cues by revisiting the problem in a spaced fashion, and keep getting episodes sleep in between attempts. You may also find it helpful to try explaining the problem to others (Needham & Begg, 1991; Nestojko et al., 2014), and to identify similarities with other problems (Cummins, 1992).

You may think that experts in a field have what seems like a magical ability to make mental leaps. But there is nothing magical at all. Experts who are at the forefront of their fields are constantly reading and adding to their expert knowledge in their field. They are constantly attempting to solve new problems to address new research questions. This means that their very careers are set up to allow them

> **BOX 11.1 HELPING OTHERS WITH UNDERSTANDING**
>
> How can you inspire insight in others? Instructors often do this by using analogies to facilitate their students' understanding. Consider teaching these two concepts: *central tendency* and *variability*. Central tendency refers to the center of a set of observations, often given as the average. Variability is a tougher concept and refers to the spread of observations. The following analogy should help: "A general wants to march his army across a river with an average depth of only two feet. The entire army drowns in the process." How could an entire army drown in a river that on average is only two feet deep? To solve the problem, you must come up with the idea that some parts of the river must be shallow while other parts must be deep. That is, although the average depth is two feet, there is a great deal of variability in depth.
>
> Research in this area indicates that explicit use of analogies and drawing attention to the critical deep relations is probably a good technique for instructors to use to enhance understanding among students (e.g., Glynn & Duit, 1995; Richland, Stigler, & Holyoak, 2012; Yuan, Uttal, & Gentner, 2017).

to continually space out attempts at making small breakthroughs. Experts' deep knowledge of their domain also allows them to detect many potential analogical relationships in problems that enhance understanding (e.g., Chi & VanLehn, 2012). Thus, experts are often well poised to make mental leaps within their domain of expertise (see Box 11.1 for another example of how experts can use analogies to facilitate insight in others).

Can You Sense an Impending Moment of Insight?

Research suggests that you cannot sense when you are about to have a moment of insight. For example, in one study (Metcalfe & Wiebe, 1987), researchers asked participants to rate their feelings of warmth (for how close they thought they were to arriving at the solution to a problem) every 15 seconds until they finally solved a problem. As you can see in Figure 11.4, whereas people did have a sense of their nearness to the solution for noninsight problems (i.e., algebra), they did not for those requiring insight. Feelings of warmth did not escalate before arriving at the solution to insight problems. Instead, the solution seemed to happen suddenly and unpredictably to the participants. Although you

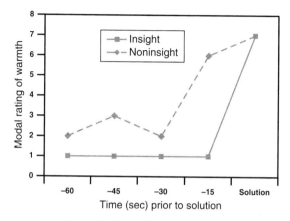

FIGURE 11.4 Most frequent (modal) ratings of closeness to solving an insight and noninsight problem (adapted from Metcalfe & Wiebe, 1987).

cannot predict the precise moment that insight will hit you, you can increase your trajectory toward getting there by following the steps to good understanding.

Putting It All Together

A major goal of acquiring knowledge is to use this knowledge in novel applications. A cardiologist learns about the circulatory system so that she can develop fresh insights to promote her patients' heart health. An engineer learns key principles of building so that she can design new structures. An astrophysicist trains to make new discoveries about the universe. Key ideas from the science learning can contribute to both goals, helping the doctor learn the ins and outs of the circulatory system, the engineer to fully grasp key components of design, and the astrophysicist to create a full understanding that can lead to important breakthroughs. And it can help you as you seek greater knowledge and understanding.

Tips You Can Use

1. **When at an impasse, take a break.** By setting a problem or difficult task aside for awhile, you may be providing yourself with a fresh start to think of new connections that you weren't able to see previously.
2. **Space out your attempts.** Distributing repeated attempts at solving a problem or understanding a difficult concept may not only help to

provide you with a fresh start each time, but also helps to prime your mind to be more likely to detect relevant cues when they come along. Not only do people tend to remember problems that they have failed to solve (Patalano & Seifert, 1994), but research suggests that spending more time during initial attempts at solving a problem can increase the chances of eventual success when you come back (see Sio & Ormerod, 2009, for a review). In addition, getting sleep between attempts permits you to harness the power of spacing and to gain the benefits of sleep for learning and insight.

3. **Ask an expert to provide you with an analogy.** When you are at an impasse in your problem-solving or understanding, ask an expert (like your instructor) if he or she can provide you with a helpful analogy. It might take some time, but most experts should be able to think of an analogy to use in explaining it to you. The analogy might help you to make the leap between something that is already in your knowledge-base (i.e., something that you already do understand) and the new concept.

4. **Actively seek out (and make) connections.** Having more knowledge at your disposal puts you in better position to detect analogies and mappings between different situations. As a general practice, actively seek out connections between things. The mere act of doing this will also involve deep processing or thinking about what you are trying to learn, which should help you better learn and remember the information (see Chapter 6 on elaboration). To do this, you could try asking yourself, "How does this relate to something that I already know and understand?" That is, continually seek to make connections between new material that you are trying to learn and things that you already know and understand.

5. **Solidify your understanding.** Try explaining the concept to another person. This aids memory (see Nestojko et al., 2014), helping to increase your own understanding and also helps you to identify what you do not yet understand very well (see Chapter 4 on metacognition). For example, if you think you have grasped the helical structure of DNA, try explaining it to someone else. To create an analogy in your description, you might use the example of a winding staircase. As you explain it, you may find yourself asking additional questions that you had not considered before.

Discussion Questions

1. One way to increase understanding is to link what you are currently studying to prior knowledge. Can you think of ways that the methods of increasing understanding that are described in this chapter overlap with techniques that you learned in prior chapters?
2. Everyone encounters blocks when they do not feel they are understanding a concept or idea. The next time you have the feeling that you are not understanding something, what things can you do to try to help yourself understand?
3. What types of daily life habits do you think could help you to become better at understanding things in the future?
4. Learning is often enhanced when you elaborate, space your studying out over time, and frequently test yourself. How would you explain this to someone entirely unfamiliar with the science of learning? Can you think of an effective analogy you could use to explain each concept?

Suggestions for Further Reading

Ut No Sio and Thomas Ormerod's in-depth review of the literature on insight is highly recommended (2009). John Kounios and Mark Beeman (2009) likewise provide an excellent review of cognitive neuroscience research on "aha" experiences, and their book *The Eureka Factor: Aha Moments, Creative Insight, and the Brain* (Kounios & Beeman, 2015) is an excellent read. On the general subject of analogies, Dedre Gentner and Linsey Smith (2013) do an admirable job of clearly synthesizing much of the latest research. For an entertaining treatment of "aha" experiences, read *The "Aha" Moment* by Robert Mankoff (2014). Also, see "Eureka? Yes, Eureka!" by John Kounios in the *New York Times* (June 10, 2017). Finally, Kevin Dunbar's (2001; see also Dunbar & Isabelle Blanchett, 2001) work observing scientists in their "habitat" provides a number of unique perspectives on analogies and scientific breakthroughs. If this chapter gets you interested in human innovation and creativity, you might also enjoy *Explaining Creativity: The Science of Human Innovation* (2011) by Keith Sawyer.

Credits

Page 214: (top) Sarah_Baird / Shutterstock
Page 214: (bottom) Mochipet / Shutterstock
Page 220: paulaphoto / Shutterstock
Page 222: taveesak srisomthavil / Shutterstock
Page 223: (top) no credit line stipulated
Page 223: (bottom) no credit line stipulated
Page 224: (left) Meowu / Shutterstock
Page 224: (right) Owls Photography / Shutterstock
Page 228: no credit line stipulated

CHAPTER 12

....

Social Aspects of Learning

Learning in a Group Context

....

Learning Objectives
- Reading this chapter will help you:
  + Understand the benefits and limits of collective knowledge.
  + Appreciate the benefits of collaboration in learning.
  + Identify the drawbacks of collaboration in learning.
  + Know how to learn in groups.

....

W hy did the chicken cross the road? If this question made you roll your eyes and immediately think, "To get to the other side," you were demonstrating two things. One, you have already suffered through one the lamest jokes known to the world. Two, you have a bit of knowledge shared by most other members of your society. Indeed, if you are reading this chapter, it is because you have already acquired a shared body of knowledge with others. From your ability to read these sentences in the English language, to your ability to understand your authors' jokes, to your knowledge of movies, everyone has knowledge that they share with one another.

In fact, when broken down to its basics, education is how knowledge is created and shared among human beings. Education, and the process of learning itself, is a social endeavor. Even when your learning does not happen in a classroom or training setting with other people, learning still involves information transmission among people. For

Even reading a book alone is a social process.

example, imagine that you are reading a book by yourself. That might not feel very social. However, another human being wrote that book that you are reading so that those ideas could be communicated to you, even if that communication is not face to face.

In other words, information is still being transmitted among people and you are learning from others. This is the case whether you are learning by searching for information on the Internet, quietly reading a book, sifting through an instruction manual, learning a piece of sheet music on the piano, trying out a new recipe, learning new software, playing a game, or solving a puzzle. Knowledge is being shared among people. Someone else created all of those things that you are learning from, from the books to the sheet music to the recipe to the software to the games, and you are receiving and processing this information. Even on the rare occasion when one person happens to stumble upon an amazing discovery never before known (an "aha!" moment like that described in Chapter 11 on understanding), much of the excitement in the discovery is in

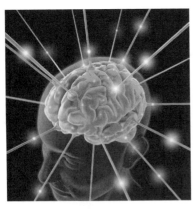

Learning is a social process and does not occur in isolation.

telling the world about it. From that perspective, almost all learning ultimately involves the transmission of information across people.

While this book has primarily focused on how an individual learns, there are entire fields of research devoted to studying how information is transmitted across people. Given that most forms of learning are social endeavors, it is worth considering this aspect of learning as a final component to your newly acquired repertoire of study skills. For example, is it better to study alone or with others? Does collaboration increase the likelihood of innovation? When collaborating, is there an ideal way to work with others?

The Promises and Perils of Collective Knowledge at the Individual Level

The idea that people share a collective knowledge, and that education plays a role in this collective knowledge, has been studied in recent years in an area of work known as **collective memory** (Roediger & Abel, 2015). Your existing knowledge-base, often referred to as semantic memory, is formed and shaped by your culture and your interactions with others. For example, try answering these two questions.

> What is the last name of the actor who played Rhett Butler in Gone with the Wind?
> What is the name of the dog from The Wizard of Oz?

If you had more trouble with the first question than the second, it may be because the first query came from a pool of questions aimed at studying general knowledge back in 1980 (from Nelson & Narens, 1980). In all likelihood, your grandparents (or maybe even your parents) would have been able to answer that first question with ease, because it probes knowledge that would have been shared among people of their generation. If you could not answer that question, it may be because the question comes from a different era—the name was commonly known in previous generations, but is not as widely known in modern times. The second question regarding The Wizard of Oz came from the same paper, but also from an updated pool of questions meant to be relevant to current or more recent generations of college students than those in 1980 (Tauber et al., 2013). Chances are, you could more easily answer the second question because it still reflects culturally relevant, shared knowledge in your generation. Indeed, nearly 80% of college students in that 2013 study could answer the second question. (Incidentally, the answers were Clark Gable and Toto.)

In fact, as you have also seen, individuals have trouble learning and understanding information if they are unable to easily connect it to prior knowledge. Consider the passage on washing laundry from Demonstration 3.1. As you may remember from this demonstration, memory for the passage is much better when people know what the passage is about (see Demonstration 3.1). Taken more broadly, the collective knowledge that people share helps you remember new events and new pieces of information. This is why, throughout the book, you are encouarged to make connections between new information that you are trying to learn and existing knowledge that you already have.

That said, while necessary to your continued ability to learn throughout life, your collective knowledge has some pitfalls, too. First, just as this collective knowledge can help you learn new information, it can also lead you down the path of remembering the wrong information if that information just so happens to fit your collective knowledge. Your mind has a tendency to fill in the blanks with what your existing knowledge suggests *should* be there.

For example, in one famous study (Brewer & Treyens, 1981), researchers had participants wait in a professor's office prior to participating in a memory study. Unbeknownst to the participants, the study actually involved testing their memory for what was in that room (the professor's office) where they had waited. The researchers found that participants often mistakenly "remembered" items that were not there. For instance, most of the participants remembered seeing books, but none were in the office. Why would they make that error? Probably because their collective knowledge suggested that most professors have books in their office, and it is reasonable to "remember" that at least a few books were in this office. Although the books were not there, people filled in the gaps with information that would be expected based on collective knowledge.

Second, collective knowledge is far from perfect. All individuals have shared beliefs and knowledge that do not stand up to close scrutiny. For instance, how do you determine the age of a dog in "human years"? One of your authors confidently believed the most common answer to the question—just take the dog's age and multiply it by seven. As it turns out, there is no simple formula to create a human equivalent of a dog's age. Age varies greatly across different types of dogs (e.g., larger dogs age more quickly), and dogs achieve key developmental milestones (such as the ability to reproduce) far earlier than humans.

Miscalculating dog years is probably a relatively harmless mistake, but errors in collective knowledge can have much more serious consequences. For example, people may rapidly and unfairly judge an individual based on a shared collective knowledge that feeds into unjustified stereotypes.

A particularly awful example of this was evident when a serious medical emergency occurred during a flight from Detroit to Minneapolis (Levin, 2016). Flight attendants asked if there was a doctor on board, and a 28-year old physician by the name of Dr. Tamika Cross offered to help. However, Dr. Cross was told by a flight attendant, "Oh no, sweetie put your hand down; we are looking for actual physicians or nurses or some type of medical personnel. We don't have time to talk to you." In the wake of this incident, a number of other female African American doctors came forward to describe having experienced similar discriminating situations for not fitting the stereotype of a doctor. Why do female African American doctors find that people are less likely to immediately believe that they are doctors? It likely has to do with the examples that people have seen of doctors throughout their lives, both in the media and all around them. This leads to a violation of expectations—expectations created by collective knowledge of what constitutes "typical."

Another facilitator of stereotypes and bias is the tendency for people to live in "information bubbles" or "echo chambers." Put another way,

Although many believe there is a simple formula, there is no easy way to translate human years to "dog years".

individuals like to seek out information that confirms what they already believe (Nickerson, 1998). For example, suppose you are absolutely adamant that the Earth is flat. You might choose to ignore clear data contrary to this (e.g., satellite photos of the Earth), and instead spend your time with other fellow flat-Earthers. You might also curate your social media feeds so that you only receive pro-flat Earth news (but see Flaxman, Goel, & Rao, 2016, for a perspective that social media may also enhance exposure to different views).

The scenario posed is not nearly as fantastical as it might seem on first glance. Indeed, social media consumption allows people to exist in just this sort of echo chamber, fed by algorithms that detect and learn a person's likes and dislikes based on online behavior that then feed news and information to the person accordingly. Although this may hold some appeal (e.g., flat-Earthers would not have to hear from those proclaiming a spherical Earth), it also limits the chances of being exposed to alternative perspectives, contributing to more polarization of views.

Indeed, one product of not seeking different views is that what people take to be "fact" can differ greatly among individuals. For example, one group of researchers (Roediger, Abel, Umanath, Shaffer, & Wertsch, 2016; see also Roediger & Wertsch, 2015; Zaromb, Butler, Agarawal, & Roediger, 2014) tested people from 11 different countries on their knowledge of World War II. They discovered that the known "facts" about World War II differed based on where you asked the question. For instance, the tank battle of Kursk was mentioned by almost all Russians queried about World War II, but is virtually unknown in the United States (Roediger & Wertsch, 2015). Further, perceptions of which country won the war differed depending on the home country of the participants (Abel, Umanath, Wertsch, & Roediger, 2018).

This is certainly not to suggest that all facts or knowledge are relative (cf. Lewandowsky, Ecker, & Cook, 2017). To the contrary, seeking truth regarding the nature of reality requires making efforts to expand your thinking, critically evaluate information, and combat your natural inclinations toward cognitive biases. And, as you learned in Chapter 2, science is particularly well suited to handle this task. In addition to the tips offered in that chapter, here are several other ideas to consider in combating cognitive bias:

1. **Take it slow.** One way to overcome cognitive biases is to avoid making quick decisions based on gut reactions (but see e.g.,

Gigerenzer & Gaissmaier, 2011, for a different view). Slow it down and try to be deliberate in your decision-making. Although this is not always possible, an abundance of research suggests that relying on more deliberate, conscious processes can help you override your more immediate reactions and tendencies (e.g., Kahneman, 2011).

2. **Keep returning to objective standards.** Particularly in situations where hiring or evaluation are occurring, return to the objective standards of the evaluation to counter potential biases in decision-making. For example, if a job requires that someone has previously managed large budgets, find the record and determine the types of budgets this person has managed. Better yet, when applicable, consider using well-developed measures as a basis for your judgment and cut out human decision-making (Dawes, Faust, & Meehl, 1989). As an illustrative example, insurance companies do not take a look at you and then decide how much to charge for a policy. Instead, all of your data (e.g., age, driving record) is combined in a program that calculates your policy.

3. **Seek counterexamples or outside perspectives.** The beginning of this book emphasized critical thinking skills in evaluating claims that you encounter in the news and in the world. Part of critical thinking involves overcoming cognitive biases by deliberately seeking contradictory perspectives and counterexamples to the ones you happen to be considering. Actively seek differing opinions and search out news sources that you do not ordinarily read, hear, or view. Also, interact with people of differing perspectives than your own and even debate topics with them.

Before moving on, try Demonstration 12.1.

DEMONSTRATION 12.1   THE TELEPHONE GAME

For this demonstration, you will need to round up a group of five to seven people (this is always a fun activity if you are spending time with a group of friends or family). Have everyone line up in a single row. The first person should whisper a short phrase to the next person in line. If you are having trouble thinking of a phrase, try this: *The pelicans awake from their slumber in the dawn.*

Each player should whisper the phrase to the next person in line. The last player says the phrase aloud.

The Promises and Pitfalls of Social Interaction on Learning

Demonstration 12.1 gave you instructions to play the telephone game. Even if you have not played this game before, you are probably familiar with the concept. The idea is that a message starts out one way with one person whispering it to the next, then gradually changes as it transfers from person to person. By the time the final person receives the message, it has changed substantially from what was said at the start of the game. For example, the first person might say, "Like a kid in a candy store." The next person relays "The kid in the candy store took the candy," and the next person says "The kids stole candy from the candy store." By the time the final message emerges, it might have turned into "a candy store was robbed by a gang of kids." Was the final message changed in your version of the telephone game in Demonstration 12.1?

The distortion that occurs to the message when passed from person to person is a well-known phenomenon in human communication. A famous memory researcher by the name of Frederic Bartlett (1932) was among the first to study the so-called transmission chains illustrated in the game of telephone. His experiments used a technique known as serial reproduction, whereby one person's memory of a picture or story serves as the to-be-remembered information for the next participant in the study, and so on. As you might expect, based on the game of telephone, Bartlett found that his participants' memory for the information changed more with each new person receiving the information from the last.

Why does information change when transmitted across individuals? A major reason is that memory processes operating at an individual level change how memory is transmitted across a whole group of individuals. In particular, at an individual level, two properties of memory are driving the change.

Information is often distorted as it is transmitted from person to person.

BOX 12.1   MODELING INFORMATION TRANSMISSION

In recent years, researchers have tried to create mathematical models of how information is transmitted from person to person, with a focus on predicting how information will be changed. These models indicate that although transmitting information from person to person can change and distort the original information, these distortions are highly predictable. Thus, mathematical models of this sort describe in more detail the processes first demonstrated by Bartlett many years ago (e.g., Suchow, Pacer, & Griffiths, 2016).

The Malleability of Memory

First, memory is malleable, meaning that memory can be altered by what is said during a social interaction or collaboration. For example, memories are vulnerable to change in response to newer information coming along after initial learning. Consider a classic study (Loftus & Palmer, 1974) in which participants viewed slides depicting a car accident and were then asked questions about the accident. One critical question asked participants to estimate the speed of the cars. Importantly, the verb that was used in the question itself was varied across participants. Some participants received harsher, stronger verbs such as "smashed" (e.g., "How fast were the cars going when they smashed into each other?") and other received weaker, less severe verbs such as "contacted" (e.g., "How fast were the cars going when they contacted other?").

As you can see in Figure 12.1, the researchers found that the more severe the verb used to ask the question, the higher the estimate of how fast the cars were going. For example, speed estimates were markedly higher when participants were asked about cars smashing into each other (far right of Figure 12.1) than when asked about cars making contact with each other (far left of Figure 12.1). Even worse, when questioned about the slides a week later, those who had been given a more severe verb in the initial question were more likely to falsely "remember" seeing broken glass. In fact, no broken glass had been shown.

These results suggest that your memory can be influenced by information introduced after learning. Applied to working in groups, such malleability indicates that information introduced by other members of the group can influence what you remember. This can be a good thing if you happen to learn the wrong information, but is a much less positive aspect of memory if you had it right to begin with but others are presenting the wrong information.

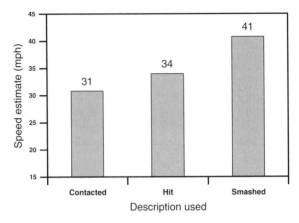

<small>FIGURE</small> 12.1 Average speed estimate for participants given the type of verb used to describe a car accident (adapted from Loftus & Palmer, 1974).

Other People Can Change What You Retrieve

Second, research on how people learn in groups indicates that other people can influence what you as an individual are able to access from your own memory. Recall from Chapter 11 on understanding that one hindrance to understanding is that sometimes having the wrong cues or the wrong information dominates your thinking, preventing you from accessing the needed information. Research on collaboration and memory suggests that something similar may take place when learning and remembering in groups.

The now classic method of studying remembering in groups was introduced in the late 1990s (Weldon & Bellinger, 1997). Participants in this study learned a list of words and then took a test, trying to remember as many of those words as possible. But there was a catch: Some participants attempted to remember these words while working alone, whereas others were put into groups of three individuals and asked to work together to remember the list. Figure 12.2 shows their data. As you might expect, the group working together (called the *collaborative group*) recalled more of the list altogether than an individual working alone. Does this mean that groups promote better memory than an individual working alone? Not quite.

Importantly, although a group of individuals working together may produce more information than an individual working alone, it is not clear whether the social process of working together helps memory. For example, imagine that Uma, Sally, and Dwayne each learn a list of words.

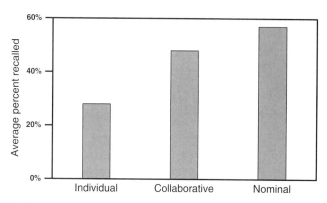

FIGURE **12.2 The percentage of information recalled by participants who worked alone (individual), in groups of three (collaborative), or by combining the output of individuals who did not work together (nominal).**

You could ask each of them to recall the words individually (see the left side of Figure 12.3) and then to pool their responses. For example, suppose that each of them individually recalled the following:

Uma recalled *harbinger, creed, route, lemur, triangle, apple*
Sally recalled *creed, credenza, orange, lemur, barrack, highway*
Dwayne recalled *kiwi, pear, orange, credenza, lemur, creed*

On an individual level, each person recalled six words. However, combined (being sure to count words recalled by more than one person, like *creed*, only once), they recalled 12 words in total. Weldon and Bellinger (1997) labeled this approach of combining the output of individuals who did not work together *nominal recall*. The influence of a social

Working alone

Working in a group

FIGURE **12.3 A depiction of the design used by studies of collaborative remembering. Groups of participants can work alone (left side) or in a group (right side).**

process on memory can be assessed by comparing nominal recall to a group of people who actually worked together to remember something. The researchers used this approach, comparing groups of people who actually worked together (right side of Figure 12.3) with results pooling together responses from people who did not work together (left side of Figure 12.3). Using this approach, Figure 12.2 shows that nominal recall was the best of all. That is, people actually working with each other recall more total information than an individual working alone will, but people working together recall less information than the combined outputs of people who worked alone, a finding termed **collaborative inhibition**. These findings show that combining outputs improves the overall amount of information recalled, but that the social process of working together hinders memory.

Data like this were something of a puzzle. One explanation researchers tested was that working in a group led people to put in less effort (perhaps assuming other group members would pick up the slack). However, getting participants to increase their effort, such as offering incentives for group performance or forcing each member to make contributions, did not change the collaborative inhibition effect (Weldon, Blair, & Huebsch, 2000).

Instead, the explanation appears to lie in the interplay between individual memory processes and social interaction, and has some lessons that you can apply in your own learning. Consider how group memory is tested. You learn some bits of information (sentences, words, scripts to bad movies) and then either recall alone or work with other people. What happens when you try to recall with other people? The most common scenario seems to be that everyone wants to contribute and starts blurting out what they know.

This is helpful if you do not know the information well (someone else may recall some information that you likely would not have remembered), but also comes at a cost. That is, by blurting out this information, it interferes with your ability to remember what you had studied (Basden, Basden, Bryner, & Thomas 1997). This is where collaborative inhibition relates to the very memory mechanisms that can prevent people from achieving a moment of understanding. Recall from Chapter 11 that when the wrong information is dominating your thought process, it can stand in the way of your access to the right information. Likewise, when other people in a group are blurting out answers, it can interfere with your ability to generate information that you otherwise would have had access to. For example, suppose you were given this short list of information to remember:

purple monkey cannon fish strawberry phone grandmother

You might learn this little sequence by elaborating and creating a story: *The purple monkey fired the cannon filled with fish and strawberries and then made a phone call to tell grandma about it.*

Note that you have learned the list in a very particular way and in a very particular sequence. When you get into a group, you are ready to recite the words by remembering your story, but another group member starts to say she envisioned a monkey in a purple shirt eating fish by the ocean while grandma fired a cannon filled with phones. It is not a bad way to learn the list, but very different from the way you learned it. However, hearing about grandma firing a cannon might now get in the way of accessing your own story, with grandma only on the other end of a phone call about a monkey firing a cannon.

The example used is a bit ridiculous, but the principle is clear: Working with others can sometimes get in the way of accessing your own memories. What can you do about this? When should you collaborate versus work alone, and what can you do to use groups effectively when you do collaborate?

To Collaborate or Not to Collaborate?

Many students have encountered this scenario: It is a few days before an exam and you definitely need more time to master some key concepts. A friend asks if you would like to study with a few other classmates. You consider politely declining so that you can study on your own, but also wonder whether you might learn by talking with others. What should you do?

The answer to this question is, "it depends." That is, whether you get a benefit from studying in groups likely depends on how effectively you have learned the material in the first place, and how you go about working with your group. Done well, working in a group can be a boon to learning.

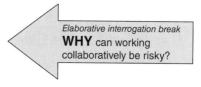
Elaborative interrogation break
WHY can working collaboratively be risky?

As you have seen, when other people talk to you about something that you have experienced, their retellings can influence your own memory for the experience. For example, suggestive questioning can alter your memory for what you learned, as in the example of participants swayed by questions about a car accident (Loftus & Palmer, 1974). Others (e.g., Marsh, 2007) note that retellings of a story in conversation are subject to memory distortions like those shown with leading questions. For example, if you join a study group to discuss material that you have read in preparation for that study group, the very discussions coming from members of the group can potentially change your memory for what you read. This could be good or it could be bad—it largely depends on how well the group members have understood the material.

If you are struggling to understand the material, surrounding yourself with others who are also struggling could lead to mutually reinforcing misunderstandings. Conversely, surrounding yourself with experts or people who excel at the topic could be beneficial. For example, one group of researchers (Meade, Nokes, & Morrow, 2009) carried out a study of collaboration among expert pilots, with extensive flying experience, and novice pilots, who were still learning to fly. Participants learned complex flight scenarios that then had to be recalled either individually or with partners of the same experience level.

When is collaboration better than studying alone?

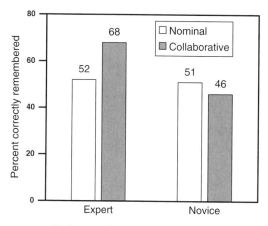

FIGURE 12.4 Percentage of flight scenarios correctly remembered by expert and novice pilots working alone on in a group (adapted from Meade et al., 2009).

The percentage of the flight scenarios remembered correctly is shown in Figure 12.4. Expert pilots (left side) recalled more of the information from the flight scenarios when they collaborated than when they worked alone. However, novice pilots performed worse when collaborating than when recalling alone. The researchers suggested that the experts were more likely than novices to elaborate on collaborator contributions, offer corrections when mistakes were made during discussion, and repeat collaborator contributions. Thus, the cases in which collaboration seems beneficial, as opposed to harmful, are when everyone in the group was knowledgeable about the material.

Indeed, there are other reasons to try to work with people who are very knowledgeable about the material. Studies of social networks suggests that human knowledge and behavior is itself almost "contagious" within social networks (Christakis & Fowler, 2009), analogous to the spread of disease in social networks. This has led to the phrase "social contagion effects."

For example, one group of researchers (Luhmann & Rajaram, 2015) examined computer simulations of how memory processes at the level of the individual affect transmission across a social network. Suppose you and a friend are in a karate club together; on a social network, these mutual interests would mean that you and your friend are closely linked, with only one degree of separation. And suppose also that you both have a friend (let's call her Ashley) you went to high school with who is not in the club, but an acquaintance (two degrees of separation).

Knowledge spreads through social networks.

And suppose further that Ashley's piano teacher also happens to belong to your church but is not someone you know well (three degrees of separation). The researchers simulated a network with just these features, individuals with different degrees of separation.

Importantly, they found that just sharing a neighbor (like Ashley) with another individual in the network led to greater similarity of the contents of memory between those two individuals than if there were at least two degrees of separation between the two individuals. In other words, within a social network, your connections' connections may have memories that are more similar than those connections' connections. Why does this matter? A major reason is that your connections' connections potentially have the ability to influence you and what resides in your knowledge-base, possibly via information transmission through the network via both communication and individual memory processes. This also means that working with experts or people high in knowledge of the material you are trying to learn has the potential to benefit your own learning.

But note, as described previously, that working with people while learning may come at a cost. In particular, when you are working collaboratively with a group, other people's remembrances can prevent you from remembering something that you would otherwise have been able to call to mind (e.g., Coman, Brown, Koppel, & Hirst, 2009; Congleton & Rajaram, 2014; Weldon & Bellinger, 1997). Collaborative inhibition of this sort is a great example of how the mechanisms of memory's operation at the individual level interact with information transmission that occurs during social interaction to affect memory.

Thus, collaboration comes with costs and benefits that you must weigh. One element to consider is the outcome you have in mind. If you are preparing for a test that you will take alone, collaboratively retrieving with a group may not necessarily be any better than attempting to retrieve alone, though it may not be harmful, either. On the one hand, while other people might think of things during collaboration that you would not have thought of yourself, doing so puts you at risk of experiencing interference with information that you might otherwise have accessed yourself had their recollections not generated interference.

If the outcome is a group product, then collaboration can be good, provided that you take steps to address collaborative inhibition. To counter collaborative inhibition, you might first have individuals attempt to retrieve information on their own and then pool together the responses. For example, one study of interior design students' team performance found that creative output was improved if students worked alone initially on the ideas before discussing as a group (King, 2016). This is a similar idea to crowdsourcing (e.g., Hertwig, 2012), which pools together the ideas and thoughts of many people who generated those thoughts on their own. In short, if the end goal is the total output of a collective group, working individually with a crowdsourcing approach in mind and pooling those responses afterward can be beneficial.

> Elaborative interrogation break
> **WHY** does team output differ?

Can groups also enhance creativity? Consider again the mechanisms thought to underlie collaborative inhibition. When people work together in a group, they collectively have the same information come to mind, which can generate interference from other potentially related thoughts coming to mind. Thus, members of a group may end up having the same ideas more accessible during and afterward with other ideas not discussed becoming less accessible. The result may be a collective, shared knowledge that emerges. This can be a good thing when what emerges as more accessible is accurate, useful information and what emerges as less accessible is inaccurate, less useful information. However, if creativity involves outside-the-box thinking, then having thoughts and ideas merge with the group could potentially impede creative ideas.

Is there a good way to capitalize on the positive elements of groups while avoiding the drawbacks? One study (Choi, Blumen, Congleton, & Rajaram, 2014) specifically examined the effects of mixing up (reconfiguring) groups during repeated attempts at retrieval. Participants first learned a set of words. Some participants worked collaboratively on the first and second retrieval attempt but as part of the same group. Others worked collaboratively on the first and second retrieval attempt, but with a different (reconfigured) group each time. The researchers found that people from reconfigured groups outperformed those who remained in the same group. Thus, reconfiguration may increase the quantity and the diversity of ideas.

Indeed, this approach is similar to what one of your authors has experienced at a number of brainstorming workshops and retreats over the years. Participants are assigned to tables of 8 to 10 people who brainstorm ideas as a group and write them down. Then, after taking a coffee break, tables are reconfigured so that everyone must work with a new set of people. The task is to continue brainstorming, but using the notes left at that table from the previous group, and now working with a new group of people at that new table. There may be something to that switching-tables method at brainstorming sessions!

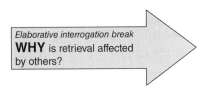

Elaborative interrogation break
WHY is retrieval affected by others?

Putting It All Together

Students frequently report studying in groups. For example, a recent survey of 463 college students found that 78% reported studying at least once in a semester in a group (McCabe & Lummis, 2018). Many of these students indicated that they studied in groups to better understand and learn the material. There is certainly a great deal of truth in this assessment—done well, groups can facilitate learning and increase creativity while conferring the positive social benefits gained by working with others. But working in groups can also introduce a set of processes that may hinder your learning, by introducing shared mistakes and misunderstandings and impeding your ability to access the correct information. These costs and benefits of groups requires that the learner carefully weigh options. The science of learning in groups will continue to be refined, but for the moment, the most prudent approach may be to view groups as an auxiliary outlet for the effective learning that you engage in on your own.

Tips You Can Use

1. **Work with experts or people who understand the material well.** To maximize gains and minimize costs associated with collaboration, work with competent people when you collaborate. Try to select people who are doing well, who seem to have a firm grasp of the material, and who will come to the meetings prepared (having done their own studying individually first before coming to the group to work).

2. **Elaborate on others' contributions.** To additionally maximize gains and minimize costs associated with collaboration, be sure to elaborate on others' contributions in the discussion. For example, if a group member is discussing Darwin's observations from his famous voyage on the *Beagle*, you might add that Darwin pondered these observations for many years before finally releasing his theory of evolution.

3. **Combine working alone first with later collaboration.** To minimize the possibility of having others interfere with your own accurate memories for the material, try testing yourself alone many times first. This strengthens access to your own accurate memories before working with a group at pooling together responses and knowledge.

4. **Pool together responses that were initially obtained individually.** Rather than trying to generate information on the spot in the group, come to the group meeting prepared with already-retrieved information that you have written down when testing yourself alone. The group can then combine and discuss these responses to come to a shared understanding.

5. **Study with different groups of people.** If you study in a group repeatedly over time, try mixing it up so that you study with a different group of people each time. If you are working in a large group, try beginning a study session by dividing into two smaller groups. Next, reconfigure the groups by having a few individuals switch between groups.

Discussion Questions

1. One theme of the chapter is that individuals have access to a collective knowledge that underlies their understanding of the world. In what ways is this knowledge a benefit to us? How much does this collective knowledge negatively affect your understanding of the world?

2. Suppose a group of students meets at the library to prepare for an upcoming exam in a biology course. What might these students do to overcome collaborative inhibition? Discuss three potential methods.
3. Describe the pros and cons of learning in a group. Under what circumstances would groups be advantageous? When would they confer a disadvantage in learning?
4. How can the fundamental principles of the science of learning, such as testing, elaboration, or spacing, be used within a group? For example, how could a group study session be used to encourage elaboration and testing?

Suggestions for Further Reading

Although the study of social processes has a rich history in psychology, it has emerged only recently a field of study in learning and memory. Mary Sue Weldon's (2000) early review of the field is a classic and provides an excellent historical overview (see also Suparna Rajaram, 2011). The recent edited compendium *Collaborative Remembering: How Remembering with Others Influences Memory* (2018) is a superb overview of the state-of-the-art from many of the leading researchers in the field. For further information on cognitive biases in decision-making, Daniel Kahneman's (2011) *Thinking, Fast and Slow* describes a decades-long program of research that resulted in a Nobel Prize in economics. Gerd Gigerenzer's ecologoical rationality approach is a compelling counterpoint to the doom and gloom of much of the cognitive biases literature and is strongly recommended (see e.g., Gerd Gigerenzer & Wolfgang Gaissmaier, 2011). Stephan Lewandowsky and colleagues (2017) also provide a strident perspective on truth and misinformation that is worth considering.

Credits

Page 236: (top) Catalin Petolea / Shutterstock
Page 236: (bottom) ktsdesign / Shutterstock
Page 239: dezy / Shutterstock
Page 248: Rawpixel.com / Shutterstock
Page 250: Szasz-Fabian Jozsef / Shutterstock
Page 245: (left) CandyBox Images / Shutterstock
Page 245: (right) Rawpixel.com / Shutterstock

GLOSSARY

....

analogy: a relationship between two similar situations, problems, or concepts.

analogical reasoning: the process of identifying the relationship between two similar situations, problems, or concepts in order to achieve understanding.

between-session spacing: a method of learning in which the presentation of information is spread out over time across multiple study sessions.

between-subjects manipulation: a method of manipulating an independent variable in which participants in an experiment are only exposed to a single level of an independent variable.

blocking: an approach to studying in which the same type of information is studied in a single session.

chunk: a meaningful unit of information.

cognitive load: the amount of effort that must be exerted to mentally process information.

cognitive offloading: a method of shifting information to external sources (e.g., notepads, models) so as to reduce the mental effort required to process information.

collaborative inhibition: the finding that a group of people will remember more information than an individual working alone will, but people working together remember less information than combining the outputs of people who worked alone.

collective memory: the memories and recollections shared by a group of people.

confound: a type of extraneous variable that occurs when an uncontrolled factor varies systematically with the manipulation of an independent variable and influences the dependent variable.

consolidation: the collective set of neurological processes that lead a memory to become stable over time.

control: a component of metacognition that refers to the actions and behaviors a learner engages in as a result of monitoring.

correlational design: an approach to observation in which researchers attempt to determine the existence, magnitude, and direction of an association between two variables.

cue: a reminder or hint used to retrieve information from memory.

deduction: the second stage of the cycle of science, in which specific predictions about data are made based on a hypothesis or theory.

deep processing: an approach to thinking about information that relies on considering the meaning of that information.

dependent variables: the outcome that is being observed or measured in experimental and descriptive research.

elaboration: the process of enriching learning by integrating information and forming associations.

elaborative interrogation: a method of encouraging elaboration that prompts an individual to ask a question about information that is being learned.

experimental research: an approach to collecting data and testing hypotheses that seeks to manipulate variables while holding all other factors constant, so as to establish the causes of behavior.

extraneous variables: factors that are uncontrolled by the experimenter that influence the outcome of an experiment.

first letter technique: an approach to learning information in which the first letter of each word an individual wishes to learn is combined to create a word or phrase. For example, IDOV represents the first letter of each of the steps of the cycle of science: induction, deduction, observation, and verification.

fluency: the degree of ease one experiences when learning or remembering information.

hypothesis: a statement, question, or theory about data that can be tested. A hypothesis is created in the first stage of the cycle of science.

independent variable: the treatment that is manipulated in an experiment. The variable is said to be independent because the experimenter determines the nature or amount of this variable independently of all other factors in the experiment.

induction: the first stage of the cycle of science, in which existing data is used to develop a statement or question that can be tested (see **hypothesis**).

insight: the term used by scientists to describe the moment when an individual achieves understanding (e.g., of a problem).

interleaving: an approach to studying in which different types of information are mixed together in a single session.

keyword mnemonic: an approach to learning information in which an individual learns a new word by first thinking of a familiar word that the new word sounds like. Next, an image is created that links the familiar word with the new word being learned. To retrieve the new word, the learner remembers the image that was created.

lag effect: the finding that when learning is spread out over time, longer gaps of time between sessions (i.e., longer lags) frequently produce better learning than shorter gaps of time.

levels: the different, specific ways that an independent variable is manipulated.

levels of processing effect: the finding that memory is influenced by how participants think about (process) information during learning. In general, considering the meaning of information (deep processing) leads to superior learning compared with other types of processing.

maintenance rehearsal: the rote (repeated) repetition of information. This is typically a highly ineffective strategy for long-term learning.

massed learning: an approach to scheduling learning in which all learning occurs in a single unit or block of time.

meta-analysis: a method of research in which the results from individual studies are combined into a single analysis.

metacognition: your knowledge and thinking about your own thought (cognitive) processes.

method of loci: an approach to learning information in which an individual mentally imagines (i.e., visualizes) each piece of information to be learned as appearing within a well-known set of locations. To later retrieve the information, the learner imagines moving through the well-known locations and attempts to picture the information that was previously imagined in each location.

monitoring: a component of metacognition that refers to an individual's observation, understanding, and assessment of his or her own learning.

narrative chaining: an approach to learning information in which an individual creates a story that links information within elements of the story. To remember the information, the individual remembers the story.

observation: the third stage of the cycle of science, in which data are collected using experimental or descriptive methods that allow a hypothesis to be tested.

quasi-experiment: an experiment for which random assignment to levels of an independent variable is not possible.

orienting questions: questions, typically used in experiments on levels of processing, that direct participants to think about information in qualitatively different ways, such as considering the appearance, sound, or meaning of information.

pegword mnemonic: an approach to learning information in which an individual uses an easy-to-learn set of information, such as a set of simple rhymes, as links (pegs) for learning a sequence of information. Information is attached to the pegs by creating an image that connects the peg with the word. To retrieve the new information, the learner recalls each peg and the image that was created.

proactive interference: the finding that previously learned information impedes learning and remembering of new information.

random assignment: the principle that all participants in an experiment are equally likely to be assigned to different levels of an independent variable in a manner that is completely unbiased. Random assignment is a necessary condition for a true experiment.

reliability: the consistency of a test or measure.

retrieval failure: the phenomena in which some bit of information has been learned (i.e., it is available) but it cannot be remembered in the moment (i.e., it is not accessible).

shallow processing: an approach to thinking about information that focuses on information unrelated to meaning, such as the appearance or sound of the information. This is typically a highly ineffective approach for long-term learning.

spacing effect: the finding that spreading learning out over multiple units of time promotes superior learning relative to engaging in all learning in a single unit of time.

spaced learning: an approach to scheduling learning in which all learning is spread out over multiple units or blocks of time.

successive relearning: an approach to learning in which an individual engages in repeated, successful retrievals of the same information, spread out across time.

testing effect: the finding that retrieving (remembering) information results in better memory than restudying (e.g., rereading) that information.

true experiment: any experiment that (1) involves the manipulation of an independent variable and (2) randomly assigns participants to levels of the independent variable. These conditions must be met to draw cause-and-effect conclusions from an experiment.

verification: the fourth stage of the cycle of science, in which the observed data are compared to the hypothesis, indicating whether that hypothesis is correct, incorrect, or in need of further testing.

within-session spacing: a method of learning in which the presentation of information is spread out across time in a single study session.

within-subjects manipulation: a method of manipulating an independent variable in which participants in an experiment are exposed to all levels of an independent variable.

REFERENCES

....

Abel, L., Umanath, S., Wertsch, J. W., & Roediger, H. L. (2018). Collective memory: How groups remember their past. In M. L. Meade, A. Barnier, P. Van Bergen, C. Harris, & J. Sutton (Eds.), *Collaborative remembering: How remembering with others influences memory.* New York: Oxford University Press.

Adesope, O. O., Trevisan, D. A., & Sundararajan, N. (2017). Rethinking the use of tests: A meta-analysis of practice testing. *Review of Educational Research, 87,* 659–701.

Agarwal, P. K., Bain, P. M., & Chamberlain, R. W. (2012). The value of applied research: Retrieval practice improves classroom learning and recommendations from a teacher, a principal, and a scientist. *Educational Psychology Review, 24,* 437–448.

Agarwal, P. K., D'Antonio, L., Roediger, H. L., McDermott, K. B., & McDaniel, M. A. (2014). Classroom-based programs of retrieval practice reduce middle school and high school students' test anxiety. *Journal of Applied Research in Memory and Cognition, 3,* 131–139.

Agarwal, P. K., Karpicke, J. D., Kang, S. H., Roediger, H. L., & McDermott, K. B. (2008). Examining the testing effect with open-and closed-book tests. *Applied Cognitive Psychology, 22,* 861–876.

Aggleton, J. P., & Waskett, L. (1999). The ability of odours to serve as state-dependent cues for real-world memories: Can Viking smells aid the recall of Viking experiences? *British Journal of Psychology, 90,* 1–7.

Ainsworth, S., Prain, V. & Tytler, R. (2011). Drawing to learn in science. *Science, 333,* 1096–1097.

Allen, I. E., & Seaman, J. (2010). *Class differences: Online education in the United States, 2010.* Needham, MA: Sloan Consortium.

Anderson, M. C., & Thiede, K. W. (2008). Why do delayed summaries improve metacomprehension accuracy? *Acta Psychologica, 128,* 110–118.

259

Atkinson, R. C. (1975). Mnemotechnics in second-language learning. *American Psychologist, 30,* 821–828.

Baddeley, A. D. (1963). A Zeigarnik-like effect in the recall of anagram solutions. *Quarterly Journal of Experimental Psychology, 15,* 63–64.

Baddeley, A., Eysenck, M. W., & Anderson, M. C. (2009). *Memory.* East Sussex: Psychology Press.

Bahrick, H. P. (1979). Maintenance of knowledge: Questions about memory we forgot to ask. *Journal of Experimental Psychology: General, 108,* 296–308.

Bahrick, H. P., & Phelps, E. (1987). Retention of Spanish vocabulary over 8 years. *Journal of Experimental Psychology: Learning, Memory, and Cognition, 13,* 344–349.

Baronchelli, A., Ferrer-i-Cancho, R., Pastor-Satorras, R., Chater, N., & Christiansen, M. H. (2013). Networks in cognitive science. *Trends in Cognitive Sciences, 17,* 348–360.

Barsalou, L. W. (1983). Ad-hoc categories. *Memory & Cognition, 11,* 211–227.

Bartlett, F. C. (1932). *Remembering: An experimental and social study.* Cambridge: Cambridge University Press.

Basden, B. H., Basden, D. R., Bryner, S., & Thomas III, R. L. (1997). A comparison of group and individual remembering: Does collaboration disrupt retrieval strategies? *Journal of Experimental Psychology: Learning, Memory, and Cognition, 23,* 1176–1189.

Beeftink, F., Van Eerde, W Rutte, C. G. (2008). The effect of interruptions and breaks on insight and impasses: Do you need a break right now? *Creativity Research Journal, 20,* 358–364.

Bell, M. C., Kawadri, N., Simone, P. M., & Wiseheart, M. (2014). Long-term memory, sleep, and the spacing effect. *Memory, 22,* 276–283.

Bellezza, F. S., & Reddy, B. G. (1978). Mnemonic devices and natural memory. *Bulletin of the Psychonomic Society, 11,* 277–280.

Benjamin, A. S., Bjork, R. A., & Schwartz, B. L. (1998). The mismeasure of memory: When retrieval fluency is misleading as a metamnemonic index. *Journal of Experimental Psychology: General, 127,* 55–69.

Benjamin, A. S., & Pashler, H. (2015). The value of standardized testing: A perspective from cognitive psychology. *Policy Insights From the Behavioral and Brain Sciences, 2,* 13–23.

Birnbaum, M. S., Kornell, N., Bjork, E. L., & Bjork, R. A. (2013). Why interleaving enhances inductive learning: The roles of discrimination and retrieval. *Memory & Cognition, 41,* 392–402.

Bjork, R. A., Dunlosky, J., Kornell, N. (2013). Self-regulated learning: Beliefs, techniques, and illusions. *Annual Review of Psychology, 64,* 417–444.

Bjork, E. L., Little, J. L., & Storm, B. C. (2014). Multiple-choice testing as a desirable difficulty in the classroom. *Journal of Applied Research in Memory and Cognition, 3,* 165–170.

Blasiman, R. N., Dunlosky, J., & Rawson, K. A. (2017). The what, how much, and when of study strategies: Comparing intended versus actual study behaviour. *Memory, 25,* 784–792.

Blake, A. B., Nazarian, M., & Castel, A. D. (2015). The Apple of the mind's eye: Everyday attention, metamemory, and reconstructive memory for the Apple logo. *Quarterly Journal of Experimental Psychology, 68*, 858–865.

Born, J., Rasch, B., & Gais, S. (2006). Sleep to remember. *The Neuroscientist, 12*, 410–424.

Bowden, E. M. (1997). The effect of reportable and unreportable hints on anagram solution and the aha! experience. *Consciousness and Cognition, 6*, 545–573.

Bower, G. H., & Clark, M. C. (1969). Narrative stories as mediators for serial learning. *Psychonomic Science, 14*, 181–182.

Bower, G. H., Clark, M. C., Lesgold, A. M., & Winzenz, D. (1969). Hierarchical retrieval schemes in recall of categorized word lists. *Journal of Verbal Learning and Verbal Behavior, 8*, 323–343.

Bower, G. H., & Winzenz, D. (1970). Comparison of associative learning strategies. *Psychonomic Science, 20*, 119–120.

Boyce, J. M., & Pittet, D. (2002). Guideline for hand hygiene in health-care settings: Recommendations of the healthcare infection control practices advisory committee and the HICPAC/SHEA/APIC/IDSA hand hygiene task force. *American Journal of Infection Control, 30*, S1–S46.

Bransford, J. D., & Johnson, M. K. (1972). Contextual prerequisites for understanding: Some investigations of comprehension and recall. *Journal of Verbal Learning and Verbal Behavior, 11*, 717–726.

Brewer, W. F., & Treyens, J. C. (1981). Role of schemata in memory for places. *Cognitive Psychology, 13*, 207–230.

Brown, P. C., Roediger, H. L., & McDaniel, M. A. (2014). *Make It Stick: The Science of Successful Learning.* Cambridge, MA: Harvard University Press.

Butler, A. C. (2010). Repeated testing produces superior transfer of learning relative to repeated studying. *Journal of Experimental Psychology: Learning,Memory, and Cognition, 36*, 1118–1133.

Butler, A. C., & Roediger, H. L. (2008). Feedback enhances the positive effects and reduces the negative effects of multiple-choice testing. *Memory & Cognition, 36*, 604–616.

Bynum, W. (2008). *A history of medicine: A very short introduction.* Oxford: Oxford University Press.

Bynum, W. (2012). *A little history of science.* New Haven, CT: Yale University Press.

Callow, N., Hardy, L., & Hall, C. (2001). The effects of a motivational general-mastery imagery intervention on the sport confidence of high-level badminton players. *Research Quarterly for Exercise and Sport, 72*, 389–400.

Callow, N., Roberts, R., & Fawkes, J. Z. (2006). Effects of dynamic and static imagery on vividness of imagery, skiing performance, and confidence. *Journal of Imagery Research in Sport and Physical Activity, 1*, 1–15.

Carpenter, S. K. (2009). Cue strength as a moderator of the testing effect: the benefits of elaborative retrieval. *Journal of Experimental Psychology: Learning, Memory, and Cognition, 35*, 1563–1569.

Carpenter, S. K., & DeLosh, E. L. (2006). Impoverished cue support enhances subsequent retention: Support for the elaborative retrieval explanation of the testing effect. *Memory & Cognition, 34*, 268–276.

Carpenter, S. K., Pashler, H., & Cepeda, N. J. (2009). Using tests to enhance 8th grade students' retention of US history facts. *Applied Cognitive Psychology, 23*, 760–771.

Castel, A. D. (2007). The adaptive and strategic use of memory by older adults: Evaluative processing and value-directed remembering. In A. S. Benjamin & B. H. Ross (Eds.), *The psychology of learning and motivation*, vol. 48, 225–270. London: Academic Press.

Castel, A. D., Vendetti, M., & Holyoak, K. J. (2012). Fire drill: Inattentional blindness and amnesia for the location of fire extinguishers. *Attention, Perception, & Psychophysics, 74*, 1391–1396.

Cepeda, N. J., Coburn, N., Rohrer, D., Wixted, J. T., Mozer, M. C., & Pashler, H. (2009). Optimizing distributed practice: Theoretical analysis and practical implications. *Experimental Psychology, 56*, 236–246.

Cepeda, N. J., Pashler, H., Vul, E., Wixted, J. T., & Rohrer, D. (2006). Distributed practice in verbal recall tasks: A review and quantitative synthesis. *Psychological Bulletin, 132*, 354–380.

Cepeda, N. J., Vul, E., Rohrer, D., Wixted, J. T., & Pashler, H. (2008). Spacing effects in learning a temporal ridgeline of optimal retention. *Psychological Science, 19*, 1095–1102.

Chase, W. G., & Ericsson, K. A. (1982). Skill and working memory. In G. H. Bower (Ed.), *The psychology of learning and motivation*, vol. 16, 1–58. Cambridge, MA: Academic Press.

Chi, M. T., Feltovich, P. J., & Glaser, R. (1981). Categorization and representation of physics problems by experts and novices. *Cognitive Science, 5*, 121–152.

Chi, M. T. H., Lewis, M. W., Reimann, P., & Glaser, R. (1989). Self-explanations: How students study and use examples in learning to solve problems. *Cognitive Science, 13*, 145–182.

Chi, M. T., & VanLehn, K. A. (2012). Seeing deep structure from the interactions of surface features. *Educational Psychologist, 47*, 177–188.

Christakis, N. A., & Fowler, J. H. (2009). *Connected: The surprising power of our social networks and how they shape our lives.* Boston: Little, Brown.

Cho, A. (2017). The unbearable lightness of neutrinos. *Science, 356*, 1322–1326.

Choi, H. Y., Blumen, H. M., Congleton, A. R., & Rajaram, S. (2014). The role of group configuration in the social transmission of memory: Evidence from identical and reconfigured groups. *Journal of Cognitive Psychology, 26*, 65–80.

Cohen, P. A. (1981). Student ratings of instruction and student achievement: A meta-analysis of multisection validity studies. *Review of Educational Research, 51*, 281–309.

Coman, A., Brown, A. D., Koppel, J., & Hirst, W. (2009). Collective memory from a psychological perspective. *International Journal of Politics, Culture, and Society IJPS, 22*, 125–141.

Congleton, A. R., & Rajaram, S. (2014). Collaboration changes both the content and the structure of memory: Building the architecture of shared representations. *Journal of Experimental Psychology: General, 143*, 1570–1584.

Cowan, N. (2001). The magical number 4 in short-term memory: A reconsideration of mental storage capacity. *Behavioral and Brain Sciences, 24*, 87–185.

Craik, F. I. (2002). Levels of processing: Past, present . . . and future? *Memory*, *10*, 305–318.

Craik, F. I. M., & Lockhart, R. S. (1972). Levels of processing: A framework for memory research. *Journal of Verbal Learning and Verbal behavior, 11*, 671–684.

Craik, F. I., Routh, D. A., & Broadbent, D. E. (1983). On the transfer of information from temporary to permanent memory. *Philosophical Transactions of the Royal Society of London. Series B, Biological Sciences, 302*, 341–359.

Craik, F. I. M., & Tulving, E. (1975). Depth of processing and the retention of words in episodic memory. *Journal of Experimental Psychology: General, 104*, 268–294.

Craik, F. I. M., & Watkins, M. J. (1973). The role of rehearsal in short-term memory. *Journal of Verbal Learning and Verbal Behavior, 12*, 599–607.

Cummins, D. D. (1992). Role of analogical reasoning in the induction of problem categories. *Journal of Experimental Psychology: Learning, Memory, and Cognition, 18*, 1103–1124.

Daniel, D. B., & Poole, D. A. (2009). Learning for life: An ecological approach to pedagogical research. *Perspectives on Psychological Science, 4*, 91–96.

Dawes, R. M., Faust, D., & Meehl, P. E. (1989). Clinical versus actuarial judgment. *Science, 243*(4899), 1668–1674.

Delaney, P. F., Verkoeijen, P. P., & Spirgel, A. (2010). Spacing and testing effects: A deeply critical, lengthy, and at times discursive review of the literature. In B. H. Ross (Ed.), *The psychology of learning and motivation*, vol. 53, 63–147. Cambridge, MA: Academic Press.

Dempster, F. N. (1987). Effects of variable encoding and spaced presentations on vocabulary learning. *Journal of Educational Psychology, 79*, 162–170.

Donovan, J. J., & Radosevich, D. J. (1999). A meta-analytic review of the distribution of practice effect: Now you see it, now you don't. *Journal of Applied Psychology, 84*, 795–805.

Dunbar, K. (2001). The analogical paradox: Why analogy is so easy in naturalistic settings, yet so difficult in the psychology laboratory. In D. Gentner, K. J. Holyoak, & B. Kokinov (Eds.), *Analogy: Perspectives from cognitive science*. Cambridge, MA: MIT Press.

Dunbar, K., & Blanchette, I. (2001). The invivo/invitro approach to cognition: The case of analogy. *Trends in Cognitive Sciences, 5*, 334–339.

Duncker, K. (1945). On problem solving. *Psychological Monographs, 58*, (no. 5, Whole No. 270).

Dunlosky, J., & Metcalfe, J. (2009). *Metacognition*. Thousand Oaks, CA: SAGE Publications.

Dunlosky, J., & Nelson, T. O. (1992). Importance of the kind of cue for judgments of learning (JOL) and the delayed-JOL effect. *Memory & Cognition, 20*, 374–380.

Dunlosky, J., Rawson, K. A., Marsh, E. J., Nathan, M. J., & Willingham, D. T. (2013). Improving students' learning with effective learning techniques promising directions from cognitive and educational psychology. *Psychological Science in the Public Interest, 14*, 4–58.

Dunlosky, J., & Tauber, S. K. (2016). *The Oxford Handbook of Metamemory*, New York: Oxford University Press.

Dunning, D., Heath, C., & Suls, J. M. (2004). Flawed self-assessment: Implications for health, education, and the workplace. *Psychological Science in the Public Interest*, 5, 69–106.

Eich, E. (1989). Theoretical issues in state dependent memory. In H. L. Roediger & F. I. M. Craik (Eds.), *Varieties of memory and consciousness: Essays in honour of Endel Tulving*, 331–354. Hillsdale, NJ: Erlbaum.

Ebbinghaus, H. (1885). *Memory: A contribution to experimental psychology* (Ruger, HA, and Bussenius, CE, trans.), New York: Columbia University, Teacher's College.

Elmes, D. G., Kantowitz, B. H., & Roediger, H. L. III. (2014). *Research methods in psychology*. Belmont, CA: Wadsworth.

Ericsson, K. A., & Polson, P. G. (1988). An experimental analysis of the mechanisms of a memory skill. *Journal of Experimental Psychology: Learning, memory and cognition, 14*, 305–316.

Eylon, B. & Reif, F. (1984). Effects of knowledge organization on task performance. *Cognition and Instruction, 1*, 5–44.

Eysenck, M. W., & Brysbaert, M. (2018). *Fundamentals of cognition*. New York: Routledge.

Fenton, J. J., Weyrich, M. S., Durbin, S., Liu, Y., Bang, H., & Melnikow, J. (2018). Prostate-specific antigen–based screening for prostate cancer: Evidence report and systematic review for the US Preventive Services Task Force. *JAMA, 319*, 1914–1931.

Festinger, L., Reicken, H. W., & Schachter, S. (1956). *When prophecy fails*. Minneapolis: University of Minnesota Press.

Flaxman, S., Goel, S., & Rao, J. M. (2016). Filter bubbles, echo chambers, and online news consumption. *Public Opinion Quarterly, 80*(S1), 298–320.

Foer, J. (2012). *Moonwalking with Einstein: The art and science of remembering everything*. New York: Penguin.

Foster, N. L., Was, C. A., Dunlosky, J., & Isaacson, R. M. (2017). Even after thirteen class exams, students are still overconfident: the role of memory for past exam performance in student predictions. *Metacognition and Learning, 12*, 1–19.

Gates, A. I. (1917). Recitation as a factor in memorizing. *Archives of Psychology, 6*, 1–104.

Geake, J. (2008). Neuromythologies in education. *Educational Research, 50*, 123–133.

Gentner, D. (2002). Analogy in scientific discovery: The case of Johannes Kepler. In L. Magnani and N. J. Nersessian (Eds.), *Model-based reasoning*, 21–39. Boston: Springer.

Gentner, D., & Smith, L. A. (2013). Analogical learning and reasoning. In D. Reisberg (Ed.), *The Oxford handbook of cognitive psychology*, 668–681. New York: Oxford University Press.

Gick, M. L., & Holyoak, K. J. (1980). Analogical problem solving. *Cognitive Psychology, 12*, 306–355.

Gigerenzer, G., & Gaissmaier, W. (2011). Heuristic decision making. *Annual Review of Psychology, 62*, 451–482.

Girón, E. C., McIsaac, T., & Nilsen, D. (2012). Effects of kinesthetic versus visual imagery practice on two technical dance movements: A pilot study. *Journal of Dance Medicine & Science, 16*, 36–38.

Glenberg, A., Smith, S. M., & Green, C. (1977). Type I rehearsal: Maintenance and more. *Journal of Verbal Learning and Verbal Behavior, 16*, 339–352.

Glynn, S. M., & Duit, R. (Eds.). (1995). *Learning science in the schools: Research reforming practice.* London: Routledge.

Godden, D., & Baddeley, A. D. (1975). Context-dependent memory in two natural environments: On land and under water. *British Journal of Psychology, 66*, 325–331.

Godefroit, P., Sinitsa, S. M., Dhouailly, D., Bolotsky, Y. L., Sizov, A. V., McNamara, M. E., & Spagna, P. (2014). A Jurassic ornithischian dinosaur from Siberia with both feathers and scales. *Science, 345*(6195), 451–455.

Goh, W. D., & Lu, S. H. (2012). Testing the myth of the encoding–retrieval match. *Memory & Cognition, 40*, 28–39.

Goodwin, D. W., Powell, B., Bremer, D., Hoine, H., & Stern, J. (1969). Alcohol and recall: State-dependent effects in man. *Science, 163*, 1358–1360.

Gorham, G. (2009). *Philosophy of science: A beginner's guide.* London: Oneworld Publications.

Green, A. E. (2016). Creativity, within reason: Semantic distance and dynamic state creativity in relational thinking and reasoning. *Current Directions in Psychological Science, 25*, 28–35.

Guillot, A., & Collet, C. (2008). Construction of the motor imagery integrative model in sport: A review and theoretical investigation of motor imagery use. *International Review of Sport and Exercise Psychology, 1*, 31–44.

Guillot, A., & Collet, C. (Eds.). (2010). *The neurophysiological foundations of mental and motor imagery.* New York: Oxford University Press.

Guthrie, J. T. (1971). Feedback and sentence learning. *Journal of Verbal Learning and Verbal Behavior, 10*, 23–28.

Guwande, A. (2002). *Better: A surgeon's notes on performance.* New York: Picador.

Hacker, D. J., Bol, L., Horgan, D. D., & Rakow, E. A. (2000). Test prediction and performance in a classroom context. *Journal of Educational Psychology, 92*, 160–170.

Hart, J. T. (1965). Memory and the feeling-of-knowing experience. *Journal of Educational Psychology, 56*, 208–216.

Hartwig, M. K., & Dunlosky, J. (2012). Study strategies of college students: Are self-testing and scheduling related to achievement? *Psychonomic Bulletin & Review, 19*, 126–134.

Hausman, H., & Kornell, N. (2014). Mixing topics while studying does not enhance learning. *Journal of Applied Research in Memory and Cognition, 3*, 153–160.

Herculano-Houzel, S. (2002). Do you know your brain? A survey on public neuroscience literacy at the closing of the decade of the brain. *Neuroscientist, 8*, 98–110.

Hertwig, R. (2012). Tapping into the wisdom of the crowd—with confidence. *Science, 336*(6079), 303–304.

Hesse, M. (1966). *Models and Analogies in Science.* Notre Dame, IN: University of Notre Dame Press.

Holmes, P. S., & Collins, D. J. (2001). The PETTLEP approach to motor imagery: A functional equivalence model for sport psychologists. *Journal of Applied Sport Psychology, 13,* 60–83.

Holyoak, K. J., & Thagard, P. (1995). *Mental Leaps: Analogy in creative thought.* Cambridge, MA: MIT Press.

Holyoak, K. J., & Thagard, P. (1997). The analogical mind. *American Psychologist, 52,* 35–44.

Hopkins, R. F., Lyle, K. B., Hieb, J. L., & Ralston, P. A. (2016). Spaced retrieval practice increases college students' short- and long-term retention of mathematics knowledge. *Educational Psychology Review, 28,* 853–873.

Howard-Jones, P. A. (2014). Neuroscience and education: myths and messages. *Nature Reviews Neuroscience, 15,* 817–824.

Huff, D. (1954). How to lie with statistics. New York: Norton.

Izawa, C. (1970). Optimal potentiating effects and forgetting-prevention effects of tests in paired-associate learning. *Journal of Experimental Psychology, 83,* 340–344.

Jacoby, L. L.,Wahlheim, C. N., & Coane, J. H. (2010). Test-enhanced learning of natural concepts: Effects on recognition memory, classification, and metacognition. *Journal of Experimental Psychology: Learning, Memory, and Cognition, 36,* 1441–1451.

Janiszewski, C., Noel, H., & Sawyer, A. G. (2003). A meta-analysis of the spacing effect in verbal learning: Implications for research on advertising repetition and consumer memory. *Journal of Consumer Research, 30,* 138–149.

Jee, B. D., Gentner, D., Uttal, D. H., Sageman, B., Forbus, K., Manduca, C. A., & Tikoff, B. (2014). Drawing on experience: How domain knowledge is reflected in sketches of scientific structures and processes. *Research in Science Education, 44,* 859–883.

Kahneman, D. (2011). *Thinking, fast and slow.* Basingstoke, UK: Macmillan.

Kang, S. H., & Pashler, H. (2012). Learning painting styles: Spacing is advantageous when it promotes discriminative contrast. *Applied Cognitive Psychology, 26,* 97–103.

Kantowitz, B., Roediger III, H., & Elmes, D. (2015). *Experimental psychology.* Stamford, CT: Cengage Learning.

Karpicke, J. D., Butler, A. C., & Roediger III, H. L. (2009). Metacognitive strategies in student learning: do students practise retrieval when they study on their own? *Memory, 17,* 471–479.

Karpicke, J. D., Lehman, M., & Aue, W. R. (2014). Retrieval-based learning: An episodic context account. In B. H. Ross (Ed), *The psychology of learning and motivation,* vol. 61, 237–284.

Karpicke, J. D., & Roediger, H. L. (2008). The critical importance of retrieval for learning. *Science, 319*(5865), 966–968.

Kasper, L. F. (1993). The keyword method and foreign language vocabulary learning: A rationale for its use. *Foreign Language Annals, 26,* 244–251.

Keller, P. E. (2012). Mental imagery in music performance: underlying mechanisms and potential benefits. *Annals of the New York Academy of Sciences, 1252,* 206–213.

Kelley, C. M., & Rhodes, M. G. (2002). Making sense and nonsense of experience: Attributions in memory and judgment. In B. H. Ross (Ed.), *The psychology of learning and motivation*, vol. 41, 293–320. Cambridge, MA: Academic Press.

Keysar, H. (2015). *1966's insane wedding gowns of the future*. Retrieved from http://mentalfloss.com/article/66531/1966s-insane-wedding-gowns-future

Kipling, R. (1901). *Kim*. Basingstoke, UK: Macmillan.

Kimball, D. R., Smith, T. A., & Muntean, W. J. (2012). Does delaying judgments of learning really improve the efficacy of study decisions? Not so much. *Journal of Experimental Psychology: Learning, Memory, and Cognition, 38*, 923–954.

King, H. S. (2016). *Team creative performance: Exploring the relationship between team diversity and conflict affecting the creative productivity of interior design student teams* (Doctoral dissertation, Colorado State University).

King, J. F., Zechmeister, E. B., & Shaughnessy, J. J. (1980). Judgments of knowing: The influence of retrieval practice. *American Journal of Psychology, 93*, 329–343.

Koriat, A. (2007). Metacognition and consciousness. In P. D. Zelazo, M. Moscovitch, and E. Thompson (Eds.), *The Cambridge Handbook of Consciousness*, 289–325. New York: Cambridge University Press.

Kornell, N. (2009). Optimising learning using flashcards: Spacing is more effective than cramming. *Applied Cognitive Psychology, 23*, 1297–1317.

Kornell, N., & Bjork, R. A. (2007). The promise and perils of self-regulated study. *Psychonomic Bulletin & Review, 14*, 219–224.

Kornell, N. & Bjork, R. A. (2008). Learning concepts and categories: Is spacing the "enemy of induction"? *Psychological Science, 19*, 585–592.

Kornell, N., & Bjork, R. A. (2009). A stability bias in human memory: Overestimating remembering and underestimating learning. *Journal of Experimental Psychology: General, 138*, 449–468.

Kornell, N., Bjork, R. A., & Garcia, M. A. (2011). Why tests appear to prevent forgetting: A distribution-based bifurcation model. *Journal of Memory and Language, 65*, 85–97.

Kornell, N., & Metcalfe, J. (2006). Study efficacy and the region of proximal learning framework. *Journal of Experimental Psychology: Learning, Memory, and Cognition, 32*, 609–622.

Kornell, N., & Rhodes, M. G. (2013). Feedback reduces the metacognitive benefit of tests. *Journal of Experimental Psychology: Applied, 19*, 1–13.

Kornell, N., Rhodes, M. G., Castel, A. D., & Tauber, S. K. (2011). The ease-of-processing heuristic and the stability bias: Dissociating memory, memory beliefs, and memory judgments. *Psychological Science, 22*, 787–794.

Kornell, N., & Son, L. K. (2009). Learners' choices and beliefs about self-testing. *Memory, 17*, 493–501.

Kosslyn, S. M., Ganis, G., & Thompson, W. L. (2001). Neural foundations of imagery. *Nature Reviews Neuroscience, 2*, 635–642.

Kosslyn, S. M., Thompson, W. L., & Ganis, G. (2006). *The case for mental imagery*. New York: Oxford University Press.

Kounios, J. (2017, June). Eureka? Yes, eureka! Retrieved from https://www.nytimes.com/2017/06/10/opinion/sunday/eureka-yes-eureka.html

Kounios, J., & Beeman, M. (2015). *The eureka factor: Aha moments, creative insight, and the brain*. New York: Random House.

Kounios, J., & Beeman, M. (2009). Aha! The cognitive neuroscience of insight. *Current Directions in Psychological Science, 18,* 210–216.

Kuhl, B. A., & Wagner, A. D. (2009). Forgetting and retrieval. In G. G. Berntson & J. T. Cacioppo (Eds.). *Handbook of Neurosciences for the Behavioral Sciences.* New York: Wiley.

Kuhn, T. S. (1970). *The structure of scientific revolutions* (2nd ed.). Chicago: University of Chicago Press.

Lee, T. D., & Genovese, E. D. (1988). Distribution of practice in motor skill acquisition: Learning and performance effects reconsidered. *Research Quarterly for Exercise and Sport, 59,* 277–287.

LePort, A. K. R., Mattfeld, A. T., Dickinson-Anson, H., Fallon, J. H., Stark, C. E. L., Frithjof, K., et al. (2012). Behavioral and neuroanatomical investigation of Highly Superior Autobiographical Memory (HSAM). *Neurobiology of Learning and Memory, 98,* 78–92.

Levin, J. R., McCormick, C. B., Miller, G. E., Berry, J. K., & Pressley, M. (1982). Mnemonic versus nonmnemonic vocabulary-learning strategies for children. *American Educational Research Journal, 19,* 121–136.

Levin, J. R., Shriberg, L. K., Miller, G. E., McCormick, C. B., & Levin, B. B. (1980). The keyword method in the classroom: How to remember the states and their capitals. *The Elementary School Journal, 80,* 185–191.

Levin, S. (2016). *Delta accused of 'blatant discrimination' by black doctor after incident on flight*. Retrieved from https://www.theguardian.com/us-news/2016/oct/13/delta-discrimination-black-doctor-incident

Levitin, D. (2014). *The organized mind: Thinking straight in the age of information overload*. New York: Penguin.

Lewandowsky, S., Ecker, U. K., & Cook, J. (2017). Beyond misinformation: Understanding and coping with the "post-truth" era. *Journal of Applied Research in Memory and Cognition, 6,* 353–369.

Light, L. L., & Carter-Sobell, L. (1970). Effects of changed semantic context on recognition memory. *Journal of Verbal Learning and Verbal Behavior, 9,* 1–11.

Lilienfeld, S. O., Lynn, S. J., Ruscio, J., & Beyerstein, B. L. (2010). *50 great myths of popular psychology: Shattering widespread misconceptions about human behavior*. West Sussex, UK: Wiley-Blackwell.

Lingham-Soliar, T. (2014). Comment on "A Jurassic ornithischian dinosaur from Siberia with both feathers and scales." *Science, 346,* 434.

Lister, J. (1867). On the antiseptic principle in the practice of surgery. *The Lancet, 90,* 353–356.

Lister, J. (1870). On the effects of the antiseptic system of treatment upon the salubrity of a surgical hospital. *The Lancet, 95,* 2–4.

Little, J. L., Bjork, E. L., Bjork, R. A., & Angello, G. (2012). Multiple-choice tests exonerated, at least of some charges: Fostering test-induced learning and avoiding test-induced forgetting. *Psychological Science, 23,* 1337–1344.

Loftus, E. F., & Palmer, J. C. (1974). Reconstruction of automobile destruction: An example of the interaction between language and memory. *Journal of Verbal Learning and Verbal Behavior, 13*, 585–589.

Luhmann, C. C., & Rajaram, S. (2015). Memory transmission in small groups and large networks: An agent-based model. *Psychological Science, 26*, 1909–1917.

M&M's obsession leads to physics discovery. (2004, February 16). Retrieved from http://www.cnn.com/2004/TECH/science/02/16/science.candy.reut/index.html

Maguire, E. A., Valentine, E. R., Wilding, J. M., & Kapur, N. (2003). Routes to remembering: the brains behind superior memory. *Nature Neuroscience, 6*, 90–95.

Mani, A., Mullainathan, S., Shafir, E., & Zhao, J. (2013). Poverty impedes cognitive function. *Science, 341*, 976–980.

Mankoff, R. (2014, March). The "aha" moment! Retrieved from https://www.newyorker.com/cartoons/bob-mankoff/the-aha-moment

Mäntylä, T., & Nilsson, L. G. (1988). Cue distinctiveness and forgetting: Effectiveness of self-generated retrieval cues in delayed recall. *Journal of Experimental Psychology: Learning, Memory, and Cognition, 14*, 502–509.

Marsh, E. J. (2007). Retelling is not the same as recalling: Implications for memory. *Current Directions in Psychological Science, 16*, 16–20.

Massa, L., & Mayer, R. (2006). Testing the ATI hypothesis: Should multimedia instruction accommodate verbalizer-visualizer cognitive style? *Learning and individual differences, 16*, 321–335.

Matlin, M. W. (2005). *Cognition*. Hoboken: John Wily & Sons.

Matlin, M. W., & Farmer, T. A. (2016). *Cognition*. New York: Wiley.

McCabe, J. (2011). Metacognitive awareness of learning strategies in undergraduates. *Memory & Cognition, 39*, 462–476.

McCabe, J. A., & Lummis, S. N. (2018). Why and how do undergraduates study in groups? *Scholarship of Teaching and Learning in Psychology, 4*, 27–42.

McDaniel, M. A., Agarwal, P. K., Huelser, B. J., McDermott, K. B., & Roediger III, H. L. (2011). Test-enhanced learning in a middle school science classroom: The effects of quiz frequency and placement. *Journal of Educational Psychology, 103*, 399–414.

McDaniel, M. A., Anderson, J. L., Derbish, M. H., & Morrisette, N. (2007). Testing the testing effect in the classroom. *European Journal of Cognitive Psychology, 19*, 494–513.

McDaniel, M. A., & Donnelly, C. M. (1996). Learning with analogy and elaborative interrogation. *Journal of Educational Psychology, 88*, 508–519.

McDaniel, M. A., Thomas, R. C., Agarwal, P. K., McDermott, K. B., & Roediger, H. L. (2013). Quizzing in middle-school science: Successful transfer performance on classroom exams. *Applied Cognitive Psychology, 27*, 360–372.

McDaniel, M. A., Roediger, H. L., & McDermott, K. B. (2007). Generalizing test-enhanced learning from the laboratory to the classroom. *Psychonomic Bulletin & Review, 14*, 200–206.

McDermott, K. B., Agarwal, P. K., D'Antonio, L., Roediger III, H. L., & McDaniel, M. A. (2014). Both multiple-choice and short-answer quizzes enhance later exam performance in middle and high school classes. *Journal of Experimental Psychology: Applied, 20*, 3–21.

Meade, M. L., Harris, C. B., Van Bergen, P., Sutton, J., & Barnier, A. J. (Eds.). (2018). *Collaborative remembering: Theories, research, and applications.* New York: Oxford University Press.

Meade, M. L., Nokes, T. J., & Morrow, D. G. (2009). Expertise promotes facilitation on a collaborative memory task. *Memory, 17*, 39–48.

Meagher, B. J., Carvalho, P. F., Goldstone, R. L., & Nosofsky, R. M. (2017). Organized simultaneous displays facilitate learning of complex natural science categories. *Psychonomic Bulletin & Review, 24*, 1987–1994.

Meister, I. G., Krings, T., Foltys, H., Boroojerdi, B., Müller, M., Töpper, R., & Thron, A. (2004). Playing piano in the mind—an fMRI study on music imagery and performance in pianists. *Cognitive Brain Research, 19*, 219–228.

Melby-Lervåg, M., & Hulme, C. (2013). Is working memory training effective? A meta-analytic review. *Developmental Psychology, 49*, 270–291.

Metcalfe, J., & Finn, B. (2008). Evidence that judgments of learning are causally related to study choice. *Psychonomic Bulletin & Review, 15*, 174–179.

Metcalfe, J., & Weibe, D. (1987). Intuition in insight and noninsight problem solving. *Memory & Cognition, 15*, 238–246.

Miles, C., & Hardman, E. (1998). State-dependent memory produced by aerobic exercise. *Ergonomics, 41*, 20–28.

Miller, G. A. (1956). The magical number seven, plus or minus two: Some limits on our capacity for processing information. *Psychological Review, 63*, 81–97.

Miller, T. M., & Geraci, L. (2011). Unskilled but aware: Reinterpreting overconfidence in low-performing students. *Journal of Experimental Psychology: Learning, Memory, and Cognition, 37*, 502–506.

Miller, T. M., & Geraci, L. (2016). The influence of retrieval practice on metacognition: The contribution of analytic and non-analytic processes. *Consciousness and Cognition, 42*, 41–50.

Mohan, L., Mohan, A., & Uttal, D. (2014). Research on thinking and learning with maps and geospatial technologies. In M. Solem, N. T. Huynh, and R. Boehm (Eds.), *GeoProgressions. Learning progressions for maps, geospatial technology, and spatial thinking: A research handbook* (9–21). Washington, DC: National Center for Research

Moore, D. W. (2005). Three in four Americans believe in paranormal. Gallup Organization, June 15. Retrieved from https://news.gallup.com/poll/16915/three-four-americans-believe-paranormal.aspx

Morehead, K., Rhodes, M. G., & DeLozier, S. (2016). Instructor and student knowledge of study strategies. *Memory, 24*, 257–271.

Morris, C. D., Bransford, J. D., & Franks, J. J. (1977). Levels of processing versus transfer appropriate processing. *Journal of Verbal Learning and Verbal Behavior, 16*, 519–533.

Moscovitch, M., & Craik, F. I. (1976). Depth of processing, retrieval cues, and uniqueness of encoding as factors in recall. *Journal of Verbal Learning and Verbal Behavior, 15*, 447–458.

Moulton, C. A. E., Dubrowski, A., MacRae, H., Graham, B., Grober, E., & Reznick, R. (2006). Teaching surgical skills: what kind of practice makes perfect?: A randomized, controlled trial. *Annals of Surgery, 244*, 400–409.

Mueller, M. L., Dunlosky, J., Tauber, S. K., & Rhodes, M. G. (2014). The font-size effect on judgments of learning: Does it exemplify fluency effects or reflect people's beliefs about memory? *Journal of Memory and Language, 70*, 1–12.

Mullet, H. G., & Marsh, E. J. (2016). Correcting false memories: Errors must be noticed and replaced. *Memory & Cognition, 44*, 403–412.

Nairne, J. S. (2002). The myth of the encoding-retrieval match. *Memory, 10*, 389–395.

Nantais, K. M., & Schellenberg, E. G. (1999). The Mozart effect: An artifact of preference. *Psychological Science, 10*, 370–373.

Needham, D. R., & Begg, I. M. (1991). Problem-oriented training promotes spontaneous analogical transfer: Memory-oriented training promotes memory for training. *Memory & Cognition, 19*, 543–557.

Nelson, T. O. (1996). Consciousness and metacognition. *American Psychologist, 51*, 102–116.

Nelson, T. O., & Dunlosky, J. (1994). Norms of paired-associate recall during multitrial learning of Swahili-English translation equivalents. *Memory, 2*, 325–335.

Nelson, T. O., & Narens, L. (1990). Metamemory: A theoretical framework and some new findings. In G. H. Bower (Ed.), *The psychology of learning and motivation*, vol. 26, 125–173. Cambridge, MA: Academic Press.

Nestojko, J. F., Bui, D. C., Kornell, N., & Bjork, E. L. (2014). Expecting to teach enhances learning and organization of knowledge in free recall of text passages. *Memory & Cognition, 42*, 1038–1048.

Nestojko, J. F., Finley, J. R., & Roediger III, H. L. (2013). Extending cognition to external agents. *Psychological Inquiry, 24*, 321–325.

Nickerson, R. S. (1998). Confirmation bias: A ubiquitous phenomenon in many guises. *Review of General Psychology, 2*, 175–220.

Nickerson, R. S., & Adams, M. J. (1979). Long-term memory for a common object. *Cognitive Psychology, 11*, 287–307.

Ozgungor, S., & Guthrie, J. T. (2004). Interactions among elaborative interrogation, knowledge, and interest in the process of constructing knowledge from text. *Journal of Educational Psychology, 96*, 437–443.

Paivio, A. (1965). Abstractness, imagery, and meaningfulness in paired-associate learning. *Journal of Verbal Learning and Verbal Behavior, 4*, 32–38.

Palmere, M., Benton, S. L., Glover, J. A., & Ronning, R. R. (1983). Elaboration and recall of main ideas in prose. *Journal of Educational Psychology, 75*, 898–907.

Parker, E. S., Cahill, L., & McGaugh, J. L. (2006). A case of unusual autobiographical remembering. *Neurocase, 12*, 35–49.

Pashler, H., Cepeda, N. J., Wixted, J. T., & Rohrer, D. (2005). When does feedback facilitate learning of words? *Journal of Experimental Psychology: Learning, Memory, and Cognition, 31*, 3–8.

Pashler, H., McDaniel, M., Rohrer, D., & Bjork, R. (2008). Learning styles: Concepts and evidence. *Psychological Science in the Public Interest, 9*, 106–119.

Patil, P., Peng, R. D., & Leek, J. T. (2016). What should researchers expect when they replicate studies? A statistical view of replicability in psychological science. *Perspectives on Psychological Science, 11*, 539–544.

Patalano, A. L., & Seifert, C. M. (1994). Memory for impasses during problem solving. *Memory & Cognition, 22*, 234–242.

Popper, K. R. (1959). *The logic of scientific discovery*. London: Hutchinson & Co.

Radvansky, G. A., Krawietz, S. A., & Tamplin, A. K. (2011). Walking through doorways causes forgetting: Further explorations. *Quarterly Journal of Experimental Psychology, 64*, 1632–1645.

Rajaram, S. (2011). Collaboration both hurts and helps memory: A cognitive perspective. *Current Directions in Psychological Science, 20*, 76–81.

Ramsey, R., Cumming, J., Edwards, M. G., Williams, S., & Brunning, C. (2010). Examining the emotion aspect of PETTLEP-based imagery with penalty taking in soccer. *Journal of Sport Behavior, 33*, 295–314.

Rauscher, F. H., Shaw, G. L., & Ky, K. N. (1993). Music and spatial task performance. *Nature, 365*, 611.

Rawson, K. A., Dunlosky, J., & Sciartelli, S. M. (2013). The power of successive relearning: Improving performance on course exams and long-term retention. *Educational Psychology Review, 25*, 523–548.

Rawson, K. A., Vaughn, K. E., Walsh, M., & Dunlosky, J. (2018). Investigating and explaining the effects of successive relearning on long-term retention. *Journal of Experimental Psychology: Applied, 24*, 57–71.

Raz A., Packard M. G., Alexander G. M., Buhle J. T., Zhu H., Yu S., et al. (2009). A slice of pi: An exploratory neuroimaging study of digit encoding and retrieval in a superior memorist. *Neurocase, 15*, 361–372.

Reed, C. L. (2002). Chronometric comparisons of imagery to action: Visualizing versus physically performing springboard dives. *Memory & Cognition, 30*, 1169–1178.

Reinhart, R. M. G. McClenahan, L. J. & Woodman, G.F. (2015). Visualizing trumps vision when training attention. *Psychological Science, 26*, 1114–1122.

Reisberg, D. (2015). *Cognition: Exploring the science of the mind*. New York: WW Norton.

Reiser, M., Büsch, D., & Munzert, J. (2011). Strength gains by motor imagery with different ratios of physical to mental practice. *Frontiers in Psychology, 2*, 194.

Rhodes, M. G. (2016). Judgments of learning. In J. Dunlosky and S. K. Tauber (Eds.), *The Oxford Handbook of Metamemory*, 65–80. New York: Oxford University Press.

Rhodes, M. G., & Castel, A. D. (2008). Memory predictions are influenced by perceptual information: Evidence for metacognitive illusions. *Journal of Experimental Psychology: General, 137*, 615–625.

Rhodes, M. G., & Castel, A. D. (2009). Metacognitive illusions for auditory information: Effects on monitoring and control. *Psychonomic Bulletin & Review, 16*, 550–554.

Rhodes, M. G., & Tauber, S. K. (2011). The influence of delaying Judgments of Learning (JOLs) on metacognitive accuracy: A meta-analytic review. *Psychological Bulletin, 137*, 131–148.

Richland, L. E., Stigler, J. W., & Holyoak, K. J. (2012). Teaching the conceptual structure of mathematics. *Educational Psychologist, 47*, 189–203.

Risko, E. F., & Dunn, T. L. (2015). Storing information in-the-world: Metacognition and cognitive offloading in a short-term memory task. *Consciousness and Cognition, 36*, 61–74.

Roediger, H. L., & Abel, M. (2015). Collective memory: A new arena of cognitive study. *Trends in Cognitive Sciences, 19*, 359–361.

Roediger, H. L., Abel, M., Umanath, S., Shaffer, R. A., & Wertsch, J. V. (2016). *Conflicting memories of World War II*. Talk presented at the 6th Meeting of the International Conference on Memory. Budapest, Hungary.

Roediger, H. L., & Guynn, M. J. (1996). *Retrieval processes*. In E. L. Bjork & R. A. Bjork (Eds.), *Human memory*, 197–236. San Diego: Academic Press.

Roediger, H. L., & Karpicke, J. D. (2006a). The power of testing memory: Basic research and implications for educational practice. *Perspectives on Psychological Science, 1*, 181–210.

Roediger, H. L., & Karpicke, J. D. (2006b). Test-enhanced learning: Taking memory tests improves long-term retention. *Psychological Science, 17*, 249–255.

Roediger, H., & Wertsch, J. (2015). Past imperfect. *New Scientist, 228*(3043), 30–31.

Rogers, T. B., Kuiper, N. A., & Kirker, W. S. (1977). Self-reference and the encoding of personal information. *Journal of Personality and Social Psychology, 35*, 677–688.

Rohrer, D., Dedrick, R. F., & Stershic, S. (2015). Interleaved practice improves mathematics learning. *Journal of Educational Psychology, 107*, 900–908.

Rohrer, D., & Taylor, K. (2006). The effects of overlearning and distributed practise on the retention of mathematics knowledge. *Applied Cognitive Psychology, 20*, 1209–1224.

Rohrer, D., & Taylor, K. (2007). The shuffling of mathematics problems improves learning. *Instructional Science, 35*, 481–498.

Rohrer, D., Taylor, K., & Sholar, B. (2010). Tests enhance the transfer of learning. *Journal of Experimental Psychology: Learning, Memory, and Cognition, 36*, 233–239.

Rosnow, R. L., & Rosenthal, R. (2012). *Beginning behavioral research: A conceptual primer* (7th ed.). New York: Pearson.

Rowland, C. A. (2014). The effect of testing versus restudy on retention: A meta-analytic review of the testing effect. *Psychological Bulletin, 140*, 1432–1463.

Rozenblit, L., & Keil, F. (2002). The misunderstood limits of folk science: An illusion of explanatory depth. *Cognitive Science, 26*, 521–562.

Rudoy, J. D., Voss, J. L., Westerberg, C. E., & Paller, K. A. (2009). Strengthening individual memories by reactivating them during sleep. *Science, 326*, 1079.

Sanders, C. W., Sadoski, M., van Walsum, K., Bramson, R., Wiprud, R., & Fossum, T. W. (2008). Learning basic surgical skills with mental imagery: Using the simulation centre in the mind. *Medical Education, 42*, 607–612.

Saufley, W. H., Otaka, S. R., & Bavaresco, J. L. (1985). Context effects: Classroom tests and context independence. *Memory & Cognition, 13*, 522–528.

Sawyer, R. K. (2011). *Explaining creativity: The science of human innovation*. New York: Oxford University Press.

Schacter, D. L. (1996). *Searching for memory: The brain, the mind, and the past.* New York: HarperCollins.

Scheck, P., Meeter, M., & Nelson, T. O. (2004). Anchoring effects in the absolute accuracy of immediate versus delayed judgments of learning. *Journal of Memory and Language, 51,* 71–79.

Schmidt, R. A., & Bjork, R. A. (1992). New conceptualizations of practice: Common principles in three paradigms suggest new concepts for training. *Psychological Science, 3,* 207–218.

Schwartz, B. L. (2018). *Memory: Foundations and Applications.* Thousand Oaks, CA: SAGE Publications.

Seifert, T. L. (1993). Effects of elaborative interrogation with prose passages. *Journal of Educational Psychology, 85,* 642–651.

Seifert, T. L. (1994). Enhancing memory for main ideas using elaborative interrogation. *Contemporary Educational Psychology, 19,* 360–366.

Seifert, C. M., & Patalano, A. J. (1991). Memory for interrupted tasks: The Zeigarnik effect revisited. In *Proceedings of the Thirteenth Annual Cognitive Science Society.*

Shermer, M. (2002). *Why people believe weird things: Pseudoscience, superstition, and other confusions of our time.* New York: W. H. Freeman and Company.

Shipstead, Z., Hicks, K. L., & Engle, R. W. (2012). Cogmed working memory training: Does the evidence support the claims? *Journal of Applied Research in Memory and Cognition, 1,* 185–193.

Short, S. E., Bruggeman, J. M., Engel, S. G., Marback, T. L., Wang, L. J., Willadsen, A., & Short, M. W. (2002). The effect of imagery function and imagery direction on self-efficacy and performance on a golf-putting task. *The Sport Psychologist, 16,* 48–67.

Shriberg, L. K., Levin, J. R., McCormick, C. B., & Pressley, M. (1982). Learning about "famous" people via the keyword method. *Journal of Educational Psychology, 74,* 238–247.

Simons, D. J., Boot, W. R., Charness, N., Gathercole, S. E., Chabris, C. F., Hambrick, D. Z., & Stine-Morrow, E. A. (2016). Do "brain-training" programs work? *Psychological Science in the Public Interest, 17,* 103–186.

Simons, D. J., & Chabris, C. F. (2011). What people believe about how memory works: A representative survey of the US population. *PloS One. 6,* e22757.

Sio, U. N., & Ormerod, T.C. (2009). Does incubation enhance problem solving? A meta-analytic review. *Psychological Bulletin, 135,* 94–120.

Sitzman, D. M., Rhodes M. G., & Tauber, S. K. (2014). Prior knowledge is more predictive of error correction than subjective confidence. *Memory & Cognition, 42,* 84–96.

Smith, B. L., Holliday, W. G., & Austin, H. W. (2010). Students' comprehension of science textbooks using a question-based reading strategy. *Journal of Research in Science Teaching, 47,* 363–379.

Smith, D., Wright, C., Allsopp, A., & Westhead, H. (2007). It's all in the mind: PETTLEP-based imagery and sports performance. *Journal of Applied Sport Psychology, 19,* 80–92.

Smith, S. M. (1979). Remembering in and out of context. *Journal of Experimental Psychology: Human Learning and Memory, 5*, 460–471.

Smith, S. M., Glenberg, A., & Bjork, R. A. (1978). Environmental context and human memory. *Memory & Cognition, 6*, 342–353.

Smith, S. M., & Vela, E. (2001). Environmental context-dependent memory: A review and meta-analysis. *Psychonomic Bulletin & Review, 8*, 203–220.

Sobel, H. S., Cepeda, N. J., & Kapler, I. V. (2011). Spacing effects in real-world classroom vocabulary learning. *Applied Cognitive Psychology, 25*, 763–767.

Soderstrom, N. C., & Bjork, R. A. (2014). Testing facilitates the regulation of subsequent study time. *Journal of Memory and Language, 73*, 99–115.

Soderstrom, N. C., & Bjork, R. A. (2015). Learning versus performance: An integrative review. *Perspectives on Psychological Science, 10*, 176–199.

Soderstrom, N. C., Kerr, T. K., & Bjork, R. A. (2016). The critical importance of retrieval—and spacing—for learning. *Psychological science, 27*, 223–230.

Soderstrom, N. C., & Rhodes, M. G. (2014). Metacognitive illusions can be reduced by monitoring recollection during study. *Journal of Cognitive Psychology, 26*, 118–126.

Sparrow, B., Liu, J., & Wegner, D. M. (2011). Google effects on memory: Cognitive consequences of having information at our fingertips. *Science*, 1207745. Retrieved from http://science.sciencemag.org/content/early/2011/07/13/science.1207745

Spitzer, H. F. (1939). Studies in retention. *Journal of Educational Psychology, 30*, 641–656.

Sternberg, R. J. (1999). The theory of successful intelligence. *Review of General Psychology, 3*, 292–316.

Stoff, D. M., & Eagle, M. N. (1971). The relationship among reported strategies, presentation rate, and verbal ability and their effects on free recall learning. *Journal of Experimental Psychology, 87*, 423–428.

Suchow, J. W., Pacer, M. D., & Griffiths, T. L. (2016). Design from zeroth principles. *Proceedings of the 38th Annual Conference of the Cognitive Science Society*, 1505–1510

Symons, C. S., & Johnson, B. T. (1997). The self-reference effect in memory: A meta-analysis. *Psychological Bulletin, 121*, 371–394.

Szpunar, K. K. (2017). Directing the wandering mind. *Current Directions in Psychological Science, 26*, 40–44.

Szpunar, K. K., Khan, N. Y., & Schacter, D. L. (2013). Interpolated memory tests reduce mind wandering and improve learning of online lectures. *Proceedings of the National Academy of Sciences, 110*, 6313–6317.

Szpunar, K. K., McDermott, K. B., & Roediger III, H. L. (2008). Testing during study insulates against the buildup of proactive interference. *Journal of Experimental Psychology: Learning, Memory, and Cognition, 34*, 1392–1399.

Talarico, J. M., & Rubin, D. C. (2003). Confidence, not consistency, characterizes flashbulb memories. *Psychological Science 14*, 455–461.

Tauber, S. K., Dunlosky, J., Rawson, K. A., Rhodes, M. G., & Sitzman, D. A. (2013). General knowledge norms: Updated and expanded from the Nelson and Narens (1980) norms. *Behavior Research Methods, 45*, 1115–1143.

Tauber, S. K., & Rhodes, M. G. (2012). Measuring memory monitoring with judgements of retention (JORs). *Quarterly Journal of Experimental Psychology*, *65*, 1376–1396.

Tauber, S. K., Witherby, A. E., Dunlosky, J., Rawson, K. A., Putnam, A. L., & Roediger, H. L. (2017). Does covert retrieval benefit learning of key-term definitions? *Journal of Applied Research in Memory and Cognition, 7*, 106–115.

Taylor, K., & Rohrer, D. (2010). The effects of interleaved practice. *Applied Cognitive Psychology, 24*, 837–848.

Teasdale, J. D., & Russell, M. L. (1983). Differential effects of induced mood on the recall of positive, negative and neutral words. *British Journal of Clinical Psychology, 22*, 163–171.

Thiede, K. W., Anderson, M. C. M., & Therriault, D. (2003). Accuracy of metacognitive monitoring affects learning of texts. *Journal of Educational Psychology, 95*, 66–73.

Thiede, K. W., & Dunlosky, J. (1994). Delaying students' metacognitive monitoring improves their accuracy in predicting their recognition performance. *Journal of Educational Psychology, 86*, 290–302.

Thiede, K. W., Dunlosky, J., Griffin, T. D., & Wiley, J. (2005). Understanding the delayed-keyword effect on metacomprehension accuracy. *Journal of Experimental Psychology: Learning, Memory, and Cognition, 31*, 1267–1280.

Thieman, T. J. (1984). A classroom demonstration of encoding specificity. *Teaching of Psychoogy, 11*, 101–102.

Thomas, A. K., & McDaniel, M. A. (2007). The negative cascade of incongruent generative study-test processing in memory and metacomprehension. *Memory & Cognition, 35*, 668–678.

Thompson, W. F., Schellenberg, E. G., & Husain, G. (2001). Arousal, mood, and the Mozart effect. *Psychological Science, 12*, 248–251.

Tullis, J. G., Finley, J. R., & Benjamin, A. S. (2013). Metacognition of the testing effect: Guiding learners to predict the benefits of retrieval. *Memory & Cognition, 41*, 429–442.

Tulving, E., & Pearlstone, Z. (1966). Availability versus accessibility of information in memory for words. *Journal of Verbal Learning and Verbal Behavior, 5*, 381–391.

Tulving, E., & Thomson, D. M. (1973). Encoding specificity and retrieval processes in episodic memory. *Psychological Review, 80*, 352–373.

Underwood, B. J. (1957). Interference and forgetting. *Psychological Review, 64*, 49–60.

Uttal, D. H., Miller, D. I., & Newcombe, N. S. (2013). Exploring and enhancing spatial thinking links to achievement in science, technology, engineering, and mathematics? *Current Directions in Psychological Science. 22*, 367–373.

Vendetti, M., Castel, A. D., & Holyoak, K. J. (2013). The floor effect: Impoverished spatial memory for elevator buttons. *Attention, Perception, & Psychophysics, 75*, 636–643.

Vul, E., & Pashler, H. (2007). Incubation benefits only after people have been misdirected. *Memory & Cognition, 35*, 701–710.

Wagner, U., Gais, S., Haider, H., Verleger, R., & Born, J. (2004). Sleep inspires insight. *Nature, 427,* 352–355.

Watkins, O. C., & Watkins, M. J. (1975). Buildup of proactive inhibition as a cue-overload effect. *Journal of Experimental Psychology: Human Learning and Memory, 1,* 442–452.

Weldon, M. S. (2000). Remembering as a social process. In D. L. Medin (Ed.), *The psychology of learning and motivation,* vol. 40, 67–120. Cambridge, MA: Academic Press.

Weldon, M. S., & Bellinger, K. D. (1997). Collective memory: Collaborative and individual processes in remembering. *Journal of Experimental Psychology: Learning, Memory, and Cognition, 23,* 1160–1175.

Weldon, M. S., Blair, C., & Huebsch, P. D. (2000). Group remembering: Does social loafing underlie collaborative inhibition? *Journal of Experimental Psychology: Learning, Memory, and Cognition, 26,* 1568–1577.

Willingham, D. T., Hughes, E. M., & Dobolyi, D. G. (2015). The scientific status of learning styles theories. *Teaching of Psychology, 42,* 266–271.

Woloshyn, V. E., Pressley, M., & Schneider, W. (1992). Elaborative interrogation and prior-knowledge effects on learning of facts. *Journal of Educational Psychology, 84,* 115–124.

Wong, R. M., Lawson, M. J., & Keeves, J. (2002). The effects of self-explanation training on students' problem solving in high-school mathematics. *Learning and Instruction, 12,* 233–262.

Wright, C., Hogard, E., Ellis, R., Smith, D., & Kelly, C. (2008). Effect of PETTLEP imagery training on performance of nursing skills: A pilot study. *Journal of Advanced Nursing, 63,* 259–265.

Wright, C. J., & Smith, D. K. (2007). The effect of a short-term PETTLEP imagery intervention on a cognitive task. *Journal of Imagery Research in Sport and Physical Activity, 2.* Retrieved from DOI: https://doi.org/10.2202/1932-0191.1014

Yates, F. A. (1966). *The art of memory.* Chicago: University of Chicago Press.

Yuan, L., Uttal, D., & Gentner, D. (2017). Analogical processes in children's understanding of spatial representations. *Developmental Psychology, 53,* 1098–1114.

Zaromb, F. M., & Roediger, H. L. (2010). The testing effect in free recall is associated with enhanced organizational processes. *Memory & Cognition, 38,* 995–1008.

Zaromb, F., Butler, A. C., Agarwal, P. K., & Roediger, H. L. (2014). Collective memories of three wars in United States history in younger and older adults. *Memory & Cognition, 42,* 383–399.

INDEX

....

7, plus or minus 2 number, 28

50 Great Myths of Psychology, 31

"1966's Insane Wedding Gowns of the Future.," 222–23

A. J. (autobiographical memory savant), 50

ad-hoc categories, 127

aerobic state cues, 198–9

airline medical emergency, 239

analogical reasoning, 224

analogy. *See* understanding, role of analogy

anecdotes are not evidence, 32

appeal to authority, 31–2

applying the scientific approach, 22

Archimedes, 224–5

articles. *See* books and publications

artists and their works, imagery, 8–10, 67, 163–5

attack-dispersion problem, 226–7

background noise, effects on studying, 42

Bartlett, Frederic, 242

between-subjects manipulation, 41

biographical information, keyword mnemonics, 111

blocking *vs.* interleaving (mixing)

imagery, 67

pros and cons of mixing, 163–5

studying artists' styles, 67

bloodletting, 18

books and publications

50 Great Myths of Psychology, 31

"1966's Insane Wedding Gowns of the Future.," 222–3

"Feats of Memory Anyone Can Do," 103, 136, 144

Guinness Book of World Records, 89, 123

"Imagery in Sport: Elite Athlete Examples and the

PETTLEP Model," 112

Journal of Imagery Research in Sport and Physical Activity, 112

Kim, 130

Memory: A Contribution to Experimental Psychology, 151

The Organized Mind, 136

brain-training, evaluating claims about, 29–30

breaks

See also spaced learning methods

elaborative interrogation, 219, 231

role in understanding, 219, 231

cancer screening, 28

causation, correlation as, 32

central tendency, 230

Chaikin, Paul, 228

chimpanzee behavior, 49

chunking memory, 28

chunks, 124
cognitive bias, 240–1
cognitive offloading,
    118–20, 136
cognitive processing,
    and organization. *See*
    organization, and
    cognitive processing
cognitive tasks,
    performance
    enhancement, 111–8
collaboration in learning
    See also group learning
    desired outcomes, 251
    elaborative
        interrogation, 247,
        251, 252
    group effects on
        retrieval, 252
    pooling individual
        responses, 253
    pros and cons, 247–52
    suggestive questioning,
        248
    working with experts,
        248–0, 253
collaborative groups, 244
collaborative inhibition,
    246–7
collective knowledge
    See also collaboration
    in learning
    cognitive bias, 240–1
    echo chambers, 239–40
    information bubbles,
        239–40
    overview, 237–8
    pitfalls, 238–40
    relative facts, 240
    stereotypes, 239–40
common sense
    See also intuition
    definition, 20
    detoxifying your body,
        20–1
    highlighting, 21
    is not evidence, 32, 35

magnetic bracelets to
    enhance blood
    flow, 21
massed *vs.* spaced
    learning methods, 21
    in a scientific approach
    to optimal learning,
    19–21
computer desktop,
    organizing, 138–9
conceptual understanding,
    99
confidence in answers,
    measuring, 58–9
confound factors, 45–6,
    55
connecting to
    other information,
        90–4, 99
    personal information,
        95–6, 99
connections, role in
    understanding, 232
consensus in the field, when
    evaluating claims, 30
consolidation of memories
    role of sleep, 157
    spaced attempts at
        understanding,
        220–1
control, metacognition,
    61–4
controlling the scientific
    approach, 22
correlation coefficient, 47
correlational designs, 47–8
correlation between
    lung cancer and
        smoking, 48
    student grades and
        instructor
        evaluations, 48
correlation is not
    causation, 32, 48
cramming, pros and cons,
    158–60, 166
Cross, Tamika, 239

cues
    matching study context
        to testing context,
        201–3, 210
    method of loci, 210
    retrieval failure, 193–4
    shared conditions, 205
    taking a break, 210
    uniqueness, 203, 205,
        216
cues, best for studying
    generated during
        studying, 208–9
    thought processes of
        learning, 207–8
    unique cues, 203, 210,
        216
    from variable learning
        contexts, 206–7
cues, elaborative
    interrogation
    distinctive properties
        of cues, 209
    importance of cues, 194
    uniqueness of cues, 203
cues, importance of
    the context of learning,
        194–5
    retrieving "forgotten"
        information, 193–4
cues, types of
    informational, 195–8
    from mental/
        physiological state,
        198–9
    from the physical
        environment, 199–201
cycle of science. *See*
    scientific approach, cycle
    of science

dance, imagery training,
    117
debate. *See* scientific
    debate
decisions about studying,
    63–4

deduction
  in the cycle of science,
    22–3
  definition, 195–6
  example, 22–3
deep processing, 87
delay effects,
  metacognition, 67–9, 73
dependent variables, 41
describing with the
  scientific approach, 21–2
descriptive methods
  combined with
    experimental
    methods, 51–4
  elaborative
    interrogation, 50
  overview, 49–50
diagramming
  organizational
  hierarchical structure,
    129
dinner orders,
  remembering, 124
dinosaurs, scales vs.
  feathers, 28
discriminating between
  similar concepts, 165
distractions from memory,
  136, 145
dog years, calculating, 239
doomsday cult, infiltrating,
  49
durable learning, 68
durian (Asian fruit), 221–2

Ebbinghaus, Hermann,
  151
echo chambers, 239–40
elaboration
  See also elaborative
    interrogation
  benefits of, 96–8
  connecting to other
    information,
    90–4, 99

connecting to personal
  information,
  95–6, 99
definition, 87–8
examples, 247
forming examples,
  94–5, 99
record for memorizing
  the most digits of pi,
  89
seeking conceptual
  understanding, 99
self-reference
  effect, 96
elaborative interrogation
  See also elaboration
  benefits of, 91, 99
  benefits of testing, 177
  collaboration in
    learning, 247, 251,
    252
  definition, xiii, 90
  imagery, 107, 120
  imagery for
    performance
    training, 111
  study of, 91–2
  taking breaks, 219,
    231
  testing, 174, 177, 183
  understanding, 216,
    219
  understanding, role of
    analogy, 228
elaborative interrogation,
  organization
  benefits to memory,
    134
  cognitive offloading,
    136
  interleaving, 132
Elaborative Interrogation
  Arrows, xiii
emotion aspect of the
  PETTLEP procedure,
  114

environmental aspect of
  the PETTLEP procedure,
  113
errors in thinking, 31–4
Eureka effect, 224
evaluating claims about
  learning
  See also scientific
    approach to
    evaluating claims
  personal learning style
    vs. learning outcome,
    51
  popularity vs. strength
    of evidence, 55
  student grades vs.
    instructor
    evaluations, 48
  tips for, 55
evidence
  anecdotes as, 32
  asking for, 14, 21, 35
  common sense as,
    32, 35
  for myths, 21
  in the scientific
    approach to optimal
    learning, 14
exam performance,
  predicting, 62–3
examples, forming,
  94–5, 99
expanding on topics. See
  elaboration
experimental methods
  See also descriptive
    methods; research
    methods
  combined with
    descriptive, 51–4
  research on learning
    and memory,
    38–40
experimental research
  goals, 38
  methods, 38–40

experimental research,
variables
between-subjects
manipulation, 41
dependent, 41
extraneous, 44
independent, 40–1
levels of independent
variables, 40–1
random assignment of,
43
reliability, 41
within-subjects
manipulation, 41
experts as resources,
248–50, 253
explaining concepts to
others, 232
explaining subject matter,
73–4, 76
extraneous variables, 44

"Feats of Memory Anyone
Can Do," 136, 144
feedback experiment, 24–7
field hockey, imagery for
athletic training, 115–16
50 Great Myths of
Psychology, 31
first letter technique for
organization, 132
flashcards, 128–9
flat-earth view, 12
fluency, 68
Foer, Joshua, 103, 136, 144
foreign language
vocabulary, learning,
68, 72
foreign or new vocabulary,
keyword mnemonics,
109
forgetting
after walking through a
doorway, 200
benefits of testing,
178–9

cues for retrieving
"forgotten"
information, 193–4

geographical information,
keyword mnemonics,
109–10
Goodall, Jane, 49
group learning
See also collaboration
in learning; collective
knowledge
effects on retrieval, 252
remembering in
groups, 244–47
Guinness Book of World
Records, 89, 123, 193
gymnasts, imagery for
athletic training, 116–7

hand washing, 17–18
hand-written notes,
organizing, 139
Haraguchi, Akira, 123
hierarchical diagrams, 145
hierarchical structure.
See organization,
hierarchical structure
highlighting, as a study
method, 10, 21
hints. See cues
humours, in ancient Greek
medicine, 18
hypotheses
collecting test data,
22–3. See also
observation.
confirming or
rejecting, 22–3. See
also verification.
definition, 22
forming, 22–3. See also
induction.
making predictions
from, 22–3. See also
deduction.

imagery
artists and their works,
8–9, 67
benefits for memory,
107
blocking vs. mixing,
9–10, 67
cognitive offloading,
118–120
for dance, 117
developing medical and
surgical skills, 117
elaborative
interrogation, 107, 120
for enhancing
understanding,
118–20, 121
pegword mnemonic,
106
in performance arts
training, 117
for performance on
cognitive tasks,
111–8
vs. repetition, 3–6
role in optimal
learning, 6
training nurses, 117
imagery, keyword
mnemonic
biographical
information, 111
description, 107–9, 120
foreign or new
vocabulary, 109
geographical
information,
109–10
unfamiliar names,
111
imagery for athletic
training
field hockey, 115–6
gymnasts, 116–7
overview, 115–7
strength-training, 115

imagery for performance
training
elaborative
interrogation, 111
imagining doing
things, 111–4
imagery for performance
training, PETTLEP
procedure
description, 113, 121
emotion aspect, 114
environmental aspect,
113
"Imagery in Sport:
Elite Athlete
Examples and the
PETTLEP Model,"
112
learning aspect, 114
perspective aspect,
114–5
physical aspect, 113
task aspect, 114
timing aspect, 114
"Imagery in Sport: Elite
Athlete Examples and
the PETTLEP Model,"
112
imagining doing
things, imagery for
performance training,
111–4
independent variables,
40–1
induction
in the cycle of science,
22–3
definition, 195–6
example, 22–3
infiltrating a doomsday
cult, 49
informational cues, 195–8
information bubbles,
239–40
innovation, spaced attempts
at understanding, 221–3

insight
definition, 215
elaborative
interrogation, 216
impending, sensing,
230–1
importance of sleep,
220–1
understanding, 215
interleaving effect, 163–5
interleaving (mixing)
vs. blocking. See
blocking vs.
interleaving
(mixing).
elaborative
interrogation, 132
with hierarchical
organization, 132–3,
145
and organization,
132–3, 145
in-the-moment
impressions
metacognition, gauge
of learning, 76
study methods, 6, 14
intuition, 6–10
See also common sense

JC, 124
jogging your memory. See
cues
Jorvik Viking Center, 204–6
journal articles. See books
and publications
Journal of Imagery
Research in Sport and
Physical Activity, 112

keyword mnemonic
biographical
information, 111
description, 107–9, 120
foreign or new
vocabulary, 109

geographical
information, 109–10
unfamiliar names,
111
Kim, 130
Kim's Game, 130–1, 138
Kind, Amy, 221–2
Kipling, Rudyard, 130–1
knowing what you need to
know, 74–5, 76
Koch, Robert, 18

lag effect, 156–8
learning
See also optimal
learning; study
methods
boosting. See
elaboration.
experimental methods,
38–40
how to learn, 13–14
illusions, 84
information in a
specific order, 106
perceived vs. actual,
2–3
research methods,
38–40
learning aspect of the
PETTLEP procedure,
114
learning retention, massed
vs. spaced learning
methods, 153
learning style myth, effects
on learning outcomes,
51–4
levels of independent
variables, 40–1
levels of processing effect,
87
Levitin, Daniel, 136

Mahadevan, Rajan, 89,
123–4, 129–30, 193–4

maintenance rehearsal,
  81–3
malleability of memory,
  243–4
massed *vs.* spaced learning
  methods
    common sense, 21
    consolidation, 157
    cramming, 158–60, 166
    discriminating
      between similar
      concepts, 165
    distributing study across
      multiple sessions,
      155–8, 166–7
    elaborative
      interrogation, 152,
      155, 158
    increasing spacing
      intervals, 155–8
    interleaving effect,
      163–5
    lag effect, 156–8
    learning retention, 153
    massed, definition, 150
    mixing methods,
      163–5, 167
    problem-solving, 161
    pros and cons of
      spacing, 149–53
    science of spaced study,
      151–2
    skill-learning, 161–3
    sleep, role of, 157, 167
    spaced, definition, 150
    spacing within sessions
      vs. between sessions,
      153–5
McClintock, Barbara, 223–4
measuring with the
  scientific approach, 21–2
medical and surgical skills,
  imagery training, 117
medicine, scientific
  approach to
    bloodletting, 18

hand washing, 17–8
humours, in ancient
  Greek medicine, 18
memorists
  A. J., 50
  Foer, Joshua, 103, 136,
    144
  Haraguchi, Akira, 123
  JC, 124
  Mahadevan, Rajan, 89,
    123–4, 129–30,
    193–4
  Molaison, Henry (H.
    M.), 49
  Simonides, 103
  World Memory
    Championships,
    105
*Memory: A Contribution to
  Experimental Psychology*,
  151
memory
  See also study methods
  7, plus or minus 2
    number, 28
  case studies, 49–50
  chunking, 28
  collective, 237–41
  connecting to other
    information, 90–4
  deep processing, 87
  distractions, 136, 145
  experimental methods,
    38–40
  forgetting after walking
    through a doorway,
    200
  hints. *See* cues.
  imagery, benefits of,
    107
  jogging. *See* cues.
  levels of processing
    effect, 87
  limits on, 28
  maintenance rehearsal,
    81–3

malleability of, 243–4
*Memory: A
  Contribution to
  Experimental
  Psychology*, 151
Miller's Magic Number,
  28
orienting questions,
  86–7
personal. *See*
  metacognition.
quality of processing,
  85–7
quantity of study time
  vs. quality of time,
  84–5
repetition, effects of,
  81–5
research methods,
  38–40
role in understanding,
  215–17
rote rehearsal, effects
  of, 81–5
shallow processing,
  87
sleep, benefits of, 27
type of learning, effects
  of. *See* levels of
  processing effect.
wealth, effects of,
  136–7
memory, elaborative
  interrogation
  benefits of imagery,
    107, 120
  connecting to other
    information, 93
  organization, 134
  rote rehearsal, effects
    of, 81, 84
memory consolidation
  role of sleep, 157
  spaced attempts at
    understanding,
    220–1

"Memory Feats that can be Accomplished by Anyone," 103
memory recall
  effect of prior knowledge, 38–40
  interference, 217
  organization and memory, 125–7
  testing effects, 171–3
mental/physiological state, cues from, 198–9
meta-analysis, 30
metacognition
  See also memory control, 61–4
  definition, 59–60
  durable learning, 68
  effects of delay, 67–9, 73
  explaining subject matter, 73–4, 76
  fluency, 68
  importance of, 62–5
  knowing what you need to know, 74–5, 76
  making decisions about studying, 63–4
  monitoring, 61–4, 65–7, 73
  monitoring illusions, 65–7
  overview, 59–60
  predicting exam performance, 62–3
  study decisions, 64–5
  testing, 71–3
  uses for, 61–5
  wait and test, 67, 73, 76
metacognition, elaborative interrogation
  delays effects of, 69
  importance of, 64
  testing, effects of, 73

metacognition, learning foreign language
  vocabulary, 68, 72
  Swahili words, 72
  text, 70–1
method of loci
  applied to cues, 210
  description, 103–7, 120–1
  learning information in a specific order, 106
  origin of, 102–3
  pegword mnemonic, 106
  public speaking, 144
  in public speaking, 144
  uses for, 120–1
Miller, George, 28
Miller's Magic Number, 28
mixing. See interleaving (mixing)
M&Ms, 228
mnemonics. See cues; keyword mnemonic; pegword mnemonic
modeling information transmission, 243
Molaison, Henry (H. M.), 49
monitoring, metacognition, 61–4, 65–7, 73
monitoring illusions, 65–7
monitoring learning, benefits of testing, 179–80
Mozart, effects on intelligence, 45
Muller-Lyer illusion, 6–7
myths
  50 Great Myths of Psychology, 31
  anecdotes are not evidence, 32

appeal to authority, 31–2
asking for evidence, 21, 35
common sense is not evidence, 32, 35
confirmation bias, 34
correlation is not causation, 32
elaborative interrogation, 21
in a scientific approach to optimal learning, 19–21
using only of your brain, 20

narrative chaining, 132
naturalistic observation, 49–50
negative correlation, 47
neutrinos, mass of, 28
Newton, Sir Isaac, 225
"1966's Insane Wedding Gowns of the Future," 222–3
nominal recall, 245
nonexperimental methods in psychology
  See also experimental research
  case studies, 49–50
  correlation coefficient, 47
  correlational designs, 47–8
  descriptive methods, 49–50
  elaborative interrogation, 50
  infiltrating a doomsday cult, 49
  Jane Goodall and chimpanzee behavior, 49

memory case studies,
49–50
naturalistic
observation, 49–50
negative correlation,
47
positive correlation, 47
surveys, 50
nurses, imagery training,
117

observation
in the cycle of science,
22–3
definition, 196
example, 22–3
optimal learning
See also study methods
artists and their works,
8–9, 67
blocking vs. mixing,
9–10, 67
learning paired words,
3–6
opinions on, 3–6
repetition vs. imagery,
3–6
scientific approach,
11–12. See also
scientific
approach to optimal
learning.
optimal learning,
elaborative interrogation
role of imagery, 6
scientific approach, 11
organization
benefits of, 124–5
chunks, 124
computer desktop,
138–9
first letter technique,
132
hand-written notes, 139
interleaving, 132–3,
145

mixing materials. See
interleaving
(mixing).
narrative chaining, 132
scheduling spaced study
sessions, 135–6, 145
silverware drawers, 138
supergroups, 124
organization, and cognitive
processing
cognitive offloading,
135–6
easing cognitive load,
134–5
hierarchical
categorization of
study materials, 138–9
natural tendency
toward organization,
133–4
nodes, 133–4
organizing study
materials, 138–9
reducing search time,
140–1
redundancy, 140–1
scheduling study
sessions, 137–8
semantic networks, 134
simultaneous display,
139–40, 145
organization, elaborative
interrogation
benefits to memory, 134
cognitive offloading,
136
interleaving, 132
organization, for effective
communication
in public speaking,
143–4
in writing, 141–2
organization, hierarchical
structure
devising and
diagramming, 129

flashcards, 128–9
hierarchical diagrams,
145
Kim's Game, 130–1
mentally applying,
129–32
organization and memory
ad-hoc categories, 127
memory and recall,
125–7
research on, 125–7
The Organized Mind, 136
orienting questions, 86–7

paired words, learning, 3–6
Pasteur, Louis, 18
pegword mnemonic, 106
performance arts
training, imagery
training, 117
personal learning style vs.
learning outcome, 51
perspective aspect of the
PETTLEP procedure,
114–15
PETTLEP procedure,
113–15
See also imagery for
performance
training, PETTLEP
procedure
physical aspect of the
PETTLEP procedure,
113
physical environment cues,
199–201
pi, record for memorizing
the most digits of, 89,
123, 193
Pluto, 28
popularity vs. strength of
evidence, 55
positive correlation, 47
practice testing, 189
predicting with the
scientific approach, 22

proactive interference, 178–9
problem-solving, massed *vs.* spaced learning methods, 161
produce during testing, 181–3, 188–9
publications. *See* books and publications
public speaking, 143–4

quality of processing, 85–7
quality of study time *vs.* quantity, 84–5
quasi experiments, 43
Quinton, Mary, 112

radiation problem, 226
random assignment of participants, 42–3
recall. *See* memory recall
record for memorizing the most digits of pi, 89, 123, 193
relative facts, 240
reliability, 41
remembering in groups, 244–7
repetition
   effects on memory, 81–5
   vs. imagery, 3–6
   learning illusions, 84
replication of studies, 30
research methods, 38–40
   See also descriptive methods; experimental methods
restudying *vs.* testing, 173–4, 189
retention of information
   benefits of testing, 174–7
   boosting. *See* elaboration.

retrieval failure, 193–4
review papers, 30
Ronaldhino, 112
rote rehearsal, effects of, 81–5

scheduling
   study sessions, 135–8, 145
   testing sessions, 186–7
scientific approach
   to apply and control, 22
   benefits of, 27–9
   common errors in thinking, 31–4. *See also* myths.
   goals of, 21–2
   hypotheses, 22
   to measure and describe, 21–2
   to understand and predict, 22
scientific approach, cycle of science
   deduction, 22–3, 195–6
   elaborative interrogation, 27
   example, 23–7
   induction, 22–3, 195–6
   observation, 22–3, 196
   overview, 22–3
   tips for, 35
   verification, 22–3
scientific approach to evaluating claims
   brain-training, 29–30
   consensus in the field, 30
   meta-analysis, 30
   replication of studies, 30
   review papers, 30
   video games improving brain function, 29–30

scientific approach to medicine
   bloodletting, 18
   hand washing, 17–18
   humours, in ancient Greek medicine, 18
scientific approach to optimal learning
   asking for evidence, 14
   belief, 19–21
   common sense, 19–21
   feedback experiment, 24–7
   flat-earth view, 12
   learning how to learn, 13–4
   myths, 19–21
scientific debate
   benefits of, 29
   cancer screening, 28
   dinosaurs, scales *vs.* feathers, 28
   elaborative interrogation, 29
   neutrinos, mass of, 28
scientific research, optimal learning. *See* scientific approach to optimal learning
self-reference effect, 96
7, plus or minus 2 number, 28
shallow processing, 87
shared conditions, 205
shared knowledge. *See* collective knowledge
silverware drawers, organizing, 138
Simonides, 103
simultaneous display experiments, 139–40, 145
skill-learning, massed *vs.* spaced learning methods, 161–3

sleep
  benefits on memory,
    27
  and consolidation of
    memory, 157, 167
  importance for insight,
    220–1
  importance to
    understanding,
    220–1
smells, as memory cues,
  204–6
smoking, dangers of, 48
snowshoe hare, 90
social aspects of learning
  See also collaboration
    in learning; collective
    knowledge; group
    learning
  collaborative groups,
    244
  collaborative
    inhibition, 246–7
  elaboration, 247, 253
  malleability of
    memory, 243–4
  modeling information
    transmission, 243
  nominal recall, 245
  overview, 235–7
  pooling individual
    responses, 253
  remembering in
    groups, 244–7
  studying in different
    groups, 253
  transmitting
    information across
    individuals, 242
spaced attempts at
  understanding
  benefits of, 231–2
  consolidation of
    memories, 220–1
  escaping a wrong
    mindset, 221–3

  importance of sleep,
    220–1
  preparing for insight,
    219–20
spaced learning methods,
  150
spaced study vs. massed.
  See massed vs. spaced
  learning methods
spacing testing,
  183–8
Star Spangled Banner,
  singing, 192
stereotypes, 239–240
strength-training,
  imagery for athletic
  training, 115
student grades vs.
  instructor evaluations,
  48
study context, matching
  to testing context,
  201–3, 210
study decisions, 64–5
studying in different
  groups, 253
study methods
  See also optimal
    learning; spaced
    learning methods
  elaborative
    interrogation, 10
  highlighting, 10
  in-the-moment
    impressions, 6, 14
  perceived vs. actual
    learning, 2–3
  perils of intuition,
    6–10
study sessions, scheduling,
  135–6, 145
successive relearning,
  183–7
suggestive questioning,
  248
supergroups, 124

Surgeon General's report
  on the dangers of
  smoking, 48
surgical skills. See medical
  and surgical skills
surveys, 50
Swahili words, learning,
  72

taking a break, 210
task aspect of the
  PETTLEP procedure,
  114
telephone game,
  241–2
testing
  demonstration, 170
  designing experiments
    about, 173–4
  effects on memory
    recall, 171–3
  elaborative
    interrogation, 174
  metacognition, 71–3
  proactive interference,
    178–9
  reasons for, 169–70
  repeated testing,
    principles of, 186,
    188
  vs. restudying, 173–4,
    189
  wait and test, 76
testing, benefits of
  elaborative
    interrogation, 177
  enhancing
    understanding,
    177–8
  monitoring learning,
    179–80
  reducing forgetting,
    178–9
  retention of
    information, 174–7
  summary of, 180–1

testing, guide to using
    elaborative
    interrogation, 183
    practice testing, 189
    produce during testing,
    181–3, 188–9
    scheduling testing
    sessions, 186–7
    spacing testing, 183–8
    successive relearning,
    183–7
testing context, matching
    to study context, 201–3,
    210
testing effect, 170
text, learning, 70–1
threats to experiments,
    44–7, 55
timing aspect of the
    PETTLEP procedure,
    114
Tombaugh, Clyde, 28
transmitting information
    across individuals, 242
trials, experiments, 126
triggering memories. See
    cues
true experiments, 41–4, 55

understanding
    benefits of testing,
    177–8
    definition, 214
    elaborative
    interrogation, 216, 219
    explaining concepts to
    others, 232
    imagery training,
    118–20, 121

insight, 215
    making connections,
    232
    mechanisms of
    memory, 215–7
    with the scientific
    approach, 22
    taking breaks, 219, 231
    wrong mindset,
    217–19
understanding, role of
analogy
    analogical reasoning,
    224
    attack-dispersion
    problem, 226–7
    central tendency, 230
    elaborative
    interrogation, 228
    Eureka effect, 224
    expert advice, 232
    overview, 223–30
    radiation problem,
    226
    Sir Isaac Newton's
    apple, 225
    variability, 230
understanding, spaced
attempts
    benefits of, 231–2
    consolidation of
    memories, 220–1
    escaping the wrong
    mindset, 221–3
    importance of sleep,
    220–1
    innovation, 221–3
    preparing for insight,
    219–20

unfamiliar names,
    keyword mnemonics,
    111
unique conditions, 205
unique cues, 203, 210, 216
unique smells, 204–6
U.S. penny, identifying,
    79–80

variability, definition, 230
variables. See experimental
    research, variables
verification
    in the cycle of science,
    22–3
    example, 22–3
video games improving
    brain function,
    evaluating claims,
    29–30
Viking smells, 204–6
vocabulary, learning with
    keyword mnemonics, 109

wait and test, 67, 73, 76
wealth, effects on memory,
    136–7
wedding gowns of the
    future, 222–3
why, asking. See
    elaborative interrogation
within-subjects
    manipulation, 41
word size in memory
    exercises, effects of, 66
World Memory
    Championships, 105
writing, organizational
    principles, 141–2